THE TRAGEDY OF AMERICAN COMPASSION

Also by Marvin Olasky

Patterns of Corporate Philanthropy (1987)

Corporate Public Relations: A New Historical Perspective (1987)

Turning Point, coauthor (1987)

The Press and Abortion, 1838–1988 (1988)

Prodigal Press (1988)

Freedom, Justice, and Hope, coauthor (1988)

More Than Kindness, coauthor (1990)

Central Ideas in the Development of American Journalism (1991)

Patterns of Corporate Philanthropy: Funding False Compassion, coauthor (1991)

Abortion Rites (1992)

Philanthropically Correct (1993)

Fighting for Liberty and Virtue (1995)

Telling the Truth: How to Revitalize Christian Journalism (1996)

Renewing American Compassion (1996)

The American Leadership Tradition (1999)

Compassionate Conservatism (2000)

Standing for Christ in a Modern Babylon (2003)

The Religions Next Door (2004)

Scimitar's Edge (2006)

The Politics of Disaster (2006)

Unmerited Mercy: A Memoir, 1968–1996 (2010)

2048, A Story of America's Future (2011)

Echoes of Eden (2012)

World View: Seeking Grace and Truth in our Common Life (2017)

Reforming Journalism (2019)

Abortion at the Crossroads (2021)

Lament for a Father (2021)

The
Tragedy of American
Compassion

MARVIN OLASKY

REGNERY GATEWAY
Washington, D.C.

Regnery Gateway™ is a trademark of Salem Communications
Holding Corporation
Regnery˙ is a registered trademark and its colophon is a trademark of
Salem Communications Holding Corporation

Cataloging-in-Publication data on file with the Library of Congress

This paperback edition published 2022

ISBN: 978-1-68451-416-8
eISBN: 978-1-68451-417-5

Published in the United States by
Regnery Gateway, an Imprint of
Regnery Publishing
A Division of Salem Media Group
Washington, D.C.
www.Regnery.com

Manufactured in the United States of America

10 9 8 7 6 5 4 3 2 1

Books are available in quantity for promotional or premium use. For
information on discounts and terms, please visit our website:
www.Regnery.com

For Susan

Contents

Acknowledgments ix

Preface to the Thirtieth Anniversary Edition
by Marvin Olasky xi

Preface
by Charles Murray xv

Introduction
The Current Impasse xxiii

Chapter One
The Early American Model of Compassion 1

Chapter Two
Turning Cities into Countryside 25

Chapter Three
First Challenge to the Charity Consensus 49

Chapter Four
The Social Darwinist Threat 73

Chapter Five
Proving Social Darwinism Wrong 99

Chapter Six
The Seven Marks of Compassion 123

Chapter Seven
And Why Not Do More? 145

Chapter Eight
Excitement of a New Century 167

CHAPTER NINE
Selling New Deals in Old Wineskins   189

CHAPTER TEN
Revolution—and Its Heartbreak   211

CHAPTER ELEVEN
Questions of the 1970s and 1980s   233

CHAPTER TWELVE
Putting Compassion into Practice   253

CHAPTER THIRTEEN
Applying History   275

NOTES   297

INDEX   351

ACKNOWLEDGMENTS

I wrote most of this book in 1990 while serving as a Bradley Scholar at the Heritage Foundation. Heritage provided not only the financial support that allowed me to spend a year in Washington, D.C., but a stimulating research and writing environment as well. Charles Heatherly, Adam Myerson, Tom Atwood, Terri Ruddy, Mark Pietrzyk, Ben and Betsy Hart, Duane Higgins, Bruce Edwards, and other colleagues were supportive.

Five years of meetings with the Villars Committee on International Relief and Development taught me much about basic causes of poverty. Discussions with Herb Schlossberg, Udo Middelmann, Ken Myers, Howard and Roberta Ahmanson, George Grant, Lane Dennis, Preston Hawkins, Ron Nash, and Ted Yamamori helped me to think about domestic applications of Villars principles.

Writing a book is like running a marathon, with many individuals handing me cups of water in the later stages. Willa Johnson, Charles Colson, Constance Horner, Charles Murray, Dan McMurry, Heather Richardson, David Bovenizer, Alfred Regnery, Patricia Bozell, Joel Belz, Bill Poole, Milton Friedman, John Perkins, O. Palmer Robertson,

Bill Smith, Jan Dennis, Guy Condon, and Robert and Vicki Goodrich all helped in different ways.

I also was impressed by the examples of compassion currently evident at the Pacific Garden Mission in Chicago, the McAuley Water Street Mission in New York, the Gospel Mission in Washington, and CityTeam in San Jose. Daily forays into the stacks of the Library of Congress allowed me to uncover numerous examples of past compassion. Collections at the Chicago Historical Society, the Chicago Public Library, the Newberry Library, the New York Public Library, and the libraries of the University of Texas at Austin also proved useful.

Finally, I thank my wife Susan, to whom this book is dedicated: she has a wise head, a gracious heart, and a loveliness that goes beyond narrative. I thank our children Peter, David, Daniel, and Benjamin: their lives teach patience and provide joy. My greatest thanks are to God, who had compassion on me almost two decades ago and pushed me from darkness into light.

PREFACE TO THE
THIRTIETH ANNIVERSARY EDITION

by Marvin Olasky

Historians say the book you're holding was influential in the passage of national welfare reform in the 1990s. If so, that's because *Tragedy* turned upside down the conventional conservative response to federal poverty programs: "They cost too much." I spent a lot of time in Washington proposing that the biggest problem of twentieth-century welfare was not its cost but its stinginess in providing what many among the poor needed most: CPS (challenging, personal, and spiritual help) rather than EBS (entitlement, bureaucracy, and secularism).

Welfare reform legislation gave only a little nudge toward CPS, so from 1995 to 2002 I tried to sow seeds by giving talks to 125 communities. The ground was often stony, the rainfall insufficient, and the sower feeble, but that work is being carried on by programs like the True Charity Initiative, based in Joplin, Missouri, and others around the country.

The book you're holding had some influence in Texas, where I became an informal, occasional advisor to Governor George W. Bush. He instructed his state bureaucracy to help rather than hinder religious poverty-fighters. When Bush ran for president, he endorsed the creation of tax credits to help local nonprofits without making them dependent on Washington. At the 2000 GOP convention his aides passed out buttons proclaiming, "I'm a compassionate conservative." Lots of delegates put them on.

They didn't stay on for long. I still like Bush, but political pressures changed the tone of his administration. To make donors happy without busting the budget, his administration dropped the tax credit idea and prioritized reducing the estate tax. Second, 9/11 led to a military budget increase. To win Democratic votes the administration also expanded domestic spending. Conservatives labeled "compassionate conservatism" merely a euphemism for "big government."

In retrospect, compassionate conservatism had its national rollout too soon: Yes, it gained a toehold, but the toe was gnarled and the nail ingrown. After three decades of a centralized "war on poverty," the decentralized approach needed more stories of street-level success and more intellectual support.

Now we have both. Community poverty-fighting successes are numerous: More than one hundred programs have won one sign of recognition, a Hope Award for Effective Compassion. Some of my favorite nonprofits, like the Bearing Bike Works in Atlanta and the WorkFaith Connection in Houston, move people from deep poverty or long prison experience to productive labor.

On the intellectual front, the book you're holding stood pretty much alone three decades ago, but dozens of others published in the twenty-first century now provide thoughtful support. Some of my favorites have clear titles: Steve Corbett and Brian Fikkert's *When Helping Hurts: How to Alleviate Poverty without Hurting the Poor…and Yourself*, Robert Lupton's *Toxic Charity: How Churches and Charities*

Hurt Those They Help (And How to Reverse It!), Lawrence Mead's *From Prophecy to Charity: How to Help the Poor*, and Howard Husock's *The Poor Side of Town: And Why We Need It.*

When I read *Tragedy* earlier this year for the first time since the 1990s, four errors jumped out at me. The first is stylistic: Young journalists I hectored during twenty-nine years of magazine editing that began soon after this book's publication will be right to hoot about my use of passive constructions. Punctuation was also semi-academic in places: I should have performed more semi-colonoscopies and bowel resections.

The second problem is deeper: colorblindness regarding the effects of segregation. The title of Gene Dattel's history, *Reckoning with Race*, is good: I didn't sufficiently reckon with it. Isabel Wilkerson's *Caste*, John McWhorter's *Losing the Race*, and Jason Riley's *Please Stop Helping Us* are books from the left and right that describe the particular problems African Americans faced and face.

A third problem: I should have done a better job of explaining two nineteenth-century terms, "worthy poor" and "unworthy poor," that today leave readers sputtering. Back then, those with biblical faith knew God creates all humans in His image, so all lives are worthy and none unworthy, but they made a pragmatic distinction: Who among the poor would use charitable funds to feed and house their families and themselves, and who would spend every available dollar on drugs or alcohol?

Josiah Quincy two centuries ago had a better nomenclature: "able" (ready and willing to work), "unable" (and thus worthy of alms), and able but "unwilling." Quincy also recognized the need to know the poor individually and not make assumptions based on appearance. He learned about "numerous and minute shades of difference" in disabilities, so he

xiv *Preface to the Thirtieth Anniversary Edition*

did not attempt to draw hard and fast distinctions. Helping the poor was and is an art, not a science.

My fourth error lay in not taking into account the decline of U.S. manufacturing that was picking up speed as I wrote. Work is important both financially and psychologically, and factory closings discouraged many workers. "College or bust" high school curricula amplified the problem: Unacademically-inclined high school students often graduated or dropped out without a skill, and some then dropped out of the workforce and into drug use.

This is a re-issue, not a rewriting, so I've left the content that follows as it was, warts and all. *Tragedy's* legacy at this point is mixed. Three decades of accomplishments in some communities have fallen far short of the original hope for a warmhearted but tough-minded approach based on historical success. But cultural change nationally and political change in Washington take a long time, and I hope some who now read this book will be prepared to take another whack at the piñata.

by Charles Murray

This is a book of hope at a time when just about everyone but Marvin Olasky has lost hope. The topic is poverty and the underclass.

The reasons for hopelessness are everywhere, but they are most obvious and most depressing in the inner city. There, in every large city in America, the family as we have known it throughout Western history seems terminal. More than 80 percent of children are born to single women. The father who fills the most ordinary of traditional roles—lives with the mother, goes to work every morning, brings home a paycheck every week, and shows his children by example how a responsible male adult is supposed to behave—has nearly vanished. It is harder to put numbers to the situation regarding mothers, but the reports from case workers and a few clear-eyed journalists reveal a world in which some substantial proportion of women play their role of mother appallingly badly, leaving the children unnurtured, undisciplined, sometimes unfed and unwashed. Children grow in a world where cause and effect are meaningless—where, for the same behavior, they are on one occasion ignored, on another laughed at indulgently, and on yet another cursed and beaten. Nor is that the only way in which cause and effect, praise and blame, can be turned topsy-turvy in the inner city. The drug dealer is lionized, the man who mops floors is scorned. The school girl who gets pregnant is envied, the school girl who studies hard is taunted.

The numbers are often secondary. What proportion of inner city adults is addicted to crack? Nobody really knows. But whatever it is, the drug trade has torn apart the social fabric of neighborhood after neighborhood. How many homeless are there? It is easy to discredit the inflated estimates that the newspapers uncritically pass on, but it takes very few homeless people sleeping in doorways to change the feel of a streetscape and soon to change the ethos of a community. Is crime as bad as people think it is? To people whose every routine of everyday life has to be altered out of fear of becoming a victim, debates over the statistical trendlines are beside the point.

These problems seem intractable because so many things, costing so much money, have been tried so often without success. Nothing new is left to try. Another jobs program? We spent tens of billions of dollars on jobs programs in the 1970s, and they failed even to dent the numbers of inner-city men who have dropped out of the job market. Another program to take women off welfare through education and training? The history of such programs is long, and they tell a monotonous story: the successes have only small effects at the margin, there are many more failures than successes, and the net number of women on the welfare rolls grows. Escalate the war on drugs? More money for inner city schools? More family planning programs? Whatever the nostrum, we have by now accumulated stacks of reports evaluating past attempts, and they document the reasons why the next effort won't work either. If you doubt the end of optimism, listen to political candidates. They know better than to talk about how to help the underclass, for no one believes them anymore.

In another sense, however, the problems of the underclass are easy to solve—if indeed the problems are a matter of too little money. As a rough-and-ready calculation, assume that the U.S. has 7.5 million families below the poverty line and that on the average it would take a $12,000 income supplement to bring those families above the poverty line. Both numbers represent the high end of the poverty problem as it has existed in the last decade. Even so, to erase poverty would cost only $90 billion, at a time when federal expenditures on "cash and noncash benefits for persons with limited income," as the federal government's *Statistical Abstract* puts it, are passing $150 billion. Without adding a dime to the federal budget, we could, right now, bring every family above the poverty line and have something on the order of $60 billion left over to fund special programs for housing, medical care, or whatever, on top of that poverty level income. So it is "easy" to cure poverty, even under the constraints of the current budget deficit. Why not do it?

In practical terms, we don't do it because much of that $190 billion is not "for persons of limited income" at all, but for the poverty industry—bureaucrats, caseworkers, service providers, and a grab-bag of vendors in the private sector who plan, implement, and evaluate social programs on government contracts. Even the money that does trickle down to the street does not go to people below the poverty line, but to persons with incomes considerably above it. All of these constituencies would block any attempt to cash out the current programs and write the monthly checks to poor people that would end poverty.

But suppose that these highly practical constraints did not apply. If we *could* put everyone above the poverty line with a check, *should* we? And in answering that question, we come face to face with the deeper questions about compassion and the poor that this book poses.

The profound truth that Marvin Olasky forces us to confront is that the problems of the underclass are not caused by poverty. Some of them are exacerbated by poverty, but we know that they need not be *caused* by poverty, for poverty has been the condition of the vast majority of human communities since the dawn of history, and they have for the most part been communities of stable families, nurtured children, and low crime. It is wrong to think that writing checks will end the problems of the underclass, or even reduce them. If tomorrow we were to adopt the plan I just outlined, giving every family enough money to put them above the poverty line, we can be confident that two things would happen.

First, the number of families that require such assistance would promptly grow by a sizable number, as families that once managed to stay above the poverty line through their own labor began to take it a little easier—a natural human reaction with disastrous long-term consequences. We might predict this outcome simply through common sense, but we don't have to rely on common sense in this instance. The United States government proved it for us back in the early 1970s with a huge demonstration project known as the Negative Income Tax Experiment. A guaranteed income will produce significant reductions in work effort. Those losses will be concentrated among young men. To end poverty by writing checks is an efficient way to increase the size of the underclass, not reduce it.

Second, the suffering that makes us despair for the inner city, especially the suffering of children, would go on. We may take the elemental case of malnourished children as an example. It is nearly impossible in the contemporary United States for a mother to be left without a way to provide her children with a decent diet. Government programs, beginning with AFDC and food stamps and working down through a long list of special food programs, not to mention churches, neighbors, and a profusion of private services, offer ways for a competent mother even in the most desperate of circumstances to make sure her child's stomach is filled with good food every day. And yet many children are malnourished nonetheless. The food is out there. Too often, a competent mother is not. More money is not going to make competent mothers of incompetent ones, nor conscientious mothers of irresponsible ones. More money is not going to bring fathers back to the children they have sired and then abandoned. Indeed, the guarantee of an income above the poverty line, no matter whether the father stays or not, is more likely to break up families than reunite them—another of the grim but commonsensical findings of the Negative Income Tax Experiment. A guaranteed income is not going to reduce drug abuse or alcoholism. It probably would not even reduce homelessness much—the number of homeless who are on the streets just because they don't have enough money for an apartment is small compared to the number who are there for complex reasons.

And so the impasse. If the social programs of the welfare state give us no way out, and if money gives us no way out, what is left? Therein lies Marvin Olasky's story.

The underclass we have always had with us. Descriptions of a subpopulation of American poor who fit the current notion of an "underclass" may be found from the inception of sociology and, as Dr. Olasky describes, appear in writings that go back to the earliest days of colonial America. But the number of people who fit that description constituted a minuscule proportion of poor people. Even in the great cities, filled with people who were miserably poor by today's standards, the neighborhoods that corresponded to today's inner cities in their crime and social disintegration—Five Points and Hell's Kitchen, for example—were isolated areas within the much larger, teeming, but energetic and functional ethnic communities that made up the social quilt of the city.

Why was the underclass so much smaller then, at a time when poverty was so much closer to real destitution than "poverty" as we know it today? Within the welter of candidate explanations is Marvin Olasky's central truth: Human needs were answered by other human beings, not by bureaucracies, and the response to those needs was not compartmentalized. People didn't used to be so foolish as to think that providing food would cure anything except hunger, nor so shallow as to think that physical hunger was more important than the other human hungers, nor so blind as to ignore the interaction between the *way* that one helps and the effects of that help on the human spirit and human behavior. *The Tragedy of American Compassion* is the recounting of an American history that today's Americans never learned.

In telling this story, Dr. Olasky concentrates appropriately on the effects on the poor, for it is there that the overridingly important message lies: *It worked.* Free societies know how to do many potentially contradictory things at the same time: create communities in which the men and women routinely understand and act on the responsibilities of adulthood, provide help to the small proportion of people who need it, and provide moral uplift—yes, "moral uplift" is the right phrase, overdue for resurrection—to the even smaller proportion of the needy who are the nucleus of an underclass.

This message runs headlong into the received wisdom. American social history of the late nineteenth and early twentieth centuries is typically taught through the texts of Lincoln Steffens and Jacob Riis and Upton Sinclair. They portrayed part of American reality, to be sure—but only part. Given the massive influx of immigrants during that period, the comparative poverty of the entire country—for America even at the opening of the twentieth century had only a tiny fraction of the wealth of contemporary America—and the unprecedented social dislocations brought about by industrialization, the achievements of earlier ages in dealing with the needy were astonishing. It was not a perfect system, and America wanted perfection. When the New Deal came along, it seemed that perfection was within our grasp if we simply used government to do more efficiently what private institutions had been doing all along. We were wrong in that belief, but we are equally wrong today in thinking that because government cannot do the job, nobody can. What is required is no more complicated, and no less revolutionary, than recognizing first, that the energy and effective compassion that went into solving the problems of the needy in 1900, deployed in the context of today's national wealth, can work wonders; and secondly, that such energy and such compassion cannot be mobilized in a modern welfare state. The modern welfare state must be dismantled.

While the potential for changing the condition of the underclass is the main story line, there is a subtext in *The Tragedy of American Compassion* that is just as important, for this is a book not just about the underclass, but about all of us. Few urban or suburban communities anywhere, including the most affluent, can be satisfied with the way their members live together. We have become a nation of subdivisions and apartment blocks, places where people eat and sleep but too seldom live together as neighbors and copartners in making their little platoons work. Bonds and affiliations—words that Marvin Olasky uses repeatedly and powerfully—are broken, and we too often have nothing of value to take their place. Dr. Olasky opens up new ways of thinking about the question that has preoccupied me in recent years, and one that I believe will increasingly be recognized as the great social question for millennium's end and beyond: How can human beings at every level of income and abilities live happily together in postindustrial urban communities?

I use the word "happily" with intent, for it is central to what Marvin Olasky has to say. We have learned in this century that the search for human happiness is not well served by egalitarian systems, let alone socialist ones. We have relearned in the last few decades the age-old lesson that narcissism and materialism are not satisfying bases for a fulfilling life. Marvin Olasky recognizes openly what most of us sense less articulately: the problems of America's social policy are not defined by economics or inequality, but by needs of the human spirit. The error of contemporary policy is not that it spends too much or too little to help the poor, but that it is fundamentally out of touch with the meaning of those needs. By reminding us that it was not always so, this badly needed history points us toward a possible and better future.

Charles Murray is the W. H. Brady Scholar at the American Enterprise Institute in Washington, D.C.

The Current Impasse

At Christmas in Washington the social pendulum swings. Stepping inside Union Station on a cold December night is like entering a magic kingdom: classical music fills the air, high-rent shops line the mall areas, and even the Amtrak waiting rooms are generally clean. But outside, over there, away from the bright light, sounds a different song. Panhandlers wait near the escalator heading down to the Metro stop. Some seem coolly efficient in their work. Some are inebriated and occasionally aggressive. Others are pathetic. And one, with a sly sense of humor, sings, "Rich folks roasting on an open fire,/ Homeless stepping on their toes."

At quitting time in America's capital two classes step on each other's toes. Most people, whether officials or clerks, head home to families and friends. Some people, volunteer doormen at the Metro, try to cadge a few more quarters from package- and guilt-laden passersby before heading toward shelters or grates. Most of the better-off avoid eye contact with these most visible poor. They know "the homeless" are with them, and they do not know how to react.

The confusion is not caused by a lack of instructors. Across the country, day after day, morning talk shows and newspapers tell us to be "compassionate" toward the poor. These days, the word "compassion" slides over tongues like a social lozenge—in one month, in five major newspapers, I found the word about three hundred times. But does "compassion" mean giving a dollar at the Metro entrance, and then appropriating a billion dollars for federal housing? Are those who refuse to do one or the other "rich folks roasting on an open fire?" In the 1990s, are they ready to be consigned—in their own minds or in social and political reality—to the circle of hell reserved for the selfish?

What should we do? One charity leader said, "The important thing to remember is that we must get involved in some way—any way"[1] But what if many points of light are actually points of darkness? If we have a cabinet full of medicine bottles, do we recommend dipping randomly into any of them? Aren't there usually warning labels, or at least suggestions that we take certain pills with food or milk? "How do we befriend the homeless?" a tipsy Washington troubadour sang. "The answer is blowing in the wind." Are we to grab a butterfly net and try to snag an answer as it flaps by?

No. The answer is not blowing in the wind, nor is it necessary to eat this and drink that, like Alice in Wonderland. The answer is sitting on pages of old magazines and reports deep in the stacks of the Library of Congress. Americans in urban areas a century ago faced many of the problems we face today, and they came up with truly compassionate solutions. We may not realize this, because only two kinds of books on the overall history of poverty-fighting in America are now available. A few of the books argue that the free market itself solves all problems of poverty. The more conventional approach stresses government intervention to restructure economic relations. But neither kind emphasizes the crucial role of truly compassionate individuals and groups in the long fight against poverty. Neither goes beyond smug rejection or neglect of pre-twentieth-century moral understandings.

Without the informed spirit that historical understanding can provide, the long debate about poverty in America has reached an impasse. In Washington, political leaders talk grandly of helping the poor, but even the word "compassion," which once had the power to compel action, is now merely a rhetorical device trotted out regularly by Republicans as well as Democrats. Around the country, "compassion fatigue" is evident as people tire of seeing generosity misused or, apparently, of no use. As columnist Ellen Goodman noted, "For many of us, there is a slow process by which...generosity can turn into resentment and sympathy can turn hard."[2]

Thoughtful journalists are throwing up their hands. Columnist William Raspberry is typical: "Washington, like cities across America, is doing a rotten job of housing its homeless. But I haven't a clue as to how to do it much better."[3] Among philosophers and political theorists, confusion reigns. James S. Fishkin ended his book on *The Limits of Obligation* with an honest abdication: "Some great revision in our assumptions or in our actions is required. But because I feel genuinely caught in this dilemma myself, I am not now advocating any particular resolution."[4] Yet, while we sit around and debate, or increasingly give up, generations are being lost. Crack babies in inner city hospitals tremble and twitch uncontrollably. Teenage mothers, alone with squalling children, fight the impulse to strike out. Women in their thirties, abandoned by husbands, wait for their numbers to be called in cold welfare offices. Homeless men line up impatiently at food wagons before shuffling off to eat and drink in alleys smelling of urine.

The good news is that the impasse can be resolved. Many lives can be saved if we recapture the vision that changed lives up to a century ago, when our concept of compassion was not so corrupt. In one sense, we have thought ourselves into this social disaster—and we can think ourselves out of it. The key to the future, as always, is understanding the past. This book, by laying out the history, attempts to suggest a new form for the debate over poverty and a new way out of the impasse.

CHAPTER ONE

The Early American Model of Compassion

In the 1980s a philanthropic trade association, the Council on Foundations, issued a press release noting several billion dollars in member contributions. Newspapers called the council "the most generous group of people in human history."[1] The superlative probably was accurate in terms of dollar amounts, but some cash-poor Americans of colonial times excelled in different measures of "generosity"—a word in those days primarily associated not with money but with nobility of character and, as in Shakespeare's *Love's Labour's Lost*, with gentleness and humility.[2]

The model of early American generosity toward those in greatest need stressed personal aid in times of disease. Pilgrim leader William Bradford, describing how sickness shrank his small band of settlers following their landing at Plymouth in 1620, commended the "6. or 7. sound persons" who could still move about and

> in ye time of most distres... spared no pains night nor day,
> but with abundance of toyle and hazard of their owne
> health, fetched them woode, made them fires, drest them

meat, made their beads, washed their lothsome cloaths,
cloathed and uncloathed them; in a word, did all ye homly
& necessarie offices for them.

Bradford wrote that they did "all this willingly and cherfully, without
any grudging in ye least, shewing herein true love unto their friends
& bretheren."[3]

This early American model also emphasized hospitality, particularly the opening of homes to those suffering destitution because of
disaster. Minutes from the Fairfield, Connecticut, town council meeting of April 16, 1673, show that "Seriant Squire and Sam moorhouse
[agreed] to Take care of Roger knaps family in this time of their great
weakness..."[4]; and minutes from the Chelmsford, Massachusetts,
town meeting in November 1753 speak of a payment to "Mr. W. Parker
for taking one Joanna Cory, a poor child of John Cory, deceased, and
to take care of her while [until] 18 years old."[5] Significantly, the honored generosity lay primarily in the giving of time, not treasure. Those
who made room for widows and orphans often received compensa-
tion for out-of-pocket expenditures from town councils or other community organizations.[6]

The model also insisted on "decent living" on the part of those who
were helped. Groups such as the Scots' Charitable Society (organized
in 1684) "open[ed] the bowells of our compassion" to widows such as
a Mrs. Stewart who had "lost the use of her left arm" and whose husband was "Wash'd Overboard in a Storm."[7] But the open hand was not
extended to all; the society ruled that "no prophane or diselut person,
or openly scandelous shall have any pairt or portione herein." The
able-bodied could readily find jobs in a growing agricultural economy;
when they chose not to, it was considered perfectly appropriate to
pressure them to change their minds.

The need to offer personal help and hospitality became a frequent subject of sermons, which in colonial days were "powerful in shaping cultural values, meanings, and a sense of corporate purpose."[8] With other media largely absent, "the sermon stood alone" as the weekly "medium of public communication," and thus would be heard and discussed. When Benjamin Colman noted in 1725 that "Acts of Compassion and Mercy to our poor and needy *Brethren* [are] esteemed by the *Lord of the Sabbath* to be *Holiness* to himself," people listened.[9] When Colman explained that "compassion and Mercy to the poor is Conformity to God," it is unlikely that many wanted to be out of conformity.[10]

Congregationalist and Presbyterian sermons regularly noted that faith without works of compassion was dead. Anglicans also argued that those blessed materially by God should "compassionate" the poor by descending into misery when necessary in order to help pull them up: "This in one order of life is right and good; nothing more harmonious."[11] And when Methodism spread in the eighteenth century, American followers propagated John Wesley's advice to "Put yourself in the place of every poor man and deal with him as you would God deal with you."[12]

The only question might be, how would we want God to deal with us? As a cold official who provides material without love? As a warm sugar daddy who gives without discipline? Cultures build systems of charity in the image of the god they worship, whether distant deist, bumbling bon vivant, or "whatever goes" gopher. In colonial America, emphasis on a theistic God of both justice and mercy led to an understanding of compassion that was hard-headed but warmhearted. Since justice meant punishment for wrongdoing, it was right for the slothful to suffer. And since mercy meant rapid response when people turned away from past practice, malign neglect of those willing to shape up also was wrong. Later, when ideas of God changed, so did systems of charity, but early on, it was considered right to place sinners in the hands of a challenging economy.

Theistic understanding led to other strong themes. First, the belief that God was not merely the establisher of principles but a personal intervenor ("God's Providence") contributed to a sense that man, created after God's image, should go beyond clockwork charity. Colman declared that

> God values our *Hearts* and *Spirits* above all our Silver or Gold, our Herds and Flocks. If *a Man would give all the Substance of his House instead of Love*, the Loves of his Soul and the Souls of his House, *it would be contemned.*[13]

Second, it was important for the better-off to know the poor individually, and to understand their distinct characters. Today's believers in "liberation theology" often argue that God is on the side of the poor, but the older distinction showed God backing the mistreated poor and chastising those who had indulged in indolence.[14]

Third, the belief that God's law overarched every aspect of life suggested that the most important need of the poor who were unfaithful was to learn about God and God's expectations for man.[15] Spiritual as well as material help was a matter of obligation rather than request, in a way parallel to what Gertrude Himmelfarb has noted in the English context:

> there was nothing invidious in being preached to. What was invidious was not being preached to, not having access to the kinds of moral, religious, and communal experiences that were a normal part of life for those not so poor as to be deprived of them.[16]

A fourth application of colonial theological understanding was an emphasis on withholding charity at times. Today, virtually everyone is prophilanthropy. Those who contribute money to charitable causes, or who give food and blankets to the homeless, are praised; even those who provide clean needles to drug addicts are usually praised. But colonial compassion was more cautious. Cotton Mather warned his church members in 1698, "Instead of exhorting you to augment your charity, I will rather utter an exhortation... that you may not *abuse* your charity by misapplying it."[17] Mather added, "Let us try to do good with as much application of mind as wicked men employ in doing evil."[18]

The difference between Mather's restraint and our exuberance indicates the difference between dominant views of human nature then and now. Mather did not assume that men (and women) naturally *want* to work. His view, and that of most leaders in both the North and the South for the next two centuries, was that many persons, given a choice between working and not working, would choose to sit. He and others viewed the poor not as standing on the bottom rung of the social ladder, with the only choices stagnation or upward movement, but as resting in the middle, capable of moving either upward to economic independence or downward to "pauperism," characterized by a defeated and dependent state of mind, as well as a lack of income.

Basing his thoughts on that understanding, Mather in 1710 gave his congregation pointed advice concerning the idle: "Don't nourish 'em and harden 'em in that, but find employment for them. Find 'em work; set 'em to work; keep 'em to work."[19] (Mather added, "If there be any base houses, which threaten debauch and poison and confound the neighborhood"—today we might call them crack houses—"let your charity to your neighbors make you do all you can for the suppression of them.")

Throughout colonial times that understanding continued to be preached. For example, Charles Chauncey in 1752 told members of the Society for Encouraging Industry and Employing the Poor that they were

> restrained as to the Distribution of [their] Charity; not being allowed to dispense it promiscuously, but obliged to take due Care to find out suitable Objects; distinguishing properly between those needy People who are *able*, and those who are *unable*, to employ themselves in Labour....[20]

Referring to the apostle Paul's famous maxim of 2 Thessalonians 3:10, "If a man will not work, he shall not eat," Chauncey added:

> The Command in my Text is plainly a *Statute of Heaven*, tying up your Hands from Charitable Distributions to the slothful poor. And, so far as appears to me, it would be an evident Breach of the Law of the Gospel, as well as of Nature, to bestow upon those the Bread of Charity, who might earn and eat their own Bread, if they did not shamefully idle away their Time.[21]

This social policy was based upon the theological view that stressed man's sinfulness, which only God's grace could change. In that the social attitude echoed a certain basic theological understanding, we might call those who espoused it "Social Calvinists." Just as ministers customarily warmed the faithful with visions of Heaven while warning sneerers of the dangers of Hell, so Social Calvinists tried to prod the poor onto the right path by using not only positive incentives ("Work, Be Independent") but negative ones as well ("Don't Work, Go Hungry"). They constantly argued that a biblical understanding of theology was the first step toward an accurate view of anthropology, which in turn was needed to keep help from turning into its opposite.

In practice, since work was readily available, there was no talk of structural unemployment; instead, the major type of poverty dealt with was caused by a calamity such as fire and earthquake, or by crippling accident or early death (often by disease). Sufferers of that kind were to receive personal care, often in neighbors' homes. For those who were alcoholics or of "disorderly" temperament, and refused to work, towns built workhouses. Rules were strict; by-laws seven through twelve of the Chelmsford workhouse noted that:

7. The master of the workhouse shall have power to reward the faithful and industrious by granting favors and…to punish at his discretion the idle, stubborn, disorderly and disobedient by immediate confinement without any food other than bread and water.

8. The master of the workhouse shall cause said house and furniture to be kept clean and in good order, and shall cause habits of cleanliness, neatness and decency to be strictly observed by all persons received into said workhouse.

9. The master of the workhouse shall cause the Lord's Day to be strictly observed.

10. Every person who may be received into said workhouse or be a member thereof must obey the orders and regulations thereof and the commands of the master, and will be required by him diligently to work and labor as he shall direct, according to age, health and capacity.

11. Every person who shall absent himself from the said workhouse...shall be deemed to be an idle, stubborn and disorderly person, and punished accordingly.
12. The use of spiritous liquors is strictly prohibited except when the master, physician or overseers of the workhouse shall otherwise order; and no person shall be allowed to have or keep in their possession or bring or receive any spiritous liquors into said workhouse.[22]

Punishment for refusal to work and continued alcoholism could include whipping. But enforcing work among the able-bodied was not seen as oppressive. The objective was to treat all as human beings, as members of the community with responsibilities, rather than as animals.

Colonial Americans hoped that the proper training of children, poor as well as rich, would forestall the need for such enforcement in later life. "Charity schools" were founded with rationales such as one offered in a sermon by Thomas Bacon of Maryland:

We are indeed, my Brethren, by God's Blessing, in Possession of a very plenteous Land. We ought to shew our Thankfulness to him by endeavouring to promote his Worship among us, which can never effectually be done without some such Provision as this, for bringing up the poorer Sort (who make up the Bulk of a People) in his Knowledge and Fear, and in the Way of providing for themselves by honest Industry. Should we neglect it, and by Vice and Immorality greatly prevail by our Negligence, may it

not justly provoke him in his Anger to dispossess us, as he
did the Israelites....[23]

This consciousness was present both within the explicitly Calvinist
church of New England and the broader church of the Middle and
Southern states.[24] Bacon's school was for poor children both white and
black, and the emphasis on equipping all children to read the Bible
continued until in the 1830s parts of the South overreacted to aboli-
tionist threats.

The idea of schools for all and work for all carried over into the
Northwest Territory, where justices of the peace appointed "overseers
of the poor." Their job was to set up poorhouses that would be maintained by the work of their inhabitants. Even the "most degraded"
person would not have to starve, for the poorhouse (miserable though
it might be) would be available. On the other hand, no one was *entitled
to* receive any material provision outside the poorhouse:

> If any poor person shall refuse to be lodged, kept, main-
> tained and employed in such house or houses, he or she
> shall not be entitled to receive relief from the overseers
> during such refusal.[25]

Individuals and churches could and did help the "worthy poor" out
of tight jams. But mandated "outdoor relief"—provision outside the
poorhouse—was seen as making it too easy to avoid the responsibilities charged to every human being.

The final pre–1800 poverty-fighting principle was an emphasis
on family relationships. Nothing that could contribute to the breakup
of families, or to the loss of the family's central role as support of its

members, was encouraged. This understanding also was reflected in the early laws in the Northwest Territory, which decreed that parents, grandparents, and children of "every poor, old, blind, lame and impotent person, or other poor person not able to work" should "relieve and maintain every such poor person," unless they themselves were economically incapable.[26] Those immediate relatives who would not offer such support were fined heavily. And thus, the final leg of a stool on which every poor person could sit—a three-legged stool of family, church, and neighborhood—was put in place.

But that stool was steadiest in the countryside and in small towns. As cities grew, more organization was necessary if those in need through no fault of their own were to be helped. When the Constitution still was young, orphanages were established in New York, Philadelphia, Baltimore, Boston, and other cities. And some groups began providing small monthly allowances to supplement the earnings of widowed mothers who worked for a livelihood. "Widows who have the charge of two, three, four or five children," a Boston association declared, "are unequivocally proper subjects of alms." Even so, the Society for the Relief of Poor Widows with Small Children (founded in New York in 1797) was cautious in distributing aid. Volunteers checked the means, character, and circumstances of each applicant to make sure that relatives were unable to help and alcoholism was not contributing to the general misery.

Aid, furthermore, almost always was in kind—food, coal, cloth—rather than in cash. During the winter of 1797–98, the society helped 98 widows with 223 children; by 1800, 152 widows, with 420 children under the age of 12, were listed on its books. The emphasis was aid to find work, because the society would accept only those clients who "would rather eat their own bread, hardly earned, than that of others with idleness." In one year widows were given nearly three thousand yards of linen, and other materials, in order to make shirts and other articles of clothing in their own homes.[27] Other groups also tried to facilitate work within the home: the Female Charitable Society of Bedford, New York, organized in 1816, distributed raw wool to the "industrious poor" among women so they could spin and weave the material into finished products.

Orphans were aided by groups such as the New York Orphan Asylum Society, which in 1806 rented a two-story frame house in Greenwich Village and hired a "pious and respectable man and his wife" as superintendent and matron. According to the society's constitution, only orphans deprived of both parents could be admitted. Their care and training also was prescribed:

> The orphans shall be educated, fed and clothed at the expense of the Society and at the Asylum. They must have religious instruction, moral example, and habits of industry inculcated on their minds.[28]

The asylum—"asylum," in those days, meant merely a place of security—opened with twelve orphans in 1806, but soon expanded to house two hundred orphans. After a few years the society received a state subsidy for its care of orphans; the records do not show that the curriculum and procedures of the asylum were compromised by such aid, nor that campaigns were launched to establish asylums under direct state control.

The decades from the Revolution to the Civil War saw a gradual extending of concern, but always in connection with the primary idea of helping those who could not help themselves. In 1791 the New York Dispensary began to care for the sick poor, and dispensaries in Baltimore and Charleston followed in 1801. In 1794 the Massachusetts Charitable Fire Society launched its work of "relieving such as suffer by fire...." And in Boston the Fragment Society, established in 1812, provided material for clothes-making and in other ways over the next three decades assisted 10,275 families faced with unanticipated problems. The society's goal was not only material aid but personal involvement: "Let us penetrate the lanes and by-ways of the city, enter the abodes of poverty and distress, and show to the destitute inmates that we sympathize in their sufferings and commiserate with them in their losses."[29]

In the growing urban areas, married women were not expected to have a paying job, and this proved vital to the expansion of voluntaristic compassion. Beginning with the establishment of a Female Humane Association to aid indigent Baltimore widows in 1798, women were often in the forefront of benevolent activity. Female Charitable Societies and Ladies Benevolent Societies, designed initially to aid widows and orphans, started up in New York City and Philadelphia, spread to smaller Northern cities such as Newburyport and Salem, Massachusetts, and finally reached the South as well. Women in Petersburg, Virginia, petitioned the legislature in 1812 to set up an orphan asylum, for they were "deeply impressed with the forlorn and helpless Situation of poor Orphan female Children... and wish to snatch [them] from ignorance and ruin."[30] A national organization founded in 1834, the American Female Guardian Society, quickly started setting up "Homes for the Friendless" in many cities.[31]

Religious beliefs underlay most activities. The Female Domestic Missionary Society for the Poor began to distribute Bibles and provide schooling in poor sections of New York City in 1816. Groups such as the Massachusetts Society for Promoting Christian Knowledge (which received funds from thirty local women's groups in 1817) and the New Hampshire Missionary Society (supported by fifty local women's organizations) saw themselves as fighting against both spiritual and material poverty.[32] And a Baltimore Female Association for the Relief of Distressed Objects, established in 1808, had a mandate that went beyond economic poverty; its members were to "search out distressed objects, to administer to their relief."[33]

These patterns prevailed in the South as well as in the North. In Charleston, the Ladies Benevolent Society, formed in 1813, aided the senile, both black and white; those the society helped in 1825 included a Mrs. Cowie who suffered from blindness and leprosy and whose body was "a perfect skeleton," Clarissa and Mary, two crippled black women, and Mary McNeile, a free black with leprosy.[34] Sometimes the rich were stunned by what they learned of conditions among the poor; one newspaper, the *Southern Evangelical Intelligencer*, reported that society members had witnessed

> scenes of distress, want, misery, and woe, scarcely to be conceived by those who have never entered the frail and unsheltered tenements of this city, where poverty, sickness and wretchedness dwell.[35]

Soon other Charleston groups, including the Female Charitable Association, were engaged in similar tasks.

The ideas spread. In Richmond, the Charitable Association of Young Men agreed in 1817 to help "indigent and distressed persons." In Columbia, South Carolina, the Ladies' Society for the Female Poor and Especially the Relief of Poor Widows with Small Children tried to have a reach as long as its name. During the 1820s, groups such as the United Female Benevolent Society of North Carolina (Fayetteville), the Female Benevolent Society (Newbern, N.C.), the Female Benevolent Society (Raleigh), and the Female Charitable Society (St. Louis) emerged. After a religious revival in 1822, the Presbyterian women of Petersburg, Virginia, established over the next several years an Education Society, a Young Ladies' Missionary Society, a Married Ladies' Missionary Society, a Tract Distribution Society, and a Dorcas Society, all devoted to aiding the poor; they also contributed to an interdenominational Female Bible Society.[36] By the 1830s so much of this kind of activity was going on that American Christendom was said to be promoting a "Benevolent Empire." The poor received Bibles, tracts, lessons at missions and Sunday schools, and material help when necessary and "rightful." Gifted but poor young men who wanted to be ministers received scholarships.

Social thought of this period did not insist on equal treatment for all who were in trouble. The goal, rather, was to serve individuals who had unavoidable problems. Along those lines the American Asylum for the Education and Instruction of the Deaf and Dumb opened in Hartford in 1817, as did a similar institution for the blind in 1829. Orphans, clearly not responsible for their plight, continued to receive major attention. During the 1830s in New York State alone, orphan asylums and societies opened their doors in Albany, Utica, New York City, Brooklyn, Troy, Buffalo, Rochester, and many other cities.[37] One incomplete list of orphanages that sprang up across the country during the 1830s included Boston; Washington; New Haven; Cincinnati; Providence; Philadelphia; Mobile; Bond Hill, Ohio; and Bangor, Maine. And in the 1840s, orphanages opened in Baltimore; Avondale, Ohio; Richmond; Savannah; Syracuse; Nashville; Natchez; Poughkeepsie;

Newark; Watertown, New York; Baton Rouge; Worcester; Chicago; Midway, Kentucky; and Hudson, New York.[38]

These activities were not restricted to Protestants; in 1827 Catholic women in Baltimore formed the Maria Marthian Society for assistance to those of "all denominations, ages, sexes, and colours."[39] As late as 1830 Catholics made up less than 4 percent of the U.S. population, but as more immigrants arrived they established St. Vincent de Paul societies along theistic principles, set up hospitals and orphanages, and built institutions such as New York's House of the Good Shepherd for "the reformation of fallen women and girls."[40] Theistic charity also was evident among Jewish pioneers who established a Hebrew Benevolent Society (1784) in Charleston, a Hebrew Benevolent and Orphan Asylum Society (1822) and Hebrew Relief Society (1831) in New York, and other societies for relief of the "poor sick" and of destitute pregnant women "before and after confinement."[41]

Meanwhile, additional problems were surfacing: What about those who were temporarily handicapped by illness or injury, or who had some other short-term problem? And how could programs be administered when small towns grew into large cities? The importance of personal involvement of rich and poor was still stressed year after year. At a time when communities were generally small, and where giver and receiver often knew each other, this was neither abstract nor unrealistic. Cities were growing throughout the antebellum period but were still generally compact, with rich and poor living near each other. Those who were better-off regularly saw different neighborhoods as they walked to work, and they worshipped among neighbors from various social and economic backgrounds. Thoroughgoing economic segregation was rare. But what would happen when that changed?

Some early attempts to strengthen American compassion against the storms to come stressed education of the charity-giving public. Each year from 1818 to 1824 the Society for the Prevention of Pauperism in the City of New York, a group whose goal was to attack destitution of all kinds, printed in its annual reports a list of ten causes of pauperism. The first three causes were ignorance, idleness, and intemperance; then came "want of economy," imprudent and hasty marriages, and lotteries; and then three specific institutions—pawnbrokers, brothels, and gambling houses.[42] This list, with its emphasis on personal failings and then-institutional lures, typified most social thought of the time, but a new element appeared: the tenth cause was "charities that gave away money too freely." There were not many of these, but in a growing economy any ease of subsidy was viewed as destructive both morally and materially.

The report also firmly distinguished between "the unavoidable necessities of the poor" and those that resulted from wrongdoing. English pauper laws that did not distinguish among different types of poverty resulted in some benefits for all, the society argued, but "stingy" ones; the society, for its part, believed that the worthy poor should be relieved "amply." Widows and orphans ought not be in absolute penury because of the sudden disaster that had befallen them. But on the other hand, barriers to independence should be avoided: "every system of charity," the society declared, should

> lay the powerful hand of moral and legal restriction upon
> every thing that contributes, directly and necessarily, to
> introduce an artificial extent of suffering; and to diminish,
> in any class of the community, a reliance upon its own

powers of body and mind for an independent and virtuous support.[43]

A report from Boston in 1835 declared similarly that charity "is abused, whenever it ministers in any way to a neglect of forethought and providence."[44]

The Boston report indicated a second kind of preparation for the anticipated storms: coalition-building among the charity organizations of the growing cities and agreement on common principles. Some twenty-three Boston charity societies declared in 1835 that recipients should believe it "disgraceful to depend upon almsgiving, as long as a capacity of self-support is retained." The societies agreed that

> to give to one who begs... or in any way to supersede the necessity of industry, of forethought, and of proper self-restraint and self-denial, is at once to do wrong, and to encourage the receivers of our alms to wrong doing.

Echoing Mather's warning of 150 years before, the societies also noted that

> a clear perception, and a faithful avoidance of the evils, of an injudicious bestowment of alms, is essential to Christian alms-giving.... We are not unnecessarily to do evil by the means by which we may, and should do good.[45]

For that reason the societies agreed that relief should be given only after a "personal examination of each case," and "not in money, but in the necessaries required in the case."

A third emphasis was cultural. It was important to promote the "right stuff" by publicizing as role models individuals who had received much and had then given of their time as well as their treasure. Merchant Stephen Girard became the subject of many popular biographical sketches.[46] Born in France in 1750, Girard left home as a boy, sailed for a dozen years, settled in Philadelphia at the start of the Revolution, and accumulated a fortune in the shipping business over the next two decades. But it was his work during the yellow fever epidemic of 1793, rather than his business acumen, that won him wide renown. Girard, who had received previous exposure to the disease, took charge of and paid bills for a hospital during that and subsequent epidemics. But he also spent months nursing the inmates himself, and supplied food and fuel to sufferers and their families. Later, he took many orphans into his own home, and upon his death made a bequest that established a school for poor orphan boys.[47]

Furthermore, it was important to impregnate American society with the idea of small-scale, personal involvement, rather than large-scale administered relief. Children from their earliest school years were given texts with concepts that taught far more than the particular subject matter. William H. McGuffey placed in an 1844 *McGuffey's Reader* a wonderful little dialogue between a "Mr. Fan-torn" and a "Mr. Goodman." Parts of it went like this:

> Mr. Fantom: I despise a narrow field. O for the reign of universal benevolence! I want to make all mankind good and happy.
>
> Mr. Goodman: Dear me! Sure that must be a wholesale sort of a job: had you not better try your hand at a *town* or *neighborhood* first?

Mr. Fantom: Sir, I have a plan in my head for relieving the miseries of the *whole world*....

Mr. Goodman: The utmost extent of my ambition at present is, to redress the wrongs of a poor apprentice, who has been cruelly used by his master....

Mr. Fantom: You must not apply to me for the redress of such petty grievances.... It is provinces, empires, continents, that the benevolence of the philosopher embraces; every one can do a little paltry good to his next neighbor.

McGuffey gave Mr. Goodman a good comeback: "Every one *can*, but I do not see that every one *does*.... [You] have such a noble zeal for the *millions*, [yet] feel so little compassion for the units."

Compassion for individuals meant avoiding stingy charity to all; instead of spreading bits of clockwork charity among those who "will not themselves toil while they can live upon the toils of others," the goal was to provide ample help to those who "were cruelly used."[48] Charity groups were aware that the task of discernment was not easy, and that sometimes extraordinarily difficult problems emerged. For example, charity societies could agree that alms

should not be given to the drunkard. But the wife and children of the drunkard...may be without food...and wholly innocent in respect to the causes of their destitution.... Let him who thinks it easy always to act wisely in [this situation] give us the light of his counsel and example.

Even in such grey cases, however, the groups could agree that families of drunkards should not be given money, and that "even relief in kind should never be given to the families of the intemperate, beyond the demands of unquestionable necessity."[49]

■   ■   ■

The emphasis on an obligation to change is criticized by many twentieth-century historians. Nineteenth-century practice is frequently described as "moralistic," "paternalistic," and "controlling." Such criticism has a point.[50] Those, for example, who established Erring Woman's Refuges did not resort to euphemism either in naming their institutions or in defining their missions: they wanted to rehabilitate young women "urged into a life of vice … at a period when the young heart is confiding and unsuspecting."[51] Refuge administrators demanded a willingness to change not by the performance of a difficult task but by the taking of one small step (such as entering the door of a building entitled "Erring…."). Their goal was not to weed out people—for they saw all as created after God's image, and thus very different from weeds—but to require the kind of self-confrontation that is evident at a modern Alcoholics Anonymous meeting when a person says, "I am an alcoholic."

There was a hardness in those days, based on the belief that some individuals needed to suffer in order to be willing to change. In 1821, Levi Woodbury and Thomas Whipple, in a report on New Hampshire's pauper laws, argued that "the poverty which proceeds from improvidence and vice ought to feel the consequences and penalties which God has annexed."[52] In the Calvinistic sense, time spent in the pit could be what was needed to save a life from permanent debauchery (and a soul from Hell). No one, however, ought to be left to starve—as a committee of the Massachusetts legislature decided in 1831, "Absolute distress and want must be relieved, whatever causes may have produced it"—but "tough love," in today's parlance, was standard.[53] Those who gave material aid without requiring even the smallest return were considered as much a threat to true compassion as those who turned their backs on neighbors and brothers.

But even at the end of the nineteenth century, it was not the toughness of earlier times that was most remembered, but the kindness. American social conditions of the past seemed almost paradisaical to charity leaders slouching through crowded urban slums. Francis Peabody told a meeting of New York's United Hebrew Charities in 1896 that the charity of several generations before "was as simple and natural a duty as the care of one's family. It was the friendly act of a well-informed neighbor."[54] Remarks by Peabody and others could, of course, be seen as nostalgia, and yet, eyewitnesses of American compassion early in the century made similar comments.

One of the little-known travelers, D. Griffiths, Jr., was amazed at the contrast between life in Ohio during the 1830s and that of the English cities and towns he had left behind. Griffiths was impressed not to see a

> signboard nailed up against the wall.... "Beggars, Gipsies, and Trampers of every description, found in a state of vagrancy in this Parish, will be dealt with according to law." The Traveller's feelings are not harrowed at every turn by the sight of some squalid, ragged, wretched object in human shape. Indeed, during the whole two years of my residence in America, I saw but one beggar.[55]

Griffiths explained the absence of beggars by citing economic growth, an open countryside, and the compassion that those who were better-off showed for those rendered destitute by unforseeable circumstances. One "disabled Scotchman," he wrote, received free "board amongst the farmers, sometimes at one house, and sometimes at another." In another town, members of a Dutch family impoverished by sickness were "provided with doctor and nurse, and in fact with everything needful for them, until they recovered."[56]

The most famous foreign observer of the early nineteenth century, Alexis de Tocqueville, noted similarly that Americans "display general compassion." In the interaction of a person doing well with a problem-laden neighbor, Tocqueville observed, "personal feeling is mingled with his pity and makes himself suffer while the body of his fellow creature is in torment."[57] Tocqueville contrasted America's "free institutions" with those of Europe, where the

> state almost exclusively undertakes to supply bread to the hungry, assistance and shelter to the sick, work to the idle, and to act as the sole reliever of all kinds of misery.

Reasons for the difference included the existence of small communities and strong religious ideas: Americans, Tocqueville observed, feel "compassion for the sufferings of one another, when they are brought together by easy and frequent intercourse."[58]

Those involved with fighting poverty gave additional explanations for the lack of "pauperism"—lackadaisical poverty—in small towns. One factor was shame: the Society for the Prevention of Pauperism observed that many were tempted to "improvidence, vice, and recklessness," but few were "indifferent to the shame and reproach of a total forfeiture of the goodwill, respect, and confidence" that such activities would bring. In a small town, the society noted, those who acted in embarrassing ways were not "overlooked, nor could [they] escape in the crowd."[59] Another factor was an expanding economy with a convenient frontier: Since the able-bodied had opportunities to work, except during short periods of business panic, and since young men could always go west and grow up with the country, it was commonly said that "no man who is temperate, frugal, and willing to work, need suffer or become a pauper for want of employment."[60]

But probably most important was the state of mind of those who gave help. In 1990 Christopher Edley, Jr., former issues director for Michael Dukakis, wrote in the *Legal Times* that he did not give money to panhandlers because "I pay taxes for social workers to determine who is truly needy."[61] Edley's decision was right, as we will see, but his rationale was wrong, and would have been horrifying to democrats of the early nineteenth century who opposed reliance on government. As Charleston minister Thomas S. Grimke argued exuberantly in 1827,

> Formerly, the community was a mere bystander, a mere spectator, as to all that was going on. The government, a few ancient, well-endowed institutions, and a handful of individuals, were the only agents.

He concluded, "Now the people are everything, and do everything, through the medium of a vast multitude of organized associations."[62]

CHAPTER TWO

Turning Cities into Countryside

As American cities began to grow, those who looked ahead studied the experience of those in the British Isles who were already tasting the future. Americans observed the establishment in England's newly industrialized cities of largely indiscriminate "outdoor relief"—subsidizing individuals living in their own homes rather than in poorhouses. They also noted with concern that the availability of such aid would lead many who did not really need it to receive help and become dependent on it. In particular, they watched the fight put up against it by Scottish theologian Thomas Chalmers, rector of St. John's Parish in Glasgow from 1819 to 1823, and later occupant of a chair in philosophy at St. Andrew's College.

Chalmers' prose was often ornate, but four key principles can be extricated. First, Chalmers insisted on a distinction between pauperism (a state of unnecessary dependence, characterized by intellectual lassitude and spiritual malaise) and poverty. Second, he argued that legal or statutory relief tended to pauperize because it removed the need for self-help and discipline. Third, he stressed the biblical obligation of the better-off to become personally involved with the poor. Fourth, he argued that those who were poor because of their own failings needed to indicate a willingness to change modes of thinking or acting that were dragging them down; if they did not, those who wished to help were to step away for a time, renew the offer, and be willing to step away again for a time if hearts had not changed.[1]

Chalmers lost the political battle in Glasgow generally but gained permission to try out his alternative plan in a specially created ten thousand-person district—an early enterprise zone—officially titled the Parish of St. John. Chalmers said he would meet the expenses of all *needed* relief in the district, one of the poorest in Glasgow, by asking parishioners for donations. His only stipulation was that state authorities and others who wanted to give indiscriminately agree to stay out. They did, and Chalmers divided his parish into twenty-five districts, putting a deacon in charge of each. When anyone asked for relief, the appropriate deacon investigated in order "to discriminate and beneficially assist the really necessitous and deserving poor...."[2]

The result was extraordinary. Chalmers' Sunday evening church collections for deaconal purposes increased, for givers were confident that the funds would be used wisely. The cost of relief also dropped as better-off church members used personal counseling and established savings banks and work exchanges to "foster amongst the poor the habits of industry, providence, frugality, saving and honest desire to rise in the world, and simple dependence on their own exertions."[3] Lives changed:

> In a few years the established pauperism of the parish sank from 164 to 99...in a population of ten thousand, but twenty new cases arose in four years, of which five were the results of illegitimate births or family desertion, and two of disease.[4]

Ripples were visible: savings in relief combined with the charity of the parishioners allowed St. John's to endow a parish school and pay the salaries of three teachers.

Chalmers himself attributed success to God's blessings and man's management. Chalmers' program was described as "thoroughly Christian in its severity and its generosities."[5] He argued that God blessed his desire to avoid stinginess with the worthy poor and demoralization among those who needed a push. He also explained that dividing up his parish into what he called "manageable portions of civic territory" was crucial, for

> there is a very great difference in respect to its practical influence between a task that is indefinite and a task that is clearly seen to be overtakable.[6]

The need to provide relief to a large city "has the effect to paralyze," Chalmers noted. But personal knowledge of those who needed help in one small area of the city tended to "quicken exertion."

The Chalmers idea was not, in fact, foreign to American thinking. Shortly before Chalmers put his plan into effect in Glasgow, the Society for the Prevention of Pauperism in the City of New York announced a plan

> To divide the city into very small districts, and to appoint, from the members of the Society, two or three Visitors for each district, whose duty it shall be to become acquainted with the inhabitants of the district, to visit frequently the families of those who are in indigent circumstances ... [and] to administer encouragement or admonition, as they may find occasion.[7]

But the New York group had problems in execution, and in any event the concept was ahead of its time. New York was still a small city, and Americans accustomed to small towns and pastoral settings felt little need of organization, since those in need would be known to their potential helpers. Not until a recession in the late 1830s led to the quick rise of thirty relief agencies in New York City alone did Americans pay attention.

The effectiveness of those thirty agencies, which were devoted to passing out soup to all who asked, received careful analysis. All agreed that there was need for fast action, but an evaluation report in 1843 concluded that some, in wanting to do so much so fast, failed to establish personal relationships with recipients, and did not sufficiently discriminate between the needy and the lazy.[8] It was agreed that some of the worthy poor suffered—but observers concluded that the reason might have been too much aid indiscriminately handed out at first, rather than too little. That is because charitable individuals who wished "to improve as well as to relieve" would give confidently and generously only when they knew that the charity would help rather than harm. When they were not sure, contributions leveled off, and since those funds affected both the worthy and unworthy, the poor who did deserve support were worse off than they would otherwise have been.

A new group, the New York Association for Improving the Condition of the Poor (AICP), grew out of these concerns with promiscuous charity. It put into effect the Chalmers district plan, and thus made large projects workable. AICP volunteers promoted participation of the working poor in savings banks, benefit societies, and life insurance programs, so that families could remain independent during unemployment or after calamities. The better-off supplied materials for domestic labor of the poor and helped them to find jobs; promoted church involvement and Sunday schools; and tried to shut down liquor shops and stop the general public from giving money to beggars, who usually would spend the money in those shops.[9]

The AICP also distinguished between its "disciplined" ability to help and the limitations inevitable in a governmental program "bound to relieve all not otherwise legally provided for." AICP leaders vowed "to aid those whom it can physically and morally elevate, and no others." They asked,

> If the Institution fails in this discrimination, and has no
> higher aim than the Almshouse, why should it exist at all?
> and why should those already heavily taxed for the public
> poor intrust funds to this charity?[10]

They pointed out that contributors were entrusting them with funds "solely" to give generous help to the "worthy poor" and nothing to the lazy: "Take away this consideration, and the motives for [AICP] support would cease."[11]

To be effective with the poor and to gain the confidence of the better-off, the AICP not only fought "indiscriminate charity" but also deemphasized material distribution; instead, the AICP stressed "home visitations" designed to guide in matters of religious observance and to advise concerning thrift, hard work, and temperance.[12] The AICP, pointedly distinguishing between poverty and pauperism, worked to keep the "poverty-stricken sons and daughters of misfortune" from following "the course of pauperism."[13] Its volunteers organized district by district as in the Chalmers plan, visited applicants for assistance, ascertained the facts, and provided references for work or for grants of coal or food, along with advice concerning the importance of school attendance for children and temperance for all. The visitors dispensed no cash.

Robert M. Hartley, secretary of the AICP for over three decades, had the typical experience and understanding among charity workers of his day. Born in 1796, he volunteered as a gospel tract distributor in New York City beginning in the 1820s. Wondering why so few were receptive to his evangelical efforts, he decided that alcoholism was the problem. As a leader of the City Temperance Society, Hartley visited distilleries, debated their owners or managers, and wrote a temperance pamphlet entitled "Way to Make the Poor Rich." He pointed out that twelve-and-a-half cents a day spent on drink amounted to $45.62 a year, which at that time was enough to buy three tons of coal, 1 load of wood, 2 barrels of flour, 200 pounds of Indian meal, 200 pounds of pork, and 8 bushels of potatoes; "into a house thus supplied," Hartley wrote, "hunger and cold could not enter."[14]

But as the years went by, Hartley saw that alcoholism often was part of a bundle of spiritual and material problems. He became interested in the entire bundle. Hartley argued that since material deprivation was often the tip of the iceberg, "to remove the evil we must remove the causes; and these being chiefly moral—whatever subsidiary appliances may be used—they admit only moral remedies."[15] A booklet distributed by the AICP stated that "every able-bodied man in this country may support himself and family comfortably; if you do not, it is probably owing to idleness, improvidence, or intemperance."[16] The solution was piety, frugality, and industry; the way to help able-bodied males confront sinful tendencies was to make sure they "should be compelled to work or left to suffer the consequences of their misconduct."[17]

In this way and others, Hartley echoed (and often quoted) the apostle Paul's warning to the Thessalonians some 1800 years before: "We hear that some among you are idle. They are not busy; they are busy-bodies. Such people we command and urge in the Lord Jesus Christ to settle down and earn the bread they eat."[18]

Many urban groups attempted to find tasks for able-bodied women as well as men. Female Benevolent Societies, such as the one at Calvary Church, set up programs to help "deserving poor Protestant women" by providing them with work at "sewing paid for in cash."[19] The Ladies' Depository, the New York House and School of Industry, and the Society for the Employment and Relief of Poor Women had similar programs. The Institution of Mercy and the Ladies' Christian Union were designed for the "protection and relief of poor girls" and "to promote temporal, moral, and religious welfare of young women," while the House of Mercy was for "the shelter and reformation of fallen women." Catholic priests and volunteers from St. Patrick's, St. Joseph's, and other parishes provided relief and moral instruction.

By the 1840s and 1850s societies to help the "worthy poor" generally—and not only widows or orphans—were springing up in every major American city, mainly along Chalmers' lines. The Boston Provident Association, established in 1851, gave food, clothes, or coal, rather than money, to those willing to work and in temporary need, but it refused to aid drunkards. Association supporters were asked to give beggars not money but cards proposing a visit to association offices, where volunteers would examine their needs, make job referrals, and provide food and temporary shelter for those deserving help. It developed both a list of "the worthy" and a "black record," which in 1853 contained 201 names of "imposters"—able-bodied persons who refused to work.[20]

Those who were ill generally received help (given nineteenth-century medicine, sometimes questionable help) regardless of their background. Before the Civil War, medical relief for the poor was available in Manhattan through the New York, Eastern, Northern, and North-Western Dispensaries, the New York Eye and Ear Infirmary, and St. Luke's Hospital. Groups such as the New York Female Assistance Society also provided "relief of the sick poor...,"[21] and Jewish groups such as the Ladies' Bikur Cholim Society relieved the "poor sick."[22] Similar organizations formed in other cities, and informal help was available in small towns.

Throughout, the goal was to make city relations as much as possible like those of the countryside. The AICP in 1855 again emphasized the importance of individuals taking personal action:

> there seems to be an increasing number of families and
> individuals who are willing to take charge of one or more,
> often of several, poor families. If this could be universally
> done, the surest steps might be taken to all the ends of a
> true and full civic and Christian economy.[23]

These volunteers generally had religious motivations. Taking charge of several poor families was stressful, as the AICP explained in 1854:

> The work is vast, complex, and difficult. To visit from time
> to time all the abodes of want in a population of 650,000
> souls—to discriminate between honest poverty and
> imposture—to elevate and not debase by relief—to arrest
> the vagrant—reclaim the intemperate—sympathize with
> the suffering—counsel the erring—stimulate the

indolent—give work to the idle—...is an undertaking of
all others, one of the most arduous and difficult.[24]

Given the difficulties of helping, charity leaders believed that few
would volunteer many hours each week if they did not see themselves
as soul-savers and not just bread-providers.

Leaders and volunteers both understood, moreover, that the most
vital kind of help involved a change in world view, not just a temporary
adjustment of worldly conditions. In recent years, conventionally liberal
historians have tended to minimize the usefulness of the groups that
"often tried to spread religion along with alms" and "paid little attention
to the underlying causes of destitution or the long-term needs of their
clients."[25] But the underlying causes and long-term needs *were* religious,
early nineteenth-century charity workers consistently argued. "Until the
feelings, opinions, and practices of the great mass are governed by sound
principles, and Christianity pervades and renovates the habits of social
and civic life," the AICP declared in 1854, "there is no reliable foundation
for prosperity." The AICP's goal was to use "sacred" as well as "secular
motives, to help to rectify what was wrong in individual character...."[26]
Catholic and Jewish groups agreed.

Reports show these patterns of charity spreading across the nation.
Before the Civil War a Brooklyn AICP stood beside its Manhattan
cousin, as did a Baltimore AICP and related societies in Boston,
Philadelphia, Chicago, St. Louis, and other cities. The South had fewer
cities but similar patterns of voluntarism, as Suzanne Lebsock's detailed
look at Petersburg, Virginia, shows. Lebsock, however, is typical among
modern historians in her bewilderment at the surprising data she
found; describing Petersburg's economic difficulties during the 1830s
and 1840s and the lack of governmental response, Lebsock's continual

puzzlement causes her to sputter, "How people got by, to repeat, is a mystery."[27]

It was a mystery, but it worked.[28] The crucial understanding was simple yet profound: people got by when other people took a personal interest in them. Ministers told their congregations that it was fine to contribute money, but the larger need, and more difficult task, was personal:

> To cast a contribution into the box brought to the hand, or to attend committees and anniversaries, are very trifling exercises of Christian self-denial and devotion, compared with what is demanded in the weary perambulations through the street, the contact with filth, and often with rude and repulsive people, the facing of disease, and distress, and all manner of heart-rending and heart-frightening scenes, and all the trials of faith, patience, and hope, which are incident to the duty we urge.[29]

Churches and charity organizations understood that professionals should be facilitators of aid, not major or sole suppliers. Ruffner agreed that "[t]here must, of course, be officers, teachers, missionaries employed to live in the very midst of the wretchedness, and to supervise and direct all the efforts of the people." But he added, "Mark you! these officers are not to stand between the giver and receiver, but to bring *giver and receiver together*."[30]

The city could reflect the countryside when discipline and love were twins, not opposites; when obligations as well as rights were emphasized; when mutual obligation rather than mere transfer of material was the rule. Effective help in the cities, as in the countryside, had to be personal; those who were better-off were to *suffer with* the troubled. It had to be conditional; when the recipient was responsible for his plight, he was to indicate a willingness to change. It had to honor those among the poor who did not give up; they had to be treated not as chumps but as human beings who deserved great "respect for character."[31]

And when the countryside could not be brought to the city—move city inhabitants to the country. Robert Hartley of the AICP, responding during one recession to questions of whether the poor could find jobs in New York City, claimed they in time could, but added that there was no need to wait: "To the sober and industrious we say, 'Stay not here in idleness and want, when the wide and fertile country offers you employment and all that is needful for comfort and elevation.' " The AICP's willingness to help with moving costs gave legitimacy to the tough message to the hesitant: "You will gossip and smoke, neglect your children and beg, live in filth and discomfort, drink and carouse, do almost anything rather than work, and expect, forsooth, to be supported by charity."[32]

Some poor adults moved; most did not. The strategy was more successful when applied to orphaned or abandoned children, who often suffered grievously as large cities became centers of anonymity at the midpoint of the nineteenth century. Hundreds of homeless children—some orphaned, some abandoned by westward-bound fathers, some runaways—roamed the slum areas of New York and other cities during the 1850s, until Charles Brace and other charity leaders found a way to send the city into the country.

Brace, a Yale graduate, writer, and missionary, had felt called to gain first-hand knowledge of how the orphaned and abandoned lived.

Settling in New York City, Brace visited "centres of crime and misery" and described them colorfully:

> There was the infamous German "Rag-pickers' Den" in Pitt and Willett Streets—double rows of houses, flaunting with dirty banners, and the yards heaped up with bones and refuse.... Then came the murderous blocks in Cherry and Water Streets, where so many dark crimes were continually committed, and where the little girls who flitted about with baskets and wrapped in old shawls became familiar with vice before they were out of childhood.
>
> There were the thieves' Lodging-houses, in the lower wards, where the street-boys were trained by older pick-pockets and burglars for their nefarious calling... the notorious rogues' den in Laurens Street—"Rotten Row"—where, it was said, no drove of animals could pass by and keep its numbers intact; and further above, the community of young garroters and burglars around "Hammersley Street and Cottage Place."
>
> And, still more north, the dreadful population of youthful ruffians and degraded men and women in "Poverty Lane," near Sixteeenth and Seventeenth streets and Ninth Avenue, which subsequently ripened into the infamous "Nineteenth-street Gang."[33]

As Brace assessed problems and needs he thought about causes. Brace did not underestimate the influence of material surroundings, particularly overcrowding, which he termed "the one great misfortune of New York," an evil that "sows pestilence and breeds every species of criminal habits."[34] In response, he called for "an underground railway with cheap workman's trains" to connect Manhattan with Westchester County, New Jersey, and Long Island.[35] He hoped, that is, for a dispersal of the population as immigrants moved west and south, but he recognized that, harsh as conditions were, some people saw little alternative, and others loved "the crowd and bustle of a city."[36]

Brace also hoped for political change. Noting that high rents forced families to crowd into small apartments and sometimes take in boarders as well, Brace showed how high taxes that supported a corrupt city administration were part of the problem, not a road to solution:

> A cheap and honest government of the masses in New York would at once lower taxation and bring down rents. The enormous prices demanded for one or two small rooms in a tenement-house are a measure (in part) of the cost of our city government.[37]

Lower taxes could also spur the construction of "Model Houses," tenements with good ventilation and a limit on crowding that could still produce profits for their owners.

But Brace's major hope was for moral change. He shared Robert Hartley's understanding of charitable experience:

> Those who have much to do with alms-giving and plans of human improvement soon see how superficial and comparatively useless all assistance or organization is, which does not touch habits of life and the inner forces which form character. The poor helped each year become poorer in force and independence.

Brace argued that "the best politics and the most complete form of government are nothing if the individual morality be not there." He saw a theological base for that morality: "Christianity is the highest education of character. Give the poor that, and only seldom will either alms or punishment be necessary."[38]

When Brace founded the New York Children's Aid Society in 1853, he began by setting up religious meetings at which boys from the streets (generally aged ten through eighteen) were preached at. Some of the boys were accomplished thieves, others sold newspapers or ran errands, but none led a sheltered life. Brace frankly described the boys' reaction when

> a pious and somewhat sentimental Sunday-school brother [delivered a] vague and declamatory religious exhortation... the words "Gas! gas!" [were] whispered with infinite contempt from one hard-faced young disciple to another.[39]

Brace, while contending that no permanent reform of individual or society could succeed apart from religion, also saw the inadequacy of giving "tracts to a vagrant, who cannot earn his support without thieving."[40]

Brace then tried direct material distribution to evidently needy children, but ran into problems. He later wrote of what he learned:

> Experience soon shows that if you put a comfortable coat on the first idle and ragged lad who applies, you will have fifty half-clad lads, many of whom possess hidden away a comfortable outfit, leaving their business next day, "to get jackets for nothing."[41]

From then on Brace argued that poverty-fighters had to stifle their "first impulse," which was to offer immediate material help. Nor, he argued, was institutionalization the answer, even when material comforts were provided. "Asylum-life is not the best training for outcast children in preparing them for practical life," he wrote. "The child, most of all, needs individual care and sympathy. In an Asylum, he is 'Letter B, of Class 3,' or 'No. 2, of Cell 426.' "[42]

Having tried first the spiritual and then the material, Brace decided to merge the two: "Material Reform and Spiritual Reform, they must go on and mutually help one another."[43] His plan, for the short term, was to set up lodging houses for abandoned children that would provide not only shelter but classes in reading and industrial arts, along with Bible lessons. He soon had six lodging houses running, and over the years the number of children helped was huge; the largest of the lodging houses served 91,000 children from 1854 through 1872. House rules were designed to "discourage pauperism" and to show the rewards of honest work. Instead of handing out clothes, Brace preferred to "give the garments as rewards for good conduct, punctuality, and industry."[44] Once they came to know the children, housekeepers who spotted cases of dire want could relieve them with less likelihood of deception and without harm to the character-building process.

Newspapers praised the lodging-house movement and attributed to it a decrease in arrests of children for vagrancy and petty larceny.[45] Brace never saw lodging houses as long-term solutions, however. He believed that children could do much better by moving out of crowded Manhattan and into families in the countryside where a father and a mother could give them personal attention. The idea was not new. Hartley had urged destitute children to "escape from the city—for escape is your only recourse against the terrible ills of beggary."[46] The practical difficulty for Brace and his colleagues at the Children's Aid Society lay in finding thousands of families willing to take responsibility for children with troubled pasts. The problems seemed enormous, Brace wrote: "How were places to be found?... and when the children were placed, how were their interests to be watched over, and acts of oppression or hard dealing prevented or punished?"[47]

Brace hit upon the idea of allowing adults who took in children to do good and do well at the same time. He decided to try sending children (aged seven to seventeen) to farmers' homes where, in return for room, board, education, and personal attention, the children would work part-time. Brace began by sending out a circular that proposed the economic arrangement but also stressed the theological reasons for personal involvement:

> To the Public: This society has taken its origin in the deeply settled feeling of our citizens, that something must be done to meet the increasing crime and poverty among the destitute children of New York. As Christian men, we cannot look upon this great multitude of unhappy, deserted, and degraded boys and girls without feeling our responsibility to God for them.... We bear in mind that One died for them, even as for the children of the rich and happy.[48]

Response was enormous; as Brace wrote, "Hundreds of applications poured in at once from the farmers and mechanics all through the Union."[49]

Here, discernment was needed, since mail order arrangements, based as they were on a combination of compassion and economic appeal, provided great opportunity for abuse. Brace recorded some pleasant outcomes, such as that of a twelve-year-old orphan who had lived with his aunt, "but being a drunken woman, had at length turned him away; and for some time he had slept in a box in Twenty-second Street." Brace found him there and sent him to a man in Wilmington, Delaware, who wrote that the boy was

> covered with vermin, almost a leper, ignorant in the extreme…and altogether such a one as, by God's help, can be made something of. Such as he is, or may turn out to be, I accept the trust conferred upon me [of] becoming the instructor and trainer of a being destined to an endless life, of which that which he passes under my care, while but the beginning, may determine all the rest.[50]

That particular match worked, further letters revealed, but others did not. Overall, the arrangements seemed too open to abuse, and another plan was hit upon.

Plan B relied on local citizen committees rather than the direct mailing of circulars. Brace and his associates worked to recruit several leading citizens from a promising agricultural community. The citizens then formed a committee—usually including the mayor, a minister, a newspaper editor, a banker, and a storekeeper—that assumed responsibility for the placing of several dozen New York boys in local families. To promote interest in providing homes for orphans and abandoned children, the committees placed newspaper stories and ran advertisements that created a sense of anticipation. Ministers preached sermons that challenged "those who practically believe in Christ's words and teachings to aid us in this effort." When some citizens responded, the committee would contact Brace and plan for the temporary care of the children.

Brace's description of what happened next is worth quoting at length:

> The farming community having been duly notified, there was usually a dense crowd of people at the station, awaiting the arrival of the youthful travelers. The sight of the little company of the children of misfortune always touched the hearts of a population naturally generous.... The agent then addressed the assembly, stating the benevolent objects of the Society, and something of the history of the children. The sight of their worn faces was a most pathetic enforcement of his arguments. People who were childless came forward to adopt children; others, who had not intended to take any into their families, were induced to apply for them; and many who really wanted the children's labor pressed forward to obtain it.[51]

Demand was high because personal, theological, and economic incentives all created open doors. The committee reviewed the applicants and turned down those with a reputation for mistreating their help. It made sure, in Brace's words, that the children would "find themselves in comfortable and kind homes, with all the boundless advantages and opportunities of the Western farmer's life about them."[52]

Overall, using such methods, the Children's Aid Society placed close to one thousand children per year during the mid- and late-1850s, two thousand per year by the late 1860s, and close to four thousand per year by the late 1870s. The total between 1853 and 1893 was 91,536 youngsters, of which 42 percent went to homes in New York State, and about that same number to seven Midwestern states (Illinois, Iowa,

Missouri, Ohio, Indiana, Kansas, and Michigan). Early in the process some children were placed in New Jersey, but by 1875 more were being sent south to Virginia or west to Kansas, and by 1885 the society's reach was extending to Florida and Texas.[53]

Reports from society agents turn statistics into lives. One report, from an agent in 1868, shows some typical placement results in Illinois:

> The large boys, with two exceptions, were placed upon farms. Quite a number of boys came back to the hotel to say good-by, and thank me for bringing them out.… John Mahoney, age 16, with Mr. J————T———— (farmer); came in town Sunday to show me a fine mule his employer had given him. J————C————, age 14, went with Mrs. D————, who has a farm; came in to tell me how well pleased he is with his place; says he will work the farm as soon as he is able, and get half the profits. D———— M————, age 17, went with A————H. B———— (farmer); came back to tell me his employer had given him a pig, and a small plot of ground to work for himself.[54]

By century's end the society's limited records showed that three placed-out children had become governors, 498 were merchants, bankers, or businessmen, 81 teachers, and so on.

Testimonials of lives changed make moving reading. One college student, writing to Brace in 1871, described how he had been

> a vagrant, roaming over all parts of the city. I would often pick up a meal at the markets or at the docks, where they were unloading fruit. At a late hour in the night I would

find a resting place in some box or hogshead, or in some
dark hole under a staircase. [I would climb] upon houses
to tear the lead from around the chimneys....[55]

The student wrote how, after spending two years in an asylum,
"one of your agents came there and asked how many boys who
had no parents would love to have nice homes in the West, where
they could drive horses and oxen." The student journeyed to a
farm in Indiana:

Care was taken that I should be occupied there and not
in town. I was always treated as one of the family. In sickness I was ever cared for by prompt attention. In winter
I was sent to the Public School. The family room was a
good school to me, for there I found the daily papers and
a fair library.

The student concluded his letter by writing, "I shall ever acknowledge
with gratitude that the Children['s] Aid Society has been the instrument of my elevation. To be taken from the gutters of New York City
and placed in a college [Yale] is almost a miracle."[56]

Other children did not have such promising futures. One woman
accepted a mentally deficient child in 1858 and wrote the following year,
"I am often asked by my friends, who think the child is little more than
half-witted, why I do not 'send her back—and get a better one.' My
answer is, that she is just the one who needs the care."[57]

Soon, Brace's Children's Aid Society was flattered by widespread
imitation of its methods. Journalistic support, for which Brace worked
hard, helped to spread the message:

I made it a point, from the beginning, to keep our movements, and the evils we sought to cure, continually before
the public in the columns of the daily journals. Articles
describing the habits and trials of the poor; editorials urg-
ing the community to work in these directions [made the
public] thoroughly imbued with our ideas and a sense of
the evils which we sought to reform.[58]

The New York Foundling Hospital, unable to provide homes in New
York for all its charges, began sending some young children to the
New England and mid-Atlantic states. The Chicago Orphan Asylum
sent its charges to downstate farms on the basis of a letter from a
farmer who agreed to clothe and feed the child, treat him kindly,
provide religious instruction, and give him a new suit of clothes, a
Bible, and $20 when he reached sixteen.[59] Precautions that are taken
today in child placement—affadavits, "home study" visits by social
workers, and so on—were not used then, but protection against abuse
took several other forms. First, in small-town and rural areas, committee members had personal knowledge of applicants, and perversi-
ties were hard to keep secret. Second, as Brace wrote, the process of
placing the children "is carried on so publicly. . .that any case of positive abuse would at once be known and corrected by the community
itself."[60] Third, an agent visited newly placed children within a few
months and checked for either pampering or overwork, both of which
were seen as pernicious. In a culture that preached compassion and
practiced neighborly surveillance, it appears that cases of neglect or
abuse were rare.[61] The society did prosecute two cases of child abuse
and occasionally removed children, generally when parents reneged
on their agreement to provide education.[62] And records show some

few cases of farmers working children too long, and of a few even evicting children when the demands of the harvest were past.[63] Some children were placed several times before a good match was made.[64]

The typical result, even critics of the program admitted, was portrayed in one report of an inspection tour:

> Wherever we went we found the children sitting at the same table with the families, going to the school with the children, and every way treated as well as any other children. Some whom we had seen once in the most extreme misery, we beheld sitting, clothed and clean… and gaining a good name for themselves in their village.

One reason for success probably was the willingness of Brace and others to use economic incentives.[65] Since extra hands were so useful on farms, some observers worried that the "farmer, while he appeared to be influenced by high motives, might be thinking too much of the economic gains he would secure through the children placed in his home."[66] But Brace believed that taking in and *suffering with* a child from the slums should not be economically draining, since it was already emotionally draining: "habits are patiently corrected, faults without number are born with, time and money are expended [out of] a noble self-sacrifice for an unfortunate fellow-creature."[67]

This was particularly true because reports of "incorrigibility" were more common than reports of neglect or abuse. Some children who had spent years acting on sinful impulses did not immediately set aside bad habits; some never did.[68] J. Macy, assistant secretary of the Children's Aid Society, minimized the problem, telling a Senate committee in 1871 that out of 21,000 children placed, "not over twelve children have turned out criminals."[69] Other observers, skeptical of that figure, estimated that about 5 percent of the total of children placed committed crimes.[70] Several Midwestern prison officials, including Hiram H. Giles, chairman of the Wisconsin prison board, objected to the placing of "juvenile criminals among the peaceful homes" of their states.[71] Whatever the exact total, most observers acknowledged that many more of the abandoned children would have turned to crime had they not moved into a family home.

Informality of arrangements created both advantages and problems in other ways as well. The society retained guardianship of the children, unless they were adopted. While this left the children "free to leave, if ill-treated or dissatisfied," children without much experience of love sometimes saw the lack of formal commitment as cause for unease.[72] On the other hand, farmers frequently gave land, ponies, calves, or lambs to their charges, and in that way provided permanent material ties to supplement whatever emotional bonds were growing. The Children's Aid Society received press criticism whenever a child sent west committed a criminal act, or whenever a case of abuse was revealed. Brace once complained:

> Twenty years' virtuous life in a street-boy makes no impression on the public. A single offense is heard for hundreds of miles. A theft of one lad is imputed to scores of others about him.[73]

Overall, however, editors who saw the need for fast action played up the stories of ponies given and family bonds developed; they seemed ready to accept a few failures in order to make successes a possibility.[74]

This prompted Brace to call journalism "that profession which has done more for this Charity than any other instrumentality."[75]

CHAPTER THREE

First Challenge to the Charity Consensus

"A penny saved is a penny earned. Usually."[1] Thus began a recent harrowing newspaper tale of a scrimping mother and the wrath she called down upon herself. It seems that Grace Capetillo, a thirty-six-year-old single mother on welfare, had tried to save some money. She shopped at thrift stores and stocked up on sale items at grocery stores. She bought second-hand winter clothes during the summer and warm-weather outfits during the winter. When her five-year-old daughter Michelle's T-shirts grew tight, she snipped them below the underarm so they would last longer. When Michelle asked for "Li'l Miss Makeup" for Christmas, Mrs. Capetillo did not pay $19.99 for it at Toys "R" Us, but $1.89 at Goodwill; she cleaned it up and tied a pink ribbon in its hair before giving the doll to Michelle. At Goodwill she even found the pieces of another popular toy, Mr. Potato Head, and bought them for seventy-nine cents, thus saving $3.18. Penny by penny, dollar by dollar, she had saved $3,000 over four years.

For her efforts, Mrs. Capetillo found herself in court. It turned out that, under the federal Aid to Families with Dependent Children program, she was ineligible for assistance once her savings passed the $1,000 mark. The Milwaukee County Department of Social Services had matched its records with those supplied by her bank to the Internal Revenue Service and learned that she was saving more than regulations allowed. The department sued her for return of all she had received—$15,545—from the time she went over the savings limit. Eventually, a judge sentenced her to one-year probation and ordered her to repay $1,000. Mrs. Capetillo, having learned her lesson and needing to get rid of another $1,000 to get under the savings limit, bought a new washing machine, a used stove to replace the hotplate, a $40 refrigerator, and a new bedroom set for Michelle.

The case probably received national press attention because everyone involved seemed proud of his or her role in it. Milwaukee County welfare official Robert Davis wanted it known that he was running a tight ship: AFDC money was "to support a person's basic needs," not a savings account.[2] Mrs. Capetillo, with her daughter ready to enter first grade, was ready to enter the work force now. Circuit Court Judge Charles B. Schudson refused to fine Mrs. Capetillo the full amount due, and implied that changes in welfare rules were in order; Schudson commented, "I don't know how much more powerfully we could say to the poor in our society, 'Don't try to save.'"[3] But no one suggested that there might be inherent problems of this sort in any program where distribution of funds to able-bodied individuals is not tied to performance of work.

"A penny saved is a penny earned." The author of that maxim, Benjamin Franklin, visited London in 1766 and was struck by how a British welfare act was teaching the opposite:

> There is no country in the world in which the poor are
> more idle, dissolute, drunken and insolent. The day you

passed that act you took away from before their eyes the
greatest of all inducements to industry, frugality and so-
briety, by giving them a dependence on somewhat else
than a careful accumulation during youth and health for
support in age and sickness.... Repeal that law and you
will soon see a change in their manners. St. Monday and
St. Tuesday will cease to be holidays.[4]

Franklin's horrified reaction was a typical early American response to
government welfare programs. Concerning governmental distribution of money or food, Franklin's contemporaries typically argued that
'Very often it creates an appetite which is more harmful than the pain
it is intended to relieve."[5] A common saying, recorded by Thomas
Cooper, was, "The more paupers you support, the more you will have
to support."[6] A Delaware governor told his legislature, "If the door of
public commiseration is thrown too widely open the great stimulus
to exertion, which providence in his wisdom, has implanted in the
bosom of the community, is too apt to be weakened."[7]

The dislike of welfare was widespread. Government subsidies,
one writer argued, lead individuals to become "degraded, dissolute,
wasteful, profligate, and idle, by promising them a support if they
do so."[8] Children would learn that income came without work, and
the result would be "generation after generation of hereditary paupers."[9] In fact, any formalized right was destructive, since many
people would ignore their own obligations and do without what
should be the "necessity of industry, forethought, and a proper
self-denial."[10] New York charity worker John Griscom emphasized
"the evils arising from gratuitous aid" and noted that any "relaxation
of concern on the part of the poor to depend on their own foresight

and industry" would merely result in an "increase of helplessness and poverty."[11]

And yet, as cities began growing, complexities proliferated and questions arose. Josiah Quincy, chairman in 1821 of a Massachusetts legislative Committee on Pauper Laws, was one of the early governmental askers of hard questions. In theory, he argued, those applying for aid could readily be categorized:

> The poor are of two classes. 1. The impotent poor; in which denomination are included all, who are wholly incapable of work, through old age, infancy, sickness or corporeal debility. 2. The able poor; in which denomination are included all, who are capable of work, of some nature, or other.[12]

Quincy favored governmental alms to those who were helpless, but he was puzzled as to the exact classification: his study showed "numerous and minute shades of difference between the pauper who through impotency can do absolutely nothing and the pauper who is able to do something, but that, very little."[13] A too stringent standard of disability would exclude some who truly needed help, but a standard too loose would discourage effort by those with some capabilities.

Quincy in 1821 was confronting a problem faced by thousands of governmental social workers during the twentieth century. And he concluded that neither his legislative committee nor other governmental bodies could do the job. Given the nuances, he attested, no group that by its nature lacked flexibility would be able to set across-the-board regulations:

> There always must exist, so many circumstances of age, sex,
> previous habits, muscular, or mental, strength, to be taken
> into the account, that society is absolutely incapable to fix
> any standard, or to prescribe any rule by which the claim
> of right to the benefit of the public provision shall abso-
> lutely be determined.[14]

His report opposed provision of aid to the poor in their homes because it would make them worse off: those who needed great help
would be treated too stingily, and those who could help themselves
would be less likely to develop industrious habits.[15]

Based on such views, the typical form of limited governmental
support of the poor in the early nineteenth century continued to be
the poorhouses (sometimes known as Alms Houses or, for those capable of work, Work Houses). Their existence meant that no one would
starve, but their poor reputation also meant that no one would be attracted into pauperism. Poor houses were never the major societal
form of charity—the "worthy poor" continued to receive help through
private means, including the compassionate provision of rooms in
homes and other personal aid—but they provided a desperation safety
net and a nonenticing alternative to "outdoor relief," which was seen
as leading to ruin.

Despite the warnings, a few cities and towns set up local "outdoor
relief" programs without sufficient safeguards early in the nineteenth
century. Results raised further questions. A report on the Beverly,
Massachusetts, program showed that some able residents accepted alms
"in preference to working," and some hard-working townspeople became "discouraged by observing that bounty bestowed upon the idle,
which they can only obtain by the sweat of their brow."[16] In New York,

relief officials offering a "certainty of public provision" were said to be handing out "invitations to become beggars."[17] New York Secretary of State J. V. N. Yates told his legislature in 1824 that "poor laws had come to encourage the sturdy beggar and profligate vagrant."[18]

Such measures were particularly criticized because many governmental studies were finding that the major cause of destitution was intemperance. Baltimore Alms House officials claimed that "of the whole number admitted, more than three-fourths were positively ascertained to have been reduced to pauperism by intemperance."[19] Philadelphia officials, after visiting Baltimore, New York, Providence, Boston, Salem, and Hartford, concluded that

> the poor in consequence of vice, constitute here and every-
> where, by far the greater part of the poor. The experience
> of every Institution your committee has visited is decisive
> on this point. From three-fourths to nine-tenths of the pau-
> pers in all parts of our country, may attribute their degrada-
> tion to the vice of intemperance.[20]

This pattern continued over the decades. After Samuel Chipman during the 1830s visited every almshouse in New York to see for himself the causes of pauperism, he thought the three-fourths estimate was accurate.[21] The *American Quarterly Review* considered the higher figure, nine out of ten, more likely.[22] Worse still, the *U.S. Commercial and Statistical Register* reported that only one out of sixty-nine paupers supported by the city of Portland, Maine, in 1841–42 was poor for a reason other than intemperance.[23] In any event, the Philadelphia committee argued that government distribution of wood and provisions would be better than monetary handouts, but "even this mode is liable to great abuse."[24] The committee in 1827 asked (much as Charles Murray today has done in his recent writing), "what plan could be adopted, which trick and imposture and indolence, would not continually overreach?" It had no answer.

Government guarantees were seen as affecting not just willingness to work but other moral standards also. The Philadelphia committee worried that the City of Brotherly Love's willingness (very unusual for the time) to support women with illegitimate children was "an encouragement to vice, and offers a premium for prostitution." Today, some say that government should at least work hard to "do no harm"; then, the Philadelphia committee hemmed and hawed in roundabout eloquence:

> Though your committee are not prepared to say, that it is the particular province or duty of the Board of Guardians in their collective capacity to recall the wanderer from the error of his ways, yet we may most assuredly assert, that they are bound to afford no inducements to a departure from virtue.[25]

The committee noted that Baltimore, Boston, and Salem, where no aid was given to mothers with illegitimate children, had very few cases of illegitimacy, but there were "in Philadelphia 269!!!" (Exclamation marks in the original) Nor did the Philadelphia grants appear to help character formation. In describing recipients of largesse, committee members observed

> the unblushing effrontery, that some of them exhibit. The thanklessness with which they receive their allotted stipend;

the insolence with which they demand a further supply, ar-
rogantly exacting as a *right*, what ought never to have been
granted, even as a charity.[26]

Government guarantees were thus seen as increasing the supply of
poverty by ruining attitudes.

American officials and charity leaders also read with great interest Chalmers' warning about how governmental involvement could
lead to compassion fatigue, and an eventual reduction of the supply
of charity. Establishing what we today call entitlements, Chalmers
argued, changes

> the whole character of charity, by turning a matter of love
> into a matter of litigation.... [The imperative] calls out
> the jealousy of our nature, and puts us upon the attitude
> of surly and determined resistance. [The request] calls
> out the compassion of our nature, and inclines us to the
> free and willing movements of generosity.[27]

The needy poor, he argued, end up with less under a mandatory system than when "the fountain of human sympathy" freely operates.[28]
The Benevolent Societies of Boston concurred with that view in an
1835 report and predicted that "in our desire to gratify the benevolent
feelings of our hearts, we are laying the foundation of a greater moral
evil."[29]

Overall, that report was typical in stressing the importance of helping in precisely the right way, with precisely the right amount, in order
to avoid "holding out strong inducements to the poor to beg and de-
ceive." Private groups, the coalition concluded, were able to act with

discernment, but government organizations would find it more difficult to say "yes" to some and "no" to others.

In examining the proper function of government many American writers during the first half of the nineteenth century referred to the experience of ancient Rome, where "politicians of the time" used "doles to the poor" to obtain "positions which they were far from competent to hold." Monthly distributions of corn to all were so corrupting that "less than 150 years was sufficient to pauperize and render dependent a fearfully large proportion of one of the most manly races which have ever lived." Nathaniel Ware, after summarizing in 1845 this interpretation of Rome's fall, sadly predicted that an American governmental welfare system *would* develop, sooner or later, because officeholders liked to appeal to poor voters who would give them power to distribute large amounts of money and the patronage that accompanied expenditure. Ware noted that officers with more power would become more important and better paid.[30]

American writers also cited the English experience. They frequently quoted Thomas Chalmers' remark that "state aid had been a mighty solvent to sunder the ties of kinship, to quench the affections of the family, to suppress in the poor themselves the instinct of self-reliance and self-respect—to convert them into paupers."[31] They criticized the English program for giving everyone a "subsistence, whatever be his indolence, prodigality or vice,"[32] and they quoted criticisms of the program from those who subscribed to biblical ideas of man's natural sinfulness: "Can we wonder if the uneducated are seduced into approving a system which aims its allurements at all the weakest parts of our nature, which offer... ease to the lazy, and impunity to the profligate?"[33]

In essence, Americans were told year after year to take to heart the experience of other countries and other times, which showed that official relief "only fostered pauperism by affixing a premium to indiscriminate poverty."[34] The Association for Improving the Condition of the Poor (AICP) stressed its rule that "all relief shall be temporary." Breaking that rule, the AICP insisted, meant that

> many, once learning to lean on public or associated relief, not only neglect to exert the powers God has given them, but continue to call for aid long after it is right. This leads on the broad road to pauperism. Individuals or societies can hardly guard too watchfully against it.

All historical and contemporary study suggested that "the more that is done, the more may be done: as the supply is, so will be the demand, unless its distribution be under the outmost discrimination."[35]

Americans also heard the message from the pulpit. Minister William Ruffner in 1853 claimed that "idleness and improvidence" result whenever "there are large funds provided—and especially when provided by state taxation, and disbursed by state officers."[36] Ruffner went on to note that charity

> is a work requiring great tenderness and sympathy, and agents, who do their work for a price rather than for love, should not be trusted to execute the wishes of donors. The keepers of poor-houses (like undertakers) fall into a business, unfeeling way of doing their duties; which is wounding and often partial and cruel to the objects of their attention.[37]

Other ministers made similar remarks.

Americans heard a like message from the White House itself. In 1854 Congress responded to impassioned pleading by Dorothea Dix and passed legislation for the federal government to construct and maintain mental hospitals. But President Franklin Pierce vetoed the bill. He explained that although he wished to help the mentally ill, who were not responsible for their plight, even worthwhile appropriations would push the federal government down a slippery slope. "If Congress has the power to make provision for the indigent insane," Pierce pointed out, "it has the same power for the indigent who are not insane."[38] Pierce also contended that the law actually would be "prejudicial rather than beneficial to the noble offices of charity," since federal funds would end up substituting for local assistance: "[S]hould this bill become a law, that Congress is to make provision for such objects, the foundations of charity will be dried up at home...."[39] Pierce's veto was upheld.

Pierce's concern about "dried up" charity was typical of the era. Writers and charity workers discussed not only the effects of governmental subsidy on initiatives among the poor but also on the attitudes of those who were better-off. They argued that the stream of personal involvement and private charity would dry up as some came to believe that if they did not help, professionals would, and if they did not contribute, the government would make up the difference. Repeatedly, Americans were told through all the traditional communications media that governmental programs "damped and discourage...the powerful workings of generous and compassionate feeling."[40]

But starting in the 1840s, some communications media began to sing a different melody. Some editors of the "penny press"—newspapers that because of printing and circulation innovations could sell for one penny—became self-conscious advocates for "the poor." Unsurprisingly, the first popular challenge to the charity consensus came from the midnineteenth-century's leading American journalist, Horace Greeley.

Greeley, founder and editor of the *New York Tribune* in 1841 (at age thirty-one) was a Universalist who believed that people are naturally good and that every person has a *right* to both eternal salvation and temporal prosperity. He probably never said the words most often attributed to him—"Go West, young man"—but he did advise many young men and women to fight poverty by joining communes in which the natural goodness of humans, freed from competitive pressure, inevitably would emerge.[41] Since Greeley did not accept the prevalent religious thinking—that man's sinful nature leads toward indolence, and that an impoverished person given a dole without obligation is likely to descend into pauperism—he saw no problem with supporting the able-bodied poor who did not work.[42]

Greeley was not hypocritical. The 1840s were a time of social experimentation in America—a preview, in a limited sense, of the 1960s—and Greeley threw himself personally into three communes that were intended to be both antipoverty solutions and centers of social revolution: the Sylvania Association in Pennsylvania, the North American Phalanx in New Jersey, and Brook Farm in Massachusetts. He even became president of the American Union of Associationists, a group that believed that man, naturally good, had been corrupted by capitalist society, and that hoped to put into practice the ideas of Charles Fourier, the French Utopian socialist.[43] At a New York City banquet in 1844, Greeley was toasted by fellow communalists as the man who had "done for us what we never could have done. He has created the cause on this continent. He has done the work of a century."[44] In one sense, these were all fringe activities. And yet, Greeley and the talented young idealists—Charles Dana, Margaret Fuller, George

Ripley, and others—who surrounded him did roil the waters. If they did not do the work of a new century, they strove mightily to undo the work of the previous century. They pressed into popular discourse the notions that there was something immoral about economic competition, that everyone had a right to sustenance, and that forced redistribution of wealth through a collective agency might well be the moral way to fight poverty.

These ideas, trickled out throughout the 1840s, were presented in toto in a series of newspaper debates Greeley joyfully conducted with his former assistant editor, Henry Raymond. Raymond, twenty-six when the debates began in 1846, had moved from assisting Greeley on the *Tribune* to working on a competing newspaper; in several years Raymond would found the *New York Times*. Greeley still had high regard for him, and later wrote that he had never seen "a cleverer, readier, more generally efficient journalist" than Raymond.[45] The philosophical differences between the two were sharp, however: one journalist noted that Greeley was "naturally liberal" and Raymond "naturally conservative; the one a Universalist, the other a Presbyterian...."[46] When Raymond challenged Greeley to a duel by pen, Greeley assented, with each newspaper agreeing to publish a total of twelve articles from its own side and twelve from the other.

Greeley opened the debate series on November 20, 1846, by asserting presuppositionally that each member of "the whole Human Family" had an equal right to the earth, and that, therefore, every New York resident had "a perfect right...to his equal share of the soil, the woods, the waters, and all the natural products thereof." Instead of discussing the obligations of individuals, Greeley focused on rights and blamed "Civilized Society, as it exists in our day," for interfering with "unimpeded, unpurchased enjoyment" of that equal share. Greeley's solution was "Association," by which all property would be communal rather than private.[47]

Raymond in response argued from history that, yes, difficulties did arise out of the need for man to earn bread through strenuous, individual effort, but without such a work requirement the problems of poverty "would be increased a thousand fold.... Without it civilization would be unknown—the face of the Earth would be a desert, and mankind transformed into savage beasts."[48] Given man's nature, competition was compassionate, Raymond contended. He argued that Greeley was unwilling to confront some basic issues of man's nature—including, most particularly, the question of "sin" and its effect on social progress.[49]

Raymond kept hammering away at those themes until Greeley, in the sixth debate, was finally driven to acknowledge that social reorganization by itself was not sufficient, for "an Association of knaves and dastards—of indolent or covetous persons—could not endure without a moral transformation of its members."[50] Raymond then stated his position: the way to fight poverty was through "personal reform of individual men."[51] He argued that reformers should "*commence* their labors by making individual men *Christians*: by seeking their personal, moral transformation. When that is accomplished, all needed Social Reform will either have been effected or rendered inevitable."[52]

To this, Greeley responded by putting forward part of what a half-century later would become known as the "Social Gospel." He tried to show that the centerpiece of Christianity was communal living and material redistribution: "Association *is* the palpable dictate of Christianity—the body whereof True Religion is the soul."[53] Emphasizing the need for material change, Greeley described slum living conditions and wrote that bringing Bibles and tracts to such homes "while Bread is scanty, wholesome Air a rarity, and Decency impossible, must be unavailing[.]"[54] Greeley's statement jarred Raymond into laying out his full position on January 20, 1847. He first partially agreed that there was a need for action:

> The existence of misery, and the necessity of relieving it, are not in controversy, for we have never doubted either. It is only upon the *remedy to be applied*, that the Tribune and ourselves are at variance.[55]

But, rather than primarily calling for material transfer, Raymond emphasized individual and church action:

> Members of any one of our City Churches do more every year for the practical relief of poverty and suffering, than any Phalanx [the Associationist name for communes] that ever existed. There are in our midst hundreds of female "sewing societies," each of which clothes more nakedness, and feeds more hunger, than any "Association" that was ever formed.[56]

He praised "individuals in each ward, poor, pious, humble men and women, who never dreamed of setting themselves up as professional philanthropists," but who daily visited the sick and helped the poor.

At this point, the two debaters were focusing on the basics. Raymond had called Greeley superficial for not getting at what Raymond saw as the root, spiritual causes of material poverty, and now Greeley struck back saying that the economic environment was the culprit: 'Association proposes a way... of reaching the *causes* of the calamities, and absolutely *abolishing* Pauperism, Ignorance, and the resulting Vices."[57] Increasingly the debates hinged on the view of man that divided the two editors. When Greeley argued on February 17 that all man's problems "have their root in that *isolation of efforts* and antagonism of interests on which our present Social Order is based," Raymond replied by insisting that individual corruption rather than social oppression was the root of most social ills.[58] While Greeley stressed his belief that "the Passions, feelings, free impulses of Man point out to him the path in which he should walk," Raymond argued that evil feeds on these passions and impulses of man's natural inclination, and that channeling those inclinations into paths of work and family, rather than dependence and pauperism, was the only alternative to anarchy and barbarism.[59]

The last three debates showed even more clearly the conflict of their two faiths. Greeley's Associationist belief was that human desires are

> good in themselves. Evil flows only from their repression or subversion. Give them full scope, free play, a perfect and complete development, and universal happiness must be the result.... Create a new form of Society in which this shall be possible...then you will have a perfect Society; then will you have "the Kingdom of Heaven...."[60]

Raymond, however, insisted that emphasis on external causes of social problems

> is in the most direct and unmistakable hostility to the uniform inculcations of the Gospel. No injunction of the New

Testament is more express, or more constant, than that of *self-denial*; of subjecting the passions, the impulses of the heart to the law of conscience.[61]

And Greeley, in response, argued that "excesses and vices are not an essential part of the passions, but on the contrary depend on external circumstances, which may be removed."[62]

Who was right? Which debater understood the nature of true compassion? Greeley argued in his eleventh essay that support for a system of equal, society-wide distribution of material was "the duty of every Christian, every Philanthropist, every one who admits the essential Brotherhood of the Human Family...,"[63] Raymond, in his response, argued that Greeley was socialist in economics, antinomian in ethics, and overall a person trying to create a new god in his own image. Greeley's thought, Raymond charged,

> pretends to be religious, and even claims to be the only true Christianity. But...it rejects the plainest doctrines of the Bible, nullifies its most imperative commandments, and substitutes for them its own interpretation of the laws of *nature*.[64]

Concerning Greeley's belief, Raymond concluded:

> Its whole spirit is in the most direct hostility to the doctrines of the Bible. It recognizes no absolute distinction between right and wrong.... It is the exact antagonist of Christianity; it starts from opposite fundamental principles and aims at precisely opposite results.[65]

The key question with which all reformers and journalists should grapple, Raymond insisted, concerned the locus of evil action in humans: did evil come from within, or was it generated by social institutions? Raymond stipulated:

> Before a cure can be applied or devised, the cause of the evil must be ascertained: and here at the very outset, the theory of Association comes in direct collision with the teachings of Christianity.[66]

The cause, Raymond argued, was "the sinfulness of the heart of Man." The remedy, he argued,

> must reach that cause, or it must prove inefficient. The heart must be changed. The law of Man's nature must cease to be the supreme law of his life. He must learn to subject that law to the higher law of righteousness, revealed in his conscience and in the Word of God ... and that subjugation can only be effected by his own personal will, with the supernatural aids furnished in the Christian Scheme.[67]

And thus, finally, the lines were clearly drawn. Greeley believed that "the heart of man is not depraved: that his passions do not prompt to wrong doing, and do not therefore by their action, produce evil."[68] Greeley, in his twelfth and final essay, reiterated his faith that "social distinctions of master and servant, rich and poor, landlord and landless," were the cause of evil. The way to end evil was to redistribute wealth so that all receive an equal share; one way to begin would be to have government tax the better-off and distribute food and funds to those less well off.

Greeley's arguments produced no immediate, enormous change, but they set out the case for distributing goods to all on moral grounds. Previously, the tendency was grudgingly to allow meager governmental distributions, if any at all; previously, that is, communalistic ideology had found a press outlet only in short-lived radical newspapers and small, insignificant magazines. But the weekly edition of the *New York Tribune* reached 10 percent of all voters in Northern states from Massachusetts to Minnesota during the 1850s—and often the most socially involved 10 percent. Justifications for government welfare programs sprouted during the 1850s, in part because Greeley offered protective cover and good publicity. Newspapers such as the *Lowell Daily Journal and Courier* followed Greeley's lead,[69] as did scholars such as Andrew W. Young, who argued that "every humane government" should maintain the poor.[70] Since Society as a whole was responsible for the poor, society as a whole should pay, wrote Henry C. Carey in his *Principles of Social Science*.[71]

As some ideas changed, their consequences began to emerge: One analyst noted that in the late 1850s "[r]eports from many communities in widely separated places all agreed that the number receiving outdoor and poorhouse relief was unprecedented."[72] In part, the welfare upsurge was related to the business panic of 1857 and the temporary, involuntary unemployment that came with it, but the increase went far beyond and lasted longer than any direct connection would justify. Almost 33,000 of the residents of Kings County, New York (Brooklyn), were on the dole in 1858; that was 13 percent of the entire population. And nearly eight thousand persons out of Albany's population of sixty thousand—also 13 percent—received governmental relief. In the textile towns of southern New England, where unemployment was higher, one-fifth of Fall River's residents and one-sixth of Providence's registered for governmental assistance.

These numbers were understandably high during periods of recession, but the trend line for relief was upward in good times as well as bad. Statistics from the New York secretary of state showed that the increase in outdoor relief was not just recession-related: 11,937 residents received temporary relief in 1840, 63,764 in 1850, and 174,403 in 1860.[73] Figures from other cities showed similar tendencies, even though most observers continued to argue that 75 to 90 percent of poverty was due to alcoholism.[74] Scholar Samuel Austin Allibone, for example, was sarcastic about a book that expressed love for the poor but did not discuss intemperance, since he connected it with three-fourths of American poverty.[75] In 1852, when a Connecticut legislative committee sent out questionnaires to 132 of the state's towns, it found only one respondent stating "want of employment" as a cause of poverty; the largest number of responses put down "intemperance."[76] Some responses might have been different five years later, but not most. A New York legislative committee in 1857 found intemperance in the backgrounds of 70 percent of the inmates of the state's poorhouses.[77]

It is hard to tell at this remove how much of the need in the late 1850s was real and how much opportune, as some with pauper mentalities decided to get while the getting was good. New Haven newspaper editors, however, came to believe that most aid was going to the "unworthy poor," and proposed that aid should be private rather than governmental so that claims could be examined carefully.[78] Henry Raymond's *New York Times* argued that governmental charity was likely "to breed indifference in the hearts of those who support, and imbecility in the characters of those who profit by the machinery of benevolence."[79] And the New York AICP continued to oppose "so questionable and hazardous a mode of relief" as "soup-houses" available to all without checking.[80] "'Be ye wise as serpents, harmless as doves,' must be carried into our charities," the AICP insisted: If Greeleyite schemes of "indiscriminate charity" were followed, "[w]e might as well throw the money in the street and let the poor scramble for it, and then be astonished at the riot we create."[81]

Others nevertheless adopted the Greeleyite position. The *Providence Journal* aired the view that the city treasury was "the savings bank in which is deposited a part of the earnings of every laborer," and that it was the "equitable and Christian" right of each worker to demand "a dividend of these profits."[82] The mayor of Boston, for his part, said that the city government had "the obligation to meet whatever need exists."[83] (A committee of the Boston City Council, however, opposed relief proposals, arguing that America could lose its freedom if there were a "slow and insidious growth in large cities of claims for subsistence upon the public treasury."[84]) The debate went on: just west of Boston, the *Waltham Sentinel* maintained that the poor generally should claim government "provision as their right...."[85]

At this point, the arguments trailed off as the War Between the States captured attention. But soon after the war the competency of governmental welfare programs became an issue: the Radical Republicans established economic aid programs for blacks and Andrew Johnson opposed them, arguing that a "system for the support of indigent person...was never contemplated by the authors of the Constitution."[86] Johnson did not scorn the ex-slaves. He told a delegation of black leaders that he wished their goal of full political, social, and economic equality "could be done in the twinkling of an eye, but it is not in the nature of things, and I do not assume or pretend to be wiser than Providence."[87] Johnson preferred charitable initiatives to federal programs, and personally sent $1,000 to support a school to educate black children in Charleston.

Southern critics of Reconstruction complained about political payoffs, but corruption was probably worse in parts of the North, and with less excuse. Boss Tweed and his associates in New York were said to have robbed the city of $160 million, but they gave a bit back in aid to the poor. It became part of smart urban politics to produce programs whereby thousands of men and women in New York and Brooklyn could line up at government distributing offices on "relief days."[88] By the early 1870s one-tenth of the city's population was receiving weekly rations from public storehouses.[89] In Brooklyn, journalists and reformers led by Seth Low (later elected mayor) called the dole system "a sore on the body politic" and "a vast political corruption fraud."[90] Low's research showed that those who were not needy participated in the program because "the county gave it" and they wanted a share. One woman received help under nine different names, but "the poor did not get the chief benefit of increased appropriations. Most of it went to underlings connected with the work of distribution."[91] Still, city welfare continued.

But not only governmental programs seemed to be loosening the relationship between justice and mercy. During the recession of 1873 some philanthropists funded thirty-four free soup kitchens and lunch distribution spots at which five to seven thousand persons ate daily.[92] These points of light were helpful to many for a brief period, but one study showed that over half the money raised for "industrious victims" of the recession was spent on "feckless bums" and "imposters."[93] Much to the dismay of Robert Hartley, the programs were not means-tested, but "free to all who would partake of the charity—irrespective of their need or desert."[94] Soon a destructive pattern emerged: One charity official noted that indiscriminate, soup kitchen charity was both too much and too little, for it was "dispersed in tantalizing doles miserably inadequate for effectual succor where the need was genuine, and dealt out broadcast among the clamorous and impudent."[95]

CHAPTER FOUR

The Social Darwinist Threat

lcoholics and addicts crouching in tenements. Children without parents roaming the streets. Homeless men lining up at free soup-kitchens. Abandoned women struggling to keep hope alive. Tough times, yes—but this is a description of inner cities, not today, but a century ago. In the 1870s most Americans still lived in rural areas, true, but urban poverty-fighters faced hurdles at least as high as those of today. At that time, urban population density was often greater and life expectancy lower, leaving thousands of orphans to roam the streets; immigration and rapid urbanization made infrastructures buckle, as the population of almost every Eastern metropolis doubled between 1860 and 1890, and increased six- and tenfold in Midwestern cities like Cleveland and Chicago. American society as a whole was far poorer than now, and conditions of labor and living far more strenuous.

Those who hoped to beat back poverty had been dealt a poor hand in other ways as well. Crime in the early 1870s was regarded as severe. *Wood's Illustrated Handbook* of 1872 warned visitors to New York to beware of all "who accost you in the street" and avoid walking late at night "except in the busiest thoroughfares." *Harper's Weekly* noted the following year that "assaults and robberies are frequent."[1] Alcoholism was everywhere and drug abuse was growing: six times more opium—146,000 pounds—was brought into the United States in 1868 than in 1840, and there may have been 100,000 drug addicts in the United States. "Walk along the streets any day and you will meet opium slaves by the score," writer Lafcadio Hearn said of Cincinnati: "They are slaves, abject slaves suffering exquisite torture. Once in the fetters of opium and morphia, they are, with few exceptions, fettered for life."[2]

Furthermore, bodies in many cities were packed close as Northern wartime production turned into a postwar factory boom and more immigrants arrived. New factory chimneys made it certain, according to *Leslie's Weekly*, that "no dumping-ground, no sewer, no vault contains more filth or in greater variety than [does] the air in certain parts of" New York City. Conjested downtown traffic amazed onlookers. "What a jam!" noted one traffic report from Lower Broadway in 1872, "Stages, carriages, cartmen, expressmen, pedestrians all melted together in one agglomerate mess!"[3] Each city's service sector was catering to a variety of tastes, then as now. One journalist, Oliver Dyer, calculated that if all of New York's post-Civil War liquor shops (5,500), houses of prostitution (647, by his count), gambling halls, and other low-life establishments were placed for a night on a single street, they would reach from City Hall in lower Manhattan to White Plains thirty miles away, with a robbery every 165 yards, a murder every half mile, and thirty reporters offering sensational detail.[4]

Many of the previously charitable became sick of it all. Compassion malaise was evident everywhere. Even Horace Greeley recorded his exasperation at what his type of thinking had wrought. "The beggars of New York," he complained in 1869, "are at once very numerous and remarkably impudent."[5] After sputtering about "chronic beggars" and noting that nine-tenths of those who solicited him were "thriftless vagabonds," Greeley concluded from his "extensive, protracted experience" that,

> the poor often suffer from poverty, I know; but oftener from lack of capacity, skill, management, efficiency, than lack of money. Here is an empty-handed youth who wants [money, but] he is far more certain to set resolutely to work without than with that pleasant but baneful accommodation. Make up a square issue,—"Work or starve!"—and he is quite likely to choose work.[6]

In a remarkable but characteristic reversal Greeley decided that, except for widows, orphans, and others within the traditional categories of charity recipient, the "best response" to a person asking for help was "Nature's—'Root, hog, or die!'"[7]

Some did not go so far as the vexed Greeley, but few were happy with the new "outdoor relief" distribution plans. George McGonegal, New York state superintendant of the poor, criticized programs wherein "families are furnished a stated amount weekly or monthly, and this is continued week after week and year after year."[8] McGonegal argued that recipients soon "lose their energy and self-respect and find it easier to rely upon the industry of others to furnish them their daily bread than to exert themselves to earn a livelihood."[9] He pointed out the danger of what we today call inter-generational dependency: When parents' prayers for a daily dole were answered,

> their children learn to think that getting provisions and fuel from the overseer of the poor is perfectly right and proper,

and they are almost certain to follow in the footsteps of their parents.

McGonegal sadly concluded: "I know of nothing which does so much to encourage pauperism and educate paupers for the next generation, as this system."[10]

Others in New York shared McGonegal's concerns. Annual reports of the United Hebrew Charities claimed that giving relief to the "unscrupulous and undeserving" was leading to "pauperizing on a wholesale scale."[11] The New York State Board of Charities in 1875 attacked the idea of "official outdoor relief" and provided a warning:

> When persons, naturally idle and improvident, have experienced for a few months the convenience of existing upon the labor of others, they are very likely to resort to this means of living as often and as continuously as possible.[12]

In 1879 the New York board reported that outdoor relief was "injurious and hurtful to the unfortunate and worthy poor, demoralizing in its tendencies, a prolific source of pauperism and official corruption, and an unjust burden upon the public."[13] In 1884 the board returned with another report that called outdoor relief "not only useless, as a means to relieving actual existing suffering, but an active means of increasing present and future want and vice."[14] The charity officials did not rule out welfare programs, but recommended "maximum caution."[15]

Corruption was evident not only in New York and Brooklyn, but in other cities as well. Questionnaires distributed throughout Massachusetts by Edward L. Pierce, secretary of the commonwealth's

Board of State Charities, showed that "a large proportion of the out-door relief, sometimes one-half, is distributed to those who stand in no need of it, and is therefore worse than wasted."[16] Even those who did need some help, he added, were being led into a very harmful addiction:

> Those once receiving [aid] apply again when proper effort might have saved them from a such a resort.... With those who have once received it the second lapse is easier than the first, and with those not yet recipients, the spectacle of others receiving it, who are in the same or not substantially different circumstances, is a tempting one.[17]

Pierce concluded that the poor were developing "exaggerated notions of their claims to support," and that the better-off were becoming "demoralized" in their giving.[18] An analyst for the Associated Charities of Boston similarly noted the birth of "a dependent feeling, a dry rot, which leads the recipient of city bounty to look upon it as something due as a reward for destitution."[19]

Leaders in other states passed similar judgments. The Rhode Island Board of State Charities and Corrections argued that welfare "does more hurt than good, and makes more paupers than it relieves."[20] Pennsylvania's Board of Commissioners of Public Charities for its part claimed that "outdoor relief carelessly and prodigally administered" was going to "large numbers of persons naturally idle and improvident."[21] The Wisconsin Board of Charities and Reform agreed:

> A large amount for poor relief does not indicate a large amount of suffering which needs to be relieved, but a large

> amount of laxity or corruption on the part of officers and
> a large amount of willingness by able-bodied idlers to be
> fed at the public expense.[22]

The Ohio Board of State Charities complained that readily offered, across-the-board relief "tends rapidly to undermine habits of industry, economy, and self-reliance, and to pauperize whole families."[23]

Individual charity workers joined the chorus. It was wrong, they reiterated, to dispense welfare "as a right" so that individuals "learn to depend upon this aid in youth, middle age, and old age as a legitimate source of income."[24] Frances Smith, district agent for the Associated Charities of Boston, felt that aid to those poor people who needed to change their ways should be

> a goad to individual reform. As long as it remain[s] in the
> hands of private agencies, private individuals could affect
> personal improvement. Statutory provisions, however,
> would disarm the private citizen and render him powerless
> to restrict the growth of pauperism in the community.[25]

She was concerned with the effect of dependency-thinking not only on the unemployed but on those with regular incomes; she said her clients had begun asking, "Why should we join a saving society? The city will provide for us when we are old."[26] She predicted that young people who grew up in cities where stipends for the elderly were available would not concentrate on personal saving, but would in their own old age demand support from others.[27]

Officials and writers repeatedly argued that outdoor relief led to rampant depersonalization: "Bread, more bread, soup, more soup. One beggar, one loaf. If two beggars, two loaves," a sardonic journalist complained: "A thousand poor, one soup-house; two thousand, two soup-houses."[28] The consequent growth of fraud-made-easy weakened support for charitable work. Contributors in the 1870s rebelled against organizations that were "simply relief societies [with] no adequate safe-guards against deception."[29] Stories abounded about those who gave money to relief groups and applicants and were fooled, for a while. The stories often ended with the givers so cynical about the process that they clamped shut their purses. One clergyman, for example, initially "grudged neither time nor money," but concluded after a winter's work that he had done twice as much harm as good by bulwarking "wasteful, indolent habits."[30]

Reports also circulated of schemers hopping from agency to agency, shopping for the best dole. Some who became adept at working the system were said to receive aid from many different groups, with income related to the number of tears shed and false stories told.[31] The degree of fraud probably was minor compared to what we now are used to, but perhaps because he was not so jaun-diced, Charles Brace reacted with amazement:

> The number of poor people who enjoy a comfortable liv-
> ing, derived from a long study and experience of those
> various agencies of benevolence, would be incredible to
> any one not familiar with the facts. They pass from one to
> the other; knowing exactly their conditions of assistance
> and meeting their requirements, and live thus by a sort of
> science of alms.[32]

Brace was astounded at the hard work involved in not working—"the industry and ingenuity they employ in this pauper trade are truly remarkable"—and bemoaned the waste of talent.[33]

As the incidence of "compassion fatigue" augmented, it became easier to give in to it, for the new immigration and urbanization was producing not only a massively increased population but economic segregation as well. Sharply defined rich and poor areas emerged after the Civil War; the better-off citizens were riding to work on broad avenues instead of walking through a variety of wards.[34] Churches were becoming more class-conscious, and many from downtown followed the uptown path of their upwardly-mobile members.[35] Economic segregation, in short, meant that the more affluent were less likely to confront need directly; it had suddenly become easy to ignore the poor and rely on the mediated compassion of press reports.

Furthermore, immigration from non-West European cultures was complicating communication between "old stock" volunteers and their charges. Louise de Koven Bowen, a lady from Chicago in the 1880s, gave a hungry immigrant family a turkey and was surprised later on "to see the bird dressed up in one of the children's dresses...."[36] Other well-off ladies with little tolerance for inter-cultural communication retreated into their own social milieu, occasionally "sponsoring an opera, musicale, or play in the name of charity...."[37] Such activities rarely helped the poor, but they allowed "aspiring Society queens [to] enhance their reputations, sharpen their skills at social one-upsmanship, and fulfill their charitable obligations at a comfortable remove from misery and want."[38]

The male social elite also was drifting away from the poor. Less social contact accompanied depersonalized employer/employee relationships. Periodic strikes and violence (railroads, Haymarket, Homestead, and so on) paralleled the late nineteenth-century tendency to turn labor into just one more part of the economic equation. Andrew Carnegie, while noting the progress of manufacturing produced material benefits throughout society, acknowledged that the price we pay for this salutary change is, no doubt, great. We assemble thousands of operatives in the factory, and in the mine, of whom the employer can know little or nothing, and to whom he is little better than a myth. All intercourse between them is at an end. Rigid castes are formed, and, as usual, mutual ignorance breeds mutual distrust.[39]

Even social schemes hailed as "progressive" showed marks of depersonalization. George Pullman, for example, "cultivated the great and noble impulses of the benefactor" by building a modern suburb for his workers outside Chicago, but—as Jane Addams later wrote—he lost "the power of attaining a simple human relationship with his employe[e]s...."[40]

When personal contact was lost, social schemes became unrealistic and even destructive: the charitable equivalent of Gresham's Law rolled into motion, for bad charity was capable of driving out good. Once some groups succumbed to the pressure to give indiscriminately, other groups faced pressure to go and do likewise, or risk being castigated as Scrooges and ignored by those it hoped to help. Charles Brace described the process:

In place of waiting to carefully assist the poor, [a charity] tempts the poor to come to it. If it be a peculiar kind of school, not much needed in the quarter, it bribes the poor children by presents to abandon the rival school and fill its own seats; if an Asylum, it seeks far and near for those even not legitimately its subjects.[41]

Brace concluded, "There arises a sort of competition of charity," a search for the lowest common denominator of giving.[42]

This might seem to be an enjoyable situation for paupers, but such competitive charity was both destructive to morale and short-lived. Golden streams tended to dry up as "the public become disgusted with all organized charity, and at last fancy that societies of benefaction do as much evil as good."[43] Soon, what had been given was abruptly removed, and the pauperized were "often worse off than if they had never been helped."[44]

Furthermore, it was during the postwar period of compassion fatigue and growing economic segregation that—not coincidentally—the poisonous ideology of Social Darwinism began to pick up many adherents. Equating the economic struggle among humans with the struggle for survival among animals, Social Darwinists typically argued that

> society is constantly excreting its unhealthy, imbecile, slow, vacillating, faithless members to leave room for the deserving. A maudlin impulse to prolong the lives of the unfit stands in the way of this beneficent purging of the social organism.[45]

Herbert Spencer, the British leader of Social Darwinism, wrote, "The unfit must be eliminated as nature intended, for the principle of natural selection must not be violated by the artificial preservation of those least able to take care of themselves."[46] Americans bought 368,755 copies of Spencer's books, according to one count.[47]

Such ideas were reflected in "The Causes of Pauperism," a report to the New York State Board of Charities in 1876, which complained that "idleness" and "other forms of vicious indulgence" are

> frequently, if not universally, hereditary in character. Insufficient attention has been given to hereditary factors, and society must take positive measures to cope with

them.... vigorous efforts must be instituted to break the line of pauper descent.[48]

Social Darwinists picked up support as social anonymity grew under conditions of urbanization, and as the falsehood of glittery exteriors was harder to spot. Soon Social Darwinist ideas concerning compassion were common: they spread throughout the 1870s and received their best and purest American expression in two books published in the 1880s, William Graham Sumner's *What Social Classes Owe to Each Other* and Simon Newcomb's *Principles of Political Economy*.

Sumner, a professor at Yale University, criticized those who allowed the word "poor" to encompass both the "idle, intemperate, and vicious," and the "wage-receivers of the humblest rank, who are degraded by the combination."[49] Sumner was right to worry about the effect of propagandistic use of language, and to advise that "the reader who desires to guard himself against fallacies should always scrutinize the terms 'poor' and 'weak' as used, so as to see which or how many of these classes they are made to cover."[50] Sumner's sarcasm concerning the Mr. Fantoms of his own day was well directed:

> The friends of humanity start out with certain benevolent feelings toward "the poor," "the weak," "the laborers," and others of whom they make pets. They generalize these classes, and render them impersonal, and so constitute the classes into social pets.[51]

Sadly, however, Sumner's Social Darwinist worldview tended to overwhelm his good sense. He assumed that those whom vice had overtaken were *perpetually* corrupt. And he felt that any help given the needy would mean "that those who have gone astray, being

relieved from Nature's fierce discipline, go on to worse...."[52] Sumner
explicitly dehumanized those who had fallen:

> Nature's remedies against vice are terrible. She removes
> the victims without pity. A drunkard in the gutter is just
> where he ought to be, according to the fitness and ten-
> dency of things. Nature has set up on him the process
> of decline and dissolution by which she removes things
> which have survived their usefulness.[53]

He ended, in essence, by forming an intellectual party of
anticompassion.

Sumner was joined in his arguments by Simon Newcomb, a profes-
sor at Johns Hopkins University, and probably the most astute of the
Social Darwinist economists who wrote about charitable efforts.
Newcomb showed that a dime offered to a beggar was a transaction of

> supply and demand, belonging to the same class as the sup-
> ply of and demand for personal services. The combined
> willingness and ability of a number of persons in the com-
> munity to give dimes to beggars constitutes a demand for
> beggary, just as much as if an advertisement, "Beggars
> wanted, liberal alms guaranteed," was conspicuously in-
> serted in the columns of a newspaper.[54]

Newcomb pointed out that intentions did not change objective laws:
"The fact that the benevolent gentleman may wish that there were no
beggars, and may be very sorry to see them, does not change the
economic effect of his readiness to give them money." Newcomb was

tough and precise: "From an economic point of view the gentleman pays the beggar for being poor, miserable, idle, dirty, and worthless."[55]

But Newcomb went on to note that it was not quite correct to call beggars "idle," for

> in every community where there is a demand for bricklay-
> ers a certain portion of the young will become bricklayers,
> and will try to lay bricks in such a way as to gain the highest
> wages… [and] in a community where there is a demand
> for beggars a certain number are sure to become beggars,
> and to study the professional accomplishments which will
> be most likely to draw money from the pockets of the
> benevolent.[56]

Newcomb argued strongly that society should not encourage such conduct. Brilliantly, he threw doubt even on the traditional distinction between voluntary and involuntary misery, on the assumption that those who did not volunteer for aid deserved it; instead, he traced some current miseries to patterns of conduct learned in childhood:

> To make a decent living, even of the lowest sort, [a person]
> must take pains, practise self-denial, seek for acquaintanc-
> es, and make for himself a good character among his
> fellow-men. It is therefore not necessary, in order that the
> demand for objects of charity should be supplied, that any
> person should deliberately make up his mind to be a beg-
> gar. To become such all he needs to do is to do nothing. He
> can then with a greater or less approximation to truth say,

"I have never tried to become a burden on society, and yet I can get no work; I have nothing to do; I am nearly starved; I shall soon be naked; I have no house in which to lay my head; I cannot get money for the barest necessities of existence."[57]

Newcomb's concern for children educated to dependency was valid and, on a society-wide scale, prescient. And yet, he based his ideas on a view that man was "by nature poor, miserable, and worthless." Newcomb was fond of the word "worthless," ignoring the biblical charge that no one created in God's image is without worth.[58] Newcomb's pedagogy was harsher still. It was based on teaching children that "they will starve to death unless they learn to make a living," and he seemed willing to accept starvation to make the lesson stick.[59] The extent of Newcomb's Social Darwinist logic made him sound like a potential killer:

Love of mankind at large should prompt us to take such measures as shall discourage or prevent the bringing forth of children by the pauper and criminal classes. No measure of repression would be too severe in the attainment of the latter object.[60]

Newcomb's blindness to the possibilities of change among even the most deprived and depraved, and his Darwinian emphasis on the survival of what seemed to be the genetically fittest, led him to seek eugenic alternatives. Believing that the future would depend upon "improving" the human stock, Newcomb contended that "the consideration due to a degraded man of any class is as nothing compared with that due to the society of the future." He opposed "the tender sentiments" that emerged from a biblical world view, for "those very sentiments are a source of enduring injury in the repugnance which they generate to a really effective system of dealing with the dangerous class in our population."[61] For all his brilliance, Newcomb was so carried away by Social Darwinist ideology that he became a leader of the anticompassion party.

For a time that party appeared about to sweep the field in urban areas. But during the 1870s and 1880s Social Darwinism also picked up strong opposition, especially from church members. The Brooklyn Christian Union called Social Darwinism an enemy of "the spiritual law of sacrifice" taught in the Bible and summarized most completely in the mercy of "the Father who spared not His Son for us," while *Charities Review* attacked the belief that "the only solution of this charitable problem is to let nature eliminate the poorer classes. Heaven forbid!"[62] Christians observed that Jesus neither abandoned the needy nor fed them immediately—instead, He taught them. (In Matthew 15, Jesus feeds thousands after they have listened to Him for three days. In Mark 6, Jesus first teaches—"He had compassion on them, because they were like sheep without a shepherd"—and only late in the day multiplies five loaves and two fish, so all eat and are satisfied.)

Evangelical Christians realized that only two concurrent changes could beat back Social Darwinism and really help the poor. First, both government and individuals had to refrain from handing out the bad charity that created unnecessary dependency. Second, thousands of points of light—not points of darkness likely to demoralize, but discerning alternatives—were needed. The new charities, they maintained, must not mimic governmental giving to all comers, but must apply under the present harsher urban conditions many of the lessons of charity learned earlier in the century.

The first step—getting governments out of the welfare distribution business—was a city-by-city struggle, but not a fruitless one. There was no national welfare system and very little on the state level during the 1870s; local programs of "outdoor relief"—payments to individuals outside of institutions—were fairly new and had not sunk deep bureaucratic roots. It was easy to explain to those who really wanted to help that, as the Associated Charities of Boston put it,

> the demoralizing effect of relief administered by the hands of city officials can hardly be overestimated, no matter how excellent the officials themselves may be. It created a dependent feeling, a dry rot, which leads the recipient of city bounty to look upon it as something due as a reward for destitution....[63]

Citizens could see that problems emerged "when officials create the impression that some right has been acquired by the pauper" to an unlimited fund created by taxpayers: "It is accessible and enticing.... He regards [it] as his by right...."[64]

Winning support through both patient argument and political organization, activists in eight of the largest cities—Brooklyn, New York, Baltimore, Philadelphia, Washington, St. Louis, Kansas City, and San Francisco—were able to abolish public outdoor relief during the 1870s and 1880s. In other cities, such as Pittsburgh, Providence, Cleveland, and Jersey City, some outdoor relief continued, but programs to separate the willing from the idle were put in place.[65] Reformers hailed the results: in 1881 Seth Low wrote that in both Philadelphia and Brooklyn "public out-door relief has been found to be unnecessary."[66] A recent historian disputes that conclusion, but it is clear that, in theory, welfare was found to be unnecessary.[67] The key question—whether the theory would work in practice—was implied in Low's contention that "whenever society has agents enough to organize relief, it can give, through private sources, all the out-door relief needed."[68] The question then: Would there be organization? Would there be agents?

Here, two writers/organizers became as important to the fight against Social Darwinism as Sumner and Newcomb were for it. Josephine Lowell of New York noted that

> in a country village, the mountain springs supply the water that is a necessity of life, but in the city, unhappily, we need reservoirs and pipes, ramifying through all the streets, and branching up into every house to bring us even the water we drink.... In like manner even our love to our neighbor must be guided through organized channels, or it will lose its life-giving powers and become a source of moral disease and death.[69]

Her book, *Public Relief and Private Charity*, became the bugle of a new philanthropic era. Buffalo minister S. Humphreys Gurteen's *A Handbook of Charity Organization* showed practically how to fill in the gaps left by the reformers' defeat of outdoor relief. A look at those two books shows how the older ideas of compassion were codified, revived, and adapted to urban circumstances.

Gurteen, who founded the Buffalo Charity Organization Society (COS), had been concerned since the Civil War with the "concentrated and systematized pauperism which exists in our larger cities."[70] He was well aware of new social conditions, including the emergence of some involuntary unemployment and the special need to assist a person impoverished "by no fault of his own."[71] But Gurteen also argued, as had Mather two centuries before, that material transfer from rich to poor was, by itself, morally neutral, and could be harmful: "It is possible to do an immense amount of harm by Charity, so-called. It is possible to reduce a fellow-being to the condition of a willing pauper, by fostering habits of indolence."[72]

Gurteen criticized the Social Darwinists directly, arguing that it is wrong

> to stand aloof in haughty indifference from all the woes of our fellowmen, and to close our ears to the cries of the suffering.... If left to themselves and no kind hand is held out to assist, they will inevitably sink lower and lower, till perchance they end their course in suicide or felony.[73]

He also noted, however, that Social Darwinist ruthlessness was a natural reaction to the "misdirected love" of those who chose to "give blindly at the approach of distress, real or feigned, mistaking the flutter of satisfaction, which ever follows an act of benevolence, for the smile of Heaven."[74] Both Social Darwinism and "Social Universalism" were harmful to those on the "border-line of involuntary poverty," for if "charity is not tempered by judgment," the poor will

> learn to be dependent, till at last, though by degrees, every vestige of manliness and ambition will have been destroyed, and they will come back as skilled beggars, to torment and curse the very people whose so-called charity has made them what they are.[75]

The goal, Gurteen insisted, should be a "more rational, more philosophic, more God-like method of meeting Pauperism."

To achieve that goal Gurteen created a new, self-consciously middle-of-the-road organization:

> To avoid these two extremes, both of which are fatal, is the grand object of the Charity Organization Society [COS]. It views man as God has made him, with capability of manliness and self-respect and holy ambition.[76]

Gurteen, in asking Buffalo citizens to support his COS, maintained the traditional emphasis on compassion defined as *suffering with*. He did not turn down cash contributions, but he asked whether the chief way for the better-off to help their neighbors was "by giving a handsome subscription from a full purse to this or that charity? By small doles of money or clothing to some favored individual? By doing our charity by proxy?"[77] "No!" Gurteen thundered, and went on to insist that Buffalo citizens become "personal workers" concerned with more than "the mere relief of bodily wants."[78] He emphasized the need to deal with spiritual as well as material problems.

At the same time, Gurteen insisted on the obligation of the recipients. He knew that, in conditions of urban anonymity, personal knowledge of character could no longer be counted on to aid dispensers of help to sort out potential claimants. Yes, a solid New York law did help: the state legislature in 1875 directed each almshouse to keep, along with a general register of the inmates,

> a record as to the sex, age, birth-place, birth of parents, education, habits, occupation, condition of ancestors and

family relations, and the cause of dependence of each person at the time of admission.[79]

And yes, questions about available resources were useful: applicants
for aid often were required to take "paupers' oaths" swearing to
destitution. Yes, there could be some checking into claims by the
applicant, although this was often difficult. But "the proof was in the
pudding." Beyond records, oaths, and investigations, Gurteen's
Buffalo Charity Organization Society set up a woodyard next to its
shelter and required able-bodied applicants for aid to take what
Gurteen called the "work test."

Gurteen was not the first to use the work test, but his handbook
publicized the idea and his ways of applying it. In Buffalo, he wrote,
transients willing to chop were given two meals and a night's lodging;
married male residents received food plus pay that could go for rent
and clothing; women were asked to sew in a nearby workroom. The
purpose of the work test was twofold. One objective, of course, was
to provide basic sustenance consistent with the apostle Paul's injunction that the able-bodied who did not work were not entitled to eat.
But a second and equally important goal was to see whether a person
had the character to work and keep at it; if he or she did, COS volunteers would work hard to help the person find steady employment.

By 1894, the Buffalo COS was providing 6,286 days of work to men
with families and 11,589 days of work to homeless men. The idea caught
on across the country, and Gurteen was able to study his and their
experience:

> When the managers of a Boston charity attached thereto a
> wood-yard, and announced that relief would be given to no

able-bodied man, unless willing to do a certain amount of work, the daily number of applicants fell off at once from one hundred and sixty to forty-nine. In every city, in which the test has been applied, it has been eminently successful.[80]

The rules of the Buffalo Charity Organization Society eventually institutionalized this procedure:

> The attempt to distinguish between worthy and unworthy cases is at times extremely difficult; in all cases, however, let the "labor axiom" be the test, i.e. whether or not the applicant is willing to do as much work as his condition will allow.[81]

Those who were crippled or temporarily unable to work because of illness were excused, as were widows with young children.

Gurteen advocated other self-sorting procedures. For example, a person who had shown the willingness to work would be eligible for financial help, but money was given as a legally recorded loan rather than a grant: Buffalo COS rules stipulated that "industrious persons are aided, whenever possible, to obtain suitable employment, and many are assisted during temporary difficulties by means of loans without interest, to be repaid in easy installments."[82] The emphasis on loans was a test of good faith, an affirmation of independence rather than pauperism, and a way of recycling limited resources. The Buffalo COS experience showed that, "owing to the arrangements made, and to the care observed by the committees in selecting suitable cases for this form of relief, the loans [were], with very few exceptions, faithfully repaid."[83]

Gurteen encountered criticism from those who thought true charity should be unconditional; one critic quoted Charles Lamb's maxim from his *Essays of Elia* earlier in the century, "Give and ask no questions." But Gurteen pointed out the flaws in what sounded nice:

> Is it, we ask, a very hard-hearted thing for the public to require an equivalent of labor, from those who are able to give it, in return for the relief which they receive? Is it unchristian? Is it not in the sweat of his brow that man is to eat his bread? Is not the Commandment, "Six days shalt thou labor?" And does not the apostle lay it down as a law, that "if any will not work, neither shall he eat?"[84]

He then asked more hard questions:

> Charles Lamb did but formulate the natural axiom of a lazy religion.... Look the question face to face for one moment.... Is it charity toward our neighbor to give on the strength of every well-thumbed letter or doleful tale, when by so doing we are only rendering easier the downward path of a fellow creature? Is it obeying the apostolic injunction to "do good and sin not," when by our indiscriminate alms-giving we are destroying the will to labor...? Is it charity, is it love, is it the God-like virtue of which St. Paul speaks, to let a sickly sentimentality cloud our reason...?[85]

And he concluded with the lessons of experience, pointing out that much drunkenness was "attributable to the money which Christian people had been in the habit of giving in the sacred name of Charity."[86] He saw pressure to change, when necessary, as a key part of compassion, and asked givers to think through the consequences of their actions, rather than settling for the burst of emotional comfort they themselves might sustain.

The other major theoritician-practitioner of the late nineteenth century, Josephine Shaw Lowell, shared Gurteen's view of human nature, and set up in New York City a Charity Organization Society similar to that of Buffalo. She criticized the Social Darwinists for callousness, but also criticized indiscriminate charitable practice that

> fails to save the recipient of relief and community from moral harm, because human nature is so constituted that no man can receive as a gift what he should earn by his own labor without a moral deterioration, and the prescence in the community of certain persons living on public relief, has the tendency to tempt others to sink to their degraded level.[87]

Mrs. Lowell argued for objective measurement of actions, not applause for good intentions: "Charity must go further than kind feeling," for "no amount of good feeling could convert an injurious act into a charitable one."[88] She provided evidence that "dolegiving and almsgiving do break down independence, do destroy energy, do undermine character." Like Gurteen, she recruited volunteers willing to "supply the precious element of human sympathy and tender personal interest which must often be lacking where the care of dependence is a business and the common everyday work the means of livelihood of overtaxed officials."[89]

Apparently working independently, she established the same principles for aid—the woodpile and so on—as Gurteen had in Buffalo.

When some observers were startled by the development of what was called "tramping"—later called "hoboing," and today a part of what is called "homelessness"—Mrs. Lowell was unsurprised. If men could survive without the burden of family obligations and responsibilities, of course a certain number would go off on their own.[90] Her COS warned that "honest employment, the work that God means every man to do, is the truest basis of relief for every person with physical ability to work." She argued that "the help which needlessly releases the poor from the necessity of providing for themselves is in violation of divine law and incurs the penalties which follow any infraction of that law."[91]

As Gurteen emphasized the work test, so Mrs. Lowell stressed investigating applicants. Many charity organization societies around the country credited to her the analysis that underlay their programs; for example, the Baltimore COS acknowledged that, because of her guidance, it began sending to the homes of applicants an agent

> who visits, relieves any pressing and unusual distress, makes careful note of all circumstances that would modify judgment, and [notifies] the church or charity on whom the person in need has a natural claim....[92]

If there was no evident matchup and the applicant deserved help, the organization would follow Mrs. Lowell's suggestions and notify "some benevolent individual in the district" who had expressed a willingness to help.

Once immediate needs were taken care of, the COS moved to

> secure for each family needing it a Volunteer Visitor, who will patiently strive to remove the cause of need [and] make the

applicant self-sustaining [by providing advice and help con-
cerning] employment, medical treatment, educational advantages, provident habits....[93]

The knowledge that an investigation was likely forestalled many fraudulent and unnecessary requests, the COS noted, but in some cases the
last of its listed functions was essential to avoid pauperization and
compassion fatigue: "Exposes deliberate imposture and fraud, warns
the perpetrator and, if this proves of no avail, takes legal measures to
protect the charitable public."[94] (In 1891, out of 7,943 applications, there
were 369 cases—5 percent—of "vagrants warned, exposed or
arrested.")

Above all, Mrs. Lowell wanted to stop the spread of the dependency disease. She observed that "the presence in the community of
certain persons living on public relief" leads others to fall into the
welfare trap also. Moreover, outdoor relief "has the tendency to become
regular and permanent" unless political pressure to stop it breaks
through barriers established by those who claim compassion as their
own.[95] She concluded that public aid "can not be defended; it has none
of the redeeming features of private charity, because there is nothing
personal or softening in it."

Mrs. Lowell, while staunchly opposing the Social Darwinists
who assumed that those who had descended into dependency
would stay there, lashed out strongly against the pauperization and
compassion fatigue that resulted from universalistic subsidies.
Transfer of material without obligation to the recipient taught dependency, and that was the worst possible education:

Nothing should be done under the guise of charity, which
tends to break down character. It is the greatest wrong

that can be done to him to undermine the character of a
poor man.

Social Darwinists who saw inevitable defeat for "the degraded class"
communicated an attitude of hopelessness. Mrs. Lowell emphasized
challenge and hope, and argued that both those who ignored the poor
and those who gave unthinkingly, lacked persevering love for the
worker who was poor but still proud: "The struggle is hard, he needs
all his determination and strength of will to fight his way, and nothing
that deprives him of these qualities can be 'charitable.' "[96]

Gurteen and Lowell had shown the negatives of noncompassionate
charity—but would volunteers in city after city be capable of developing positive alternatives? By the 1880s it was clear that individual,
church, and community effort was needed to beat back Social
Darwinism and truly help the poor. To do so, citizens would have to
understand that the outdoor relief of the soup-kitchens was not generous but stingy—stingy in human contact, stingy in its estimation of
what human beings made after God's image were capable of doing and
becoming, and stingy in refusing to divide up the available amount of
material support so that those who really needed it received an ample
supply, but those who would be hurt by it received none.

CHAPTER FIVE

Proving Social Darwinism Wrong

By the mid-1880s outdoor relief was out and the works of Gurteen and Lowell were in the bookstores. But neither subtraction nor theoretical addition would solve the problem without an outpouring of volunteers for effective charitable organizations. Conventional history texts, if they mention pre-New Deal poverty fighting at all, suggest that (1) whatever happened is irrelevant to our problems because conditions were so different then, and (2) not much happened anyway. The first statement is not true, as we have seen. The second also is not true: Records in the Library of Congress show tens of thousands of points of light, including two thousand in Baltimore, Chicago, and New York alone during 1890 (a decade and a half after the drive against outdoor relief began in earnest, a decade and a half before what became known as the "social gospel" kicked in).

In Baltimore, the Association for the Improvement of the Condition of the Poor had two thousand volunteers who made 8,227 visits in 1891 to 4,025 families. Nearly half of those families were headed by widows, and they generally received material aid; most of the others were headed by able-bodied men, who generally received help in fighting alcohol and opium addiction and securing jobs. The personal involvement of rich and poor, not just material transfer, was evident in many ways. The Memorial Union for the Rescue of Homeless and Friendless Girls offered free rooms with private families where teenagers and young women were placed until long-term housing and jobs could be found. The Home for Mothers and Infants provided personal help and religious instruction to destitute women with small children. And the Presbyterian Eye, Ear and Throat Charity Hospital offered free beds and Bible readers to those unable to pay or read.[1]

The Baltimore charity groups typically emphasized self-help for most of the poor and material transfer only for those unable to work. In 1890 the Thomas Wilson Fuel-Saving Society, designed to assist "those who have but little money to lay by small sums during the summer, for the purchase of coal in the winter at reduced rates," helped 1,500 families to buy 3,000 tons of coal, and 400 families to buy sewing machines.[2] When Orville Horwitz established the Horwitz Benevolent Fund, he stipulated that money "would not be distributed among political idlers or bummers, but would be so applied as to relieve the actual distress of worthy persons."[3]

Many of the charity groups had Protestant bases, but Catholic and Jewish groups flourished along similar principles; for example, volunteers with the Society of St. Vincent de Paul of the City of Baltimore made 4,800 visits and relieved 345 families, while those with the Hebrew Benevolent Society and the Hebrew Ladies Sewing Society helped widows and provided job leads and challenge to the able-bodied.[4]

The Chicago story was similar; records for 1891 show about 200,000 families and individuals aided through the work of 124 points of light. As in Baltimore, organizations tended to fall along religious lines. The charter of the Chicago Erring Woman's Refuge for Reform, which cared for 171 girls and young women in 1891, provided "that the Board of Managers shall include not less than one member of each Protestant Church in Chicago," and the Chicago Home for the Friendless defined itself as "a Protestant institution" that gave "protection and employment or assistance" to 985 women and 929 children in 1891 (1,230 listed their religion as Protestant, 649 Roman Catholic, and 30 Jewish). Church-based organizations generally did not discriminate along religious lines; the Home for Crippled Children, for example, announced that "the home is distinctly Protestant, but no child is debarred on account of race, nationality or religious belief."[5] They generally did discriminate, and explicitly, "in favor of those in whom habits of temperance, industry and thrift give promise of permanent benefit from the aid furnished...."[6]

That emphasis on categorizing cut across religious lines. The Helping Hand agency agreed to help the able who are "willing to work" but not "drinking men or loafers,"[7] while Catholic institutions such as St. Mary's Training School for Boys were well known for their no-nonsense approach. When the United Hebrew Charities of Chicago reported the work of its employment bureau for 1990, it noted that 549 men were helped to get jobs (201 as laborers and porters, 61 as clerks, 26 as butchers, 16 as shoemakers, 15 as cabinet makers, and 23 as tailors), but "119 refused employment when offered, though the abilities of the applicants were consulted."[8] Those 119 were not welcomed back unless they indicated a willingness to work.

New York's charity organizations also tended to stress personal help and the exchange of time rather than money. The American Female Guardian Society and Home for the Friendless sheltered over a thousand children who were "not consigned to institution life but were transferred by adoption to Christian homes." The Nursery and Child's Hospital (Lexington Avenue and 51st Street) gave free medical care and support to hundreds of unmarried pregnant women in return for their agreement "to remain three months after confinement to take care of two infants." New York's 1,288 charitable organizations often employed professional managers, but one of their major tasks was to coordinate the activities of tens of thousands of volunteers who provided food, clothing, fuel, shelter, and employment, supported free schools and kindergartens, organized sea excursions and summer camps, staffed free hospitals and dispensaries, and constructed missions and reformatories, libraries and reading-rooms.[9]

Most charity groups of the day demanded that all able-bodied persons work. The St. Barnabas House typically provided "temporary help because of sickness and adversity" to 1,656 individuals in 1891, but warned that "this is not a home for rounders"; i.e., those who made the rounds of give-away places. And the Riverside Rest Association provided shelter for alcoholics or opium addicts only if they seemed determined to go straight. Those capable of working were almost always required to report to one of the dozens of organizations with names like the Christian Aid to Employment Society, the Evangelical Aid Society for the Spanish, the Olivet Helping Hand Society, and the Society for the Employment and Relief of Poor Women. Groups such as the Industrial Christian Alliance noted that they used "religious methods"—namely, prayer and worship of a God who made man little lower than the angels, and was not content to see him little higher than the animals—to "restore the fallen and helpless to self-respect and self-support."

Medical care was available at clinics throughout the city, including the Harlem Dispensary, the Bloomingdale Clinic for the Free Treatment of the Poor, the Good Samaritan Dispensary (which treated 73,363 new patients in 1891 and dispensed 85,752 prescriptions), and the North-Eastern Dispensary, which treated 22,431 persons, including 3,276 in their own homes—yes, clinic doctors even made free house calls. Descriptions of these dispensaries regularly included the words, "supported by private contributions." Other voluntary organizations served specialty interests: the Lunacy Law Reform and Anti-Kidnapping League was "for the protection of sane persons against unjust and unlawful imprisonment in insane asylums and hospitals," and the Society for the Purification of Italian Quarters worked "to drive houses of ill-fame, beer dives,... and gangs of loafers, thieves, etc., from Italian quarters, and... to stop the sale of decayed fruits and vegetables."[10]

Some of these groups were ecumenical; the New York Charity Organization placed applicants for aid "as speedily as possible under the care of their nearest religious affiliations," regardless of sect. Others, like the Asylum for the Relief of Half-Orphan and Destitute Children, described themselves as "Protestant in influence." As in other cities, however, specifically Catholic activities, usually organized on a parish basis, also were numerous. The able-bodied homeless could generally receive a bed at shelters like St. Joseph's Night Refuge, but they had to do some work. As the *Saint Vincent De Paul Quarterly* explained,

> The Vincentian must be prepared to discipline, admonish and encourage.... [Most of the poor] must be disciplined into providence, for they are seldom provident for themselves. To be their true benefactors, the visitor must admonish them...to know and appreciate their high destiny....

St. Patrick's Cathedral sponsored a free school with 1,500 students, a free library, a Young Men's Literary and Athletic Society, and many other "self-improvement" activities, and St. Alphonsus sponsored a total abstinence society. Organizations such as the Epiphany Ladies Society for Clothing Poor Children paralleled the Protestant-based Dorcas sewing circles.[11]

New York had an abundance of Jewish charitable organizations as well: the United Hebrew Charities (UHC) had workrooms and medical and employment bureaus that mirrored those of its Christian-based neighbors. The UHC medical bureau in 1899 provided 12,480 nurses' visits, 3,037 house calls by doctors, and 4,406 office visits, and gave the needy not only 5,634 prescriptions but 440 bottles of cod-liver oil.[12] An employment bureau helped find jobs for 4,176, and even provided an alternative job site for a recent immigrant cited for "violation of Sanitary Code, killing chicken in tenement house." UHC also provided detectives and lawyers to track down and bring to court husbands who abandoned wives and children. In short, thousands of volunteers pro-vided guidance to new arrivals in America.[13]

The accent on personal involvement was present in every report of the United Hebrew Charities. Knowledgeable counsel is "as impor-tant as the relieving of wants," one annual report stated:

> The conditions of success in this country may be made plain, and the insane anticipations of easy prosperity may be corrected. The best kind of life and the most available region of the country may be pointed out.[14]

Manager Nathaniel Rosenau noted that if every person possessing the capability should assume the care of a single family, there "would not be enough poor to go around."[15] Many synagogue and temple sister-hoods sponsored employment bureaus, day nurseries, "working girls' clubs," sewing rooms, and reading rooms. The Hebrew Benevolent Fuel Society, for example, distributed 250 tons of coal to the "worthy poor," the Ladies' Hebrew Lying-In Society helped 397 poor mothers in 1891, and the Achnoseth Orchim Association provided temporary lodging for Jewish immigrants and helped them find jobs and learn English, as did the American Committee for Ameliorating the Condition of Russian Refugees.

The UHC also worked hard in another area—to beat compassion fatigue. It showed that its funds went not to perpetuate pauperization but to fight it. One annual report noted that only 7 percent of individuals helped five years before were still on the rolls, since "many of those whom this organization [has] aided, [have] become self-supporting."[16] The understanding among religions of the need to challenge the poor was evident when *The American Hebrew*, a magazine representing conservative Judaism, ran declarations that "heart and hand should work in unison," for charity requires "disciplinary force as well as a free hand. It must find out the defects of an applicant and try and build up character."[17] The building-up would begin early: the Hebrew Sheltering and Guardian Society of New York helped six hundred children aged three to fourteen by "removing them from all harmful associations" and giving them "religious and moral education."

Similar charitable patterns emerged in smaller cities as well. The Women's Christian Association of Pittsburgh and Allegheny established the Pittsburgh Home for Destitute Women, the Home for Working Women, the Home for Aged Protestant Women, and the Sheltering Arms, a reformatory for the erring who wished to be reformed.[18] A small group in Utica, New York, established sewing schools for women and children, a hospital, and an employment bureau,[19] and groups in Kansas City and other cities, like those in New York and

Chicago, provided poor families with coal during the winter and penny ice during the summer, making small charges to avoid "pauperizing."[20] Discretion in giving was of course allowed: a family with a sick child could receive twenty-five pounds of ice rather than ten, a major difference under crowded conditions in urban slums.[21]

It is hard to get an overall number of the people helped by the tens of thousands of points of light, not only because of the diversity of the small organizations but also because many individual churches and synagogues carried on their own private programs and varied tremendously in their record-keeping. One analysis of activity among 112 Protestant churches in Manhattan and the Bronx alone showed that 397 social agencies were run by the churches, including 48 industrial schools, 45 libraries or reading rooms, 44 sewing schools, 40 kindergartens, 29 small-sum savings banks and loan associations, 21 employment offices, 20 gymnasia and swimming pools, 8 medical dispensaries, 7 full-day nurseries, and 4 lodging houses.[22] There were also dozens of laundries, night schools, and cooking schools, as well as a legal aid society, a medical aid society, a bowling alley, a billiard room, two woodyards, and two low-cost coal clubs.

Some of the churches located in slum areas had an enormous variety of programs. St. Bartholomew's, located in an area of New York City to which immigrants from the Middle East were flocking, sponsored a tailor shop that provided temporary work for thirty-five women and 3,600 garments for needy children, and an employment bureau that filled over 2,500 jobs annually. Volunteers fluent in Armenian, Syriac, and Turkish staffed special job-finding and evangelism programs for immigrants. The church set up a medical clinic that served nearly eight thousand patients and provided over 13,000 prescriptions, with 90 percent of the recipients paying small amounts. The church also established a Mutual Benefit Fund for low-cost insurance, a Penny Provident Fund that allowed three thousand depositors to save small amounts on a regular basis, and a Loan Association that provided access to low-cost loans.

In addition, the church ran summer camps and sports programs, and provided free classes in English composition, dressmaking, embroidering, sewing, and cooking, along with classes (for a small fee) in stenography, bookkeeping, and French. Over two thousand students enrolled in evening classes, and four thousand came to Sunday school classes offered in English, Armenian, Syriac, and Turkish. The church's community center had a library and rooms for meetings of various clubs, and even used its flat top as a gardening center where neighborhood children grew flowers and vegetables, while a Fresh Air program provided two thousand outings to countryside and beach. Soon, so many people were coming to the church for services as well as activities that the church had eighteen services in several languages on Sunday, including one in Armenian and one in Chinese.

Another New York Episcopal church, St. George's, whose membership largely dwelt in tenements, offered a nursery and an Industrial Trade School that gave courses in carpentry, drawing, printing, plumbing, and other skills to three hundred students. The church also ran a special trolley car five days per week each summer to a seaside cottage it owned on Long Island; nearly six thousand adults and an equal number of children went in the summer of 1899, with the day's trip arranged, as the church bulletin noted, so that mothers could get home in time to cook dinner. Two other Episcopal churches in New York, Grace Church and the Church of the Ascension, established the Houses of Anna and Simeon for the elderly, provided shelter to abandoned children, ran a laundry service that provided thirty-seven jobs and laundered over 200,000 articles per year, and provided the "worthy poor" with physicians, pharmacists, legal aid, and trips to museums and art galleries.[23]

Also in New York, Baptist churches on Fifth and Marcy avenues operated a day nursery, kindergarten, and community library, and sent 250 children at a time to a two-week outing on a farm. Near the Bowery, the Lodging House Missionary Society of the Broome Street Tabernacle conducted gospel meetings for those who lived in cheap lodging houses; the church itself provided a cooking school, a gymnasium, a library, and regular lectures.[24] In Cincinnati, teachers at the Ninth Street Baptist Church gave free sewing lessons to three hundred girls and free singing lessons to five hundred boys and girls, and the church provided physicians, nurses, and medicine in cases of medical emergency. Its ministers reported that God's grace and church social programs (in that order) led to eight hundred confessions of faith over a seven-year period.

In the tenement district of Boston, the Methodists' Morgan Chapel offered five-cent baths in its basement for those living in tub-less tenements, and visits from volunteer physicians to the needy. The church also provided classes (taught by volunteer instructors) in dressmaking, carpentry, tailoring, and printing, and put unemployed women to work making garments and staffing a nursery and kindergarten. Volunteers from local music conservatories taught vocal and instrumental classes and gave free Saturday evening concerts; the concerts were followed by a temperance meeting which concluded at 11 P.M.—the same time the bars closed. These activities were tied to the church's evangelical mission and helped the church accept more conversions during 1899 than in any of its previous fifty years.[25]

Many Chicago churches had their own programs, too. Grace Church (Episcopal) was typical in developing an industrial school, a

"Working Girl's Society," and a "Diet Kitchen" that prepared food for invalids. Parachurch organizations also flourished; they included the Woman's Baptist Home Mission Society, with "religious and temperance features," and the Chicago Central Woman's Christian Temperance Union, which sponsored a day nursery, a free kindergarten, a free medical dispensary, and two missions. The Anchorage Mission for Women, for its part, held prayer meetings, helped find jobs for three hundred women, and cared for fifty "unfortunate girls who have been led astray."

Across the country parallel patterns emerged. In Buffalo, eight resident helpers and eighty volunteer workers at Westminster Presbyterian Church listed nearly seven thousand appointments a year for a variety of social services tied to evangelism. In Pittsburgh, the Fourth Avenue Baptist Church was known for its visiting nurse who made 8,000 visits to 800 patients (including 43 who had typhoid fever) in three years. And the church's Toy Mission enlisted six hundred volunteers to prepare and distribute 3,600 toys to poor children at Christmas. In St. Louis, St. Stephen's Mission was known for its clothing department, kitchen, laundry room, gymnasium, library, baths, and conversions.[26]

Probably the largest set of programs was developed in Philadelphia by a minister, Russell Conwell, who had been successful in law and journalism before turning to preaching and helping his Grace Church to become the largest Protestant congregation in the United States. Hundreds of church volunteers and paid workers staffed the large assortment of benevolent organizations, including Samaritan Hospital, which became a "teaching, healing, and preaching church."[27] Conwell gave his famous lecture on individual initiative, "Acres of Diamonds," thousands of times over several decades throughout the United States, and used the profits, along with contributions, to open several reading rooms and, in 1890, the enormous Baptist Temple. By 1897-98 the night school started by that church had classes attended by 3,500 students, lectures that drew an additional four thousand, a law curriculum, and a theological seminary; the school is known today as Temple University.

One way to improve outreach as well as discernment was to institute careful training programs for volunteers. In Brooklyn, the Tabernacle Lay College offered courses on city missions, management of orphanages and prisons, establishment of Sunday schools, and so on. In New York, Bethany Institute (originally called the Training Home for Christian Workers) provided training in ministry and internships at city missions. By 1892, Bethany was drawing students from most denominations as well as from all areas of the country, and had graduated nearly four hundred women. In Chicago, the Bible School for the Training of Evangelists emphasized not only full-time but also volunteer spiritual and material work in poor areas. Similarly, the American Christian Commission worked "to educate those who would follow Christ in a life of labor among the poor, the criminal and the outcast."[28]

Churches also tried to increase outreach by distributing tracts widely through organizations such as the New York City Mission and Tract Society. The society explained that "benevolence is a Christian virtue, and hence a Christian's duty," but added that "haphazard [and] indiscriminate giving is not benevolence." The demoralized poor needed a change of heart:

> When the street-beggar tells his pitiful story, it is harder for
> a tenderhearted man to say "No," than to give him a dime
> and so get rid of him.... This wholesale, blind almsgiving

is a fruitful cause of pauperism and crime. While, therefore, true benevolence is a virtue, this false benevolence is a sin.[29]

The tract concluded, "Let no close-fisted brother hide behind our words, and find in them an excuse for not giving at all. What is censured is not giving too much, but giving in the wrong way." The right way was to distribute Bible materials and explain patiently and personally how God's teaching could change lives.

Other activities often had a denominational flavor and were designed to show particular faiths in practice. Few Christians in those days understood pluralism to mean that they should shelve their religious convictions. Presbyterians maintained over one hundred missions and industrial training schools; a church such as Bethany Presbyterian in Philadelphia sponsored homes for women and children, a cooperative society that provided health and death benefits, kindergartens, a day nursery, employment bureau, workingmen's club, savings bank, dispensary, and Bethany College.[30] The Methodists' Bureau of Local Missionary Work had about fifty missions operating in 1890, including Glenn Home in Cincinnati and the E. E. March Home in Chicago.[31] A typical Methodist church in the 1890s emphasized both person-to-person evangelism and established a building association in which people were taught and helped to save toward a home.[32] As for Lutherans, by 1894 they were operating at least 75 orphanages and hospitals. A new denomination, the Christian and Missionary Alliance, became particularly known for urban evangelism.

New York's church directories from the 1870s through the 1890s also show an enormous number of Catholic activities, parish by parish. Our Lady of Mercy, for example, had a circulating library and mutual benevolent association; St. Alphonsus advertised a Beneficial Society, a reading room, and a men's total abstinence society; and St. Vincent de Paul's had a free sewing class and a free school and day nursery.[33] Annual reports and directories also describe the employment bureaus, sewing schools, day nurseries, "working girls' clubs," and other organizations set up by the sisterhoods of Jewish congregations such as Beth-El, Ahawath Chesed, Shaarat Zedek, Rodef Sholom, Shaarai Hashomayim, Shearith Israel, B'nai Jeshurun, Emanu-El, and Shaaray Tefila.[34]

The traditional efforts to help orphans and abandoned children led many churches to join in building asylums for some and placing others. By 1890 Baltimore Catholics were funding St. Vincent's Infant Asylum (for children up to six), the Dolan Children's Aid Asylum (under the supervision of the Young Catholic's Friend Society and the Sisters of the Holy Cross), St. Patrick's Orphan Asylum, St. Joseph's House of Industry, St. Peter's Asylum for Female Children, and (separate and perhaps equal) the St. Elizabeth Home for Colored Children.[35] And in Boston, Chaplain Rufus R. Cook of the Suffolk County Jail interviewed boys arrested for petty theft or similar offenses who expressed a desire to reform. If they seemed determined, he gained their probation to the custody of the Society, sent them to a farm in West Newton (about ten miles from Boston), and trained them there for several months.[36] If their conduct was good, they were placed at approved family farms throughout New England. The farmers were responsible for schooling, clothing, and feeding the boys; the goal was to let the boys see life in an intact family, while they learned a trade.

Success rates for the programs varied, and statistics were not always reliable. A Massachusetts Board of Charities study in 1869 showed that 80 percent of the four hundred boys placed by Cook were doing well. Another study showed that 20 of 95 boys placed had run back to their old urban haunts—but that left 75 still leading changed lives on the farms. Work with children became one of the two most publicized late nineteenth-century charitable activities. The other—and probably the most dramatic theater of the late nineteenth-century's war on poverty and Social Darwinism—was the mission movement.

It was remarkable, to begin with, that the mission movement picked up the support it did, for when the better-off peered into the worst slums of New York and other large cities, even the best intentioned were put off. Alfred S. Hatch, a president of the New York Stock Exchange who espoused Social Darwinism before converting to Christianity, noted that

> theoretically all Christians believe that the vilest sinner may be saved, yet there is much practical unbelief and skepticism on the subject, when they are brought face to face with some of the worst forms of human depravity.[37]

It was also remarkable that it began where it did, on Water Street in New York City, for nowhere in America did skepticism seem more warranted.

The Water Street/Fourth Ward area, just below the Bowery, was a place with "the poorest sort of poor homes and some of the worst of saloons," dozens of them.[38] Alcoholic men slept at low tide in pits that turned into salty pools when the tide rolled in. Desperate prostitutes huddled in basements, dashed out to grab the hats of passing sailors, and ran back into their unlit quarters, waiting for the sailors to come in to retrieve and perhaps stay, in the shadows where diseased faces could not be seen.

The Water Street way of life was perhaps best symbolized by its most famous attraction, Kit Burns' Rat Pit. The Rat Pit, at 273 Water Street, was a combination bar and amphitheater where dogs fought rats while men laid down bets. Inside, hollering was heavy as one dog and up to one hundred rats were turned loose in the pit and wages were placed on the rate of rat death. When that grew tiring Burns's son-in-law would jump into the pit and fight the rats unarmed except for teeth (and may the better bite win). When even that grew tedious the denizens of Water Street could toast the exploits of a six-foot Englishwoman known as Gallus Mag, who fought frequently with pistol and club and liked to bite off the ears of opponents. She displayed the trophies in a jar of alcohol.[39]

Several New York clergymen in 1868 had tried to strike at the heart of Water Street hell-raising. They had contracted with Kit Burns to rent his rat pit for an hour a day at the rate of $150 per month (the equivalent of ten times that amount now). When the preachers and choristers arrived each day, Burns cleaned the blood from the floor of the arena and put a table in the center with a pitcher of ice water on it. Reporters and church members from uptown filled the seats, heard a sermon, and were hurried out by Burns, who told reporters, "Them fellows has been making a pulpit out of my rat pit and I'm going to purify it after them. Jim! Bring out them varmints."[40] Nothing had changed, and the rats scurried around.

The reasons for the failure were not hard to fathom. As the *New York Herald* pointed out, professional preachers were orating over the heads of Water Street listeners: "What is wanted is a man of enthusiasm... rough language and homely bits of philosophy, who intuitively knows exactly the emotions which govern his hearers."[41] Kit Burns himself described the problem succinctly:

I don't want to say a word against them preachers for they've paid me a pretty fair rent for the pit, but if they ever want to reform the girls in Water Street and shut up its rum mills they've got to do it in some other way than by howling for it.[42]

The man who found the other way was Jerry McAuley, a prime candidate for any Social Darwinist least-wanted list. McAuley's father, a counterfeiter, abandoned his family. McAuley's mother, unable to control her son, sent him off to other relatives, and by nineteen, when Jerry McAuley was sent off to the state penitentiary for highway robbery, he was known as a riotous drunkard and an accomplished local bandit.

A change seemed to occur during the next several years: McAuley attended gospel meetings in prison and read the Bible, a copy of which was placed in every cell. But when he was let out after serving half of his fifteen-year sentence, McAuley was soon back to his old pursuits—in his own estimate, a more vicious thief than ever before.[43] Yet, a seed of reformation had been planted, in soil more fertile than anyone might have guessed. McAuley *would* listen to the volunteer missionaries who came through the neighborhood; he *would* resolve, again and again, to do better, only to fall back, again and again, and perform a vicious act in anger against his own "weakness." Finally, after four years of sporadic action but increasingly fervent prayer, he was able to stay straight.[44]

McAuley, however, did not know what to do with his new life. He no longer wanted to be a "river thief," yet he needed not only something to be, but something to do. His progress was erratic until finally, in his own words,

I had a sort of trance or vision.... It seemed as if I was working for the Lord down in the Fourth Ward. I had a house
and people were coming in. There was a bath and they came
in and I washed and cleansed them outside and the Lord
cleansed them inside. They came at first by small numbers,
then by hundreds, and afterwards by thousands.... Something
said to me, "Would you do that for the Lord if He should call
you?" I answered, "Yes, Lord, open the way and I will go." I
felt that I could go down there where I had always lived. I was
used to the filth and felt sure I should be called to work for
Jesus there.[45]

McAuley now had a goal in life: to establish a mission and help others
who were as he had been and still, to some extent, was.

Getting started was hard. McAuley's friends and advisors initially
tried to discourage him. One minister said, "You're wild, Jerry, to try
to start a mission down there. Why, they'll kill you the first thing and
fire you and the benches outdoors together." McAuley replied that he
had "taken and given a good many hard knocks," and would set up the
mission "where I am most needed and where no one else wants to go."[46]
He did that in 1872 by renting a small, Water Street room with personal
help and funds provided by church leaders who were unwilling to give
up, even though their plan of importing middle-class ecclesiastical
style into the Rat Pit had failed.[47]

McAuley's services were different from anything Water Street had
ever seen. He invited in tough guys and stumblers-by for cheap, hot
food and lots of hot stories. Tales of destitution and depravity were on
the menu every night, but so was dessert—stories by McAuley and
others of how God's grace had changed their own lives. Men coming

off the street "were a terrible degraded set, hungry and alive with vermin, but we looked beyond all that and saw only souls," McAuley said. "Every now and then God found a real jewel among them."[48]

The McAuley Mission grew. Night after night, in a narrow, stuffy hall, between four walls filled with verses from the New Testament, a crowd of thieves, ex-convicts, and drunkards who had hit bottom, gathered from 7:30 to 9:00 o'clock for hymns, a Bible reading, a short statement by McAuley, and then—the most exciting part of the evening—individual confessions and testimonies. A burglar told of his crimes and desire to change.[49] A longshoreman detailed corruption and explained why he had to get out.[50] An engineer, a printer, and a steamship officer told their stories in frank language.[51] People from wealthy families also came to tell and be told. A Dartmouth student who had become a drunken lawyer told how he was sinking deeper and deeper until God transformed his life.[52] In the Victorian age there was nothing sheltered about such talk and the worship that arose as lives were transformed.

The goal, of course, was to let those who had stumbled in see that dramatic change in their lives was possible, and to challenge them to speak up also. McAuley believed in *challenge*; he wanted each individual to recognize his own "sin" and his own need for the grace to change. One night a man stood and began praying, in a stereotyped way, for "the heathen," for sinners everywhere, for everyone except himself. McAuley interrupted and said, "Look here, my friend, you had better ask God to have mercy on *your* soul."[53]

The emphasis was always on individual responsibility and the need to change, and McAuley did not readily accept excuses. "You know you're living in the gutter and you know it's your own fault," he said one night. "God didn't put you in the gutter. You went there of your own accord."[54] Then he asked the pointed question:

> Are you satisfied? Of course you're not. I know because I've
> tried the devil's service myself. I've been a thief. I've been
> in jail.... I crawled up out of the gutter at last, with God's
> help, and now I want to get you out ... [but you'll never] be
> any better until you stop sinning and come to Christ. Now
> if there's any one of you who has manliness enough left to
> say to me, to this company, and to Almighty God that he's
> going to try to stop sinning and live a new life, let him get
> up and say so.[55]

And several dozen of the several hundred in the audience would, speaking briefly but often movingly.

The mission was also careful to celebrate "anniversaries"—when a convert had stood fast for one year, he would lead the service and tell his story at length for the first time. One night a Scottish immigrant named Andy, celebrating his anniversary, told of how he had been a drunkard, gambler, and drifter, until the night he wandered into the mission, drunk. Then, through God's grace, his life was changed: he prayed and resolved to change, took a job as a cook, and was now reconciled with his family in Scotland, to which he planned to return shortly. McAuley urged such testimony, for he said that "those of us whom God has taken out of the dirty hole ought to be always telling of his goodness."[56]

The McAuley Mission had an effect not only on the down-and-out but on wealthy Christians who had been sliding toward Social Darwinism. Helen E. Brown, who put McAuley's reminiscences into book form, wrote:

> I have been taught, while preparing this simple biogra-
> phy...deep and sweet lessons of faith in work with the

outcast and fallen, both men and women. No erring
fellow-creature has sunk so low in grovelling vice, but that
now I believe, however my faith was formerly staggered,
that Jesus is "able to save to the uttermost." And this is a
lesson of priceless value to the Christian worker.[57]

And Reverend William M. Taylor, pastor of the Broadway Tabernacle
Church, told the skeptical, "The world's outcasts can be saved by
Christ. If Jerry could be saved, who not?"[58]

Undeniably, radical changes did take place; only the cause was debated. William James' *The Varieties of Religious Experience* records the
conversion at the mission of Samuel Hadley, an alcoholic who was over-
come by guilt for his sins as he heard the testimonies of others. James
recounted how Hadley fell to his knees in front of all and shook with
fear, until his face suddenly relaxed as a sense of rebirth swept through
him. James added one telling fact: Hadley never drank again, and went
on to become first the director of the Water Street Mission, and then of
another mission that he opened himself. This, according to James, was
abnormal psychology, explicable as a natural phenomenon. But for
McAuley, the cause of change among others was the same as his own: "I
have been a great sinner, and have found Jesus a great Saviour, and that
is why I would tell my story, that others may be led to adore and seek the
blessed Friend who saved, and has thus far kept me by his grace."[59]

In any event, many individuals helped by McAuley went on to help
others. When Michael Dunn, a fifty-two-year-old ex-convict who had
spent two-thirds of his life in prison, crossed the threshold into the
Water Street mission in 1878, McAuley told him,

> You've got brains and you've used them for naught since
> God gave them to you but to do rascality and teach the

same to others. It's time now to turn round and see if you can't undo some of your wicked work. Do you like it? Do you want to keep on serving terms till you go up to your last Judge? I believe you can be an honest man and a happy one if you will.[60]

Dunn was "born again," and the following year set up a halfway house, the House of Industry and Home for Discharged Convicts. By 1881 Dunn had enough support to establish a home with room to feed and lodge twenty-seven ex-convicts. The men made brooms or worked at other tasks in return for their room and board, and spent evenings in the reading room or at religious meetings held three nights a week.

During the 1880s, as McAuley's autobiography was distributed widely throughout the United States, other leaders tried to prove the Social Darwinists wrong. Chicago's Pacific Garden Mission (founded in 1877), Washington, D.C.'s, Central Union Mission, and Boston's North End Mission became three of the best-known inner-city efforts. The North End Mission even spun off associates—Elliot Christian Mission, Women's Mission, Portland Street Mission, Pitts Street Mission, Kneeling Street Mission—throughout Boston. Some missions were for all comers, and others had particular appeal; John Jaegar's "Mission of the Living Waters," for example, on Chrystie and then Delancey streets in New York's lower east side, became a refuge for German-speaking immigrants.[61] But the goal of all the missions was the challenge to change, not subsidy of sordidness: in New Haven the Union Gospel Mission worked to help "pauperized humanity" become "self-respecting, self-supporting, upright Godfearing citizens."[62]

The missions relied on volunteer help and contributions from individuals such as Alfred Hatch of the Stock Exchange. Missions also were aided by favorable stories in the *Christian Herald* and other evangelical magazines.[63] The *Herald* described shelter missions such as the Friendly Inn of Boston, which from 1884 through 1893 provided 120,000 nights of lodging, 275,000 meals, and several hundred thousand hours of work in the woodyards to homeless men. The *Herald* noted how work provided not only meals but a future, for when supervisors saw men sober and faithful in their work, they helped them find permanent jobs.[64] Other urban missions built model tenements and lodging houses, equipped libraries and reading rooms, and provided job training.[65]

Nor were missions confined to the larger cities. In Germantown, Pennsylvania, William Raws was converted to Christianity at a revival meeting in 1888, and soon began urban evangelical work of his own. He opened the Whosoever Gospel Mission in 1892 in the space that had housed a saloon, and then added to the basic gospel service a lodging house, dining hall, and woodyard.[66] At first those who needed food and lodging were put to work chopping wood and manufacturing brooms, but by 1897 over one hundred men could choose among brushmaking, shoemaking, upholstering, printing, or chaircaning by day, and enjoy gospel meetings and safe lodging at night. The mission continued to grow until, by 1914, 125 persons were working there daily and attending services.[67] Some seeds of the mission movement even spread around the world, with results such as the Helping Hand Mission of Auckland, New Zealand.[68]

McAuley himself opened a second mission, the Cremorne on West 32nd Street, as a beachhead in the area of New York known as "the Tenderloin." By the time McAuley died in 1884, almost every American urban area had its missions and a common goal: challenge to change. Other children of the mission movement—"retreats for women," "homes for the friendless," and hope halls for released convicts—had the same purpose. By the 1890s the New York mission list was long, and included names such as the Catherine Mission, Christ's Rescue Mission, the Gospel Temperance Mission, the Jewish Mission, the Beulah Mission and Free Employment Bureau, the Gospel Mission to The Tombs, and so on. Low-cost hotels with regular Bible teaching and names such as the Galilee Coffee House and the Madison Square Church House, also drew in wanderers. What they all tried to remember, even when they grew, was the lesson McAuley had taught and the Reverend E. Stuart Dodge noted at a memorial meeting for him ten days after his death: "Jerry believed in hand-picked souls. The best fruit is not shaken from the tree, but picked by hand, one by one."[69]

CHAPTER SIX

The Seven Marks of Compassion

E ven if it is acknowledged that the late nineteenth-century war on poverty is relevant to our own, and that much happened, a third question remains: What exactly did the charity of that era accomplish? That question is difficult to answer with certitude. Most overall statistics of the period are not thorough enough to be particularly useful. One of my favorite pages of the 1890 census report makes up in candor what it misses in accuracy by noting three times that "the results of this inquiry are comparatively valueless" and "the returns are so scanty that general conclusions can not be based on them."[1]

Often we have to fall back on eyewitness reports and journalistic assessments, which are abundant. Author Edward Everett Hale analyzed the success of the Boston Industrial Aids Society in reforming alcoholics: "These women were most of them poor creatures broken down with drink, or with worse devils, if there are worse. But...five hundred people in a year take five hundred of these broken-down women into their homes, sometimes with their babies, and give them a new chance."[2] A middle-class volunteer in the slums was astounded when "with my own eyes I saw men who had come into the mission sodden with drink turn into quiet, steady workers.... I saw foul homes, where dirty bundles of straw had been the only bed, gradually become clean and respectable; hard faces grow patient and gentle, oaths and foul words give place to quiet speech."[3] Writer Josiah Strong concluded in 1893, "Probably during no hundred years in the history of the world have there been saved so many thieves, gamblers, drunkards and prostitutes as during the past quarter of a century."

Strong and others were favorably inclined toward theistic values—but even some who were deeply skeptical of the theology were impressed by the practice. Muckraker Ray Stannard Baker was struck by testimonies such as that of a former "drunken wretch" whose life was transformed when he stumbled into the McAuley Mission and came to believe "that Jesus Christ had the power to save me when I could not save myself." Baker did not know quite what to make of the account and many others like it, but he was a good-enough journalist, and a curious-enough soul, to conclude that

> a mere report of what is said cannot convey the earnestness and simplicity with which the words are spoken. Carping criticism may say what it will about such a story, but it cannot touch that man. He knows what he has got, and those wretches who hear him—do they not understand intimately what he has suffered? And do they not also long blindly for the power...?[4]

Baker also saw that "it apparently makes not the slightest difference whether the man is an unlettered Chris or a university graduate; the power of reconstruction is the same." Baker called the McAuley Mission "one of the most extraordinary institutions in the country," and noted his surprise that once the individuals "surrendered" to Christ, they were able to escape alcoholism, find jobs, and be reconciled with their families.[5]

For those who scoff at both believers and skeptics, the most credible observer of the entire era may be liberal reformer Jacob Riis, author in 1890 *of How the Other Half Lives*. Riis lived his concern for the New York poor by hauling heavy cameras up dozens of flights of tenement stairs day after day to provide striking photographs of dull-eyed families in crowded flats. After seeing much misery, Riis concluded that "New York is, I firmly believe, the most charitable city in the world. Nowhere is there so eager a readiness to help, when it is known that help is worthily wanted; nowhere are there such armies of devoted workers."[6] Riis described how one charity group over eight years raised "4,500 families out of the rut of pauperism into proud, if modest, independence, without alms."[7] He noted that another "handful of noble women…accomplished what no machinery of government availed to do. Sixty thousand children have been rescued by them from the streets."[8]

These reflections are not exceptional—newspapers and magazines of the 1890s contained many similar stories. Jacob Riis and his contemporaries were not arguing that the war on poverty a century ago was won, or was even winnable in any final sense: Riis wrote that "the metropolis is to lots of people like a lighted candle to the moth."[9] Those who climbed out of urban destitution were replaced quickly by others awaiting trial by fire. But poverty-fighters then saw movement and hope. They saw springs of fresh water flowing among the poor, and not just blocks of ice sitting in a perpetual winter. This sense of movement contrasts with the frustrating solidity of American poverty during recent decades, which have seen multigenerational welfare dependency become common. And the optimism back then contrasts sharply with the demoralization among the poor and cynicism among the better-off that is so common now.

What was their secret? As we have seen, it was not neglect, either benign or malign; in the late nineteenth century, Social Darwinism did not sink deep roots. Nor was the secret of their success a century ago the showering of money on the poor, nor the triumph of an anti-statist spirit: they knew that private agencies could be just as bad as government ones. No, charity workers a century ago were fired up by seven ideas that recent welfare practice has put on the back burner. For convenience of memory these seven seals of good philanthropic practice can even be put in alphabetical order, A through G: Affiliation, Bonding, Categorization, Discernment, Employment, Freedom, God. If we understand how these seven were applied, we will at least be able to ask the right questions about our recent wrong turn.

Let's begin where poverty-fighting a century ago began, by emphasizing *affiliation*. Many men a century ago, as now, were abandoning their families. Both church groups and the United Hebrew Charities fought the trend. Many young people were running away from home, and some of the elderly were out of contact with their children. Charity organizations responded by instructing all volunteers to work hard at "restoring family ties that have been sundered" and "strengthening a church or social bond that is weakened." The prime goal of relief, all agreed, was not material distribution but "affiliation... the reabsorption in ordinary industrial and social life of those who for some reason have snapped the threads that bound them to the other members of the community."[10]

In practice, when individuals or families with real needs applied for material assistance, charity workers began by interviewing applicants and checking backgrounds in order to answer one question: "Who is bound to help in this case?" Charity workers then tried to call in relatives, neighbors, or former coworkers or coworshippers. "Relief given without reference to friends and neighbors is accompanied by moral loss," Mary Richmond of the Baltimore Charity Organizing Society noted. "Poor neighborhoods are doomed to grow poorer and more sordid, whenever the natural ties of neighborliness are weakened by our well-meant but unintelligent interference."[11] When material support was needed, charities tried to raise it from relatives and others with personal ties instead of appropriating funds from the general income.[12] "Raising the money required specially on each case, though very troublesome, has immense advantages," one minister wrote. "It enforces family ties, and neighborly or other duties, instead of relaxing them."[13]

Affiliation was important for both old and young. A typical case from the files of the Associated Charities of Boston notes that when an elderly widower applied for help, "the agent's investigation showed that there were relatives upon whom he might have a claim." A niece "was unable to contribute anything," but a brother-in-law who had not seen the old man for twenty-five years "promised to send a regular pension," and he did.[14] The brother-in-law's contribution paid the old man's living expenses and reunited him with his late wife's family. "If there had been no careful investigation," the caseworker noted, the man would have received some bread, but would have remained "wretched in his filthy abode."[15] Similarly, abandoned young people were to be placed in alternative families, not institutionalized. Orphans were to be placed with families as quickly as possible—a century ago that meant days or weeks, not months or years in foster care.

Affiliation could also mean reinvolvement with religious or ethnic groups. The New York Charity Organization Society asked applicants what they professed or how they had been raised, and then referred them to local churches and synagogues. Some groups emphasized ethnic ties. The Belgium Society of Benevolence, the Chinese Hospital Association, the French Benevolent Society, the German Ladies' Society, the Hungarian Association, the Irish Immigrant Society, and many similar groups all had New York offices and did not want to see their people act in shameful ways. On an individual level, members of the same immigrant groups helped each other out.

When adult applicants for help were truly alone, then it was time for *bonding* with volunteers, who in essence became new family members. Charity volunteers a century ago usually were not assigned to paper-pushing or mass food-dispensing tasks, but were given the opportunity to make a large difference in several lives over several years. Each volunteer had a narrow but deep responsibility: the Philadelphia Society for Organizing Charitable Relief noted that "a small number of families, from three to five, are enough to exhaust all the time, attention, and friendly care which one visitor has."[16] The thousands of volunteers were not babied by promises of easy satisfaction and warm feelings.[17] Instead, the Philadelphia Society warned that volunteers would have "discouraging experiences, and, perhaps for a time little else," but would nevertheless be expected to maintain "the greatest patience, the most decided firmness, and an inexhaustible kindness."[18]

There were failures, but success stories also emerged. The magazine *American Hebrew* in 1898 told how one man was used to dependency, but volunteers "with great patience convinced him that he must earn his living"; soon he did, and regained the respect of his family and community. Similarly, a woman had become demoralized, but "for months she was worked with, now through kindness, again through discipline, until finally she began to show a desire to help herself."[19] A man who had worked vigorously could no longer do so because of sickness, but was helped to develop a new trade in mending broken china. Speakers at the Indiana State Conference on Social Work regularly told of those "transformed from dependent to respectable citizen."[20]

The key was personal willingness to become deeply involved. Nathaniel Rosenau of the United Hebrew Charities noted that good charity could not be based on the "overworked and somewhat mechanical offices of a relieving society."[21] The charity magazine *Lend a Hand* regularly reminded readers that they could not "discharge duties to the poor by gifts of money alone.... Let us beware of mere charity with the tongs."[22] Philanthropic groups such as the Associated Charities of Boston saw their role not as raising more money, but as helping citizens to go beyond "tax-bills [or] vicarious giving" by serving "as a bureau of introduction between the worthy poor and the charitable."[23] *Charities Review* paid close attention to language abuse and stressed the importance of understanding "charity in its original meaning of 'love,' not charity in its debased meaning of 'alms.' "[24]

But such contact was not uninformed. Volunteers—typically, middle-class church members—were helped in their tasks by the careful *categorization* that charities required upon initial contact with applicants. Charities did not treat everyone equally—and, since they were private, they did not have to. Instead, charity organization societies considered "worthy of relief" only those who were poor through no fault of their own and unable to change their situation quickly. In this category were orphans, the aged, the incurably ill, children with "one parent unable to support them," and adults suffering from "temporary illness or accident." Volunteers who were tender-hearted but not particularly forceful served as helpers to the helpless.

Other applicants for aid were placed in different categories and received different treatment. Jobless adults who showed themselves "able and willing" to work, or part-time workers "able and willing to do more," were sent to employment bureaus and classified as "Needing Work Rather Than Relief." Help in finding work also was offered to "the improvident or intemperate who are not yet hopelessly so." But the "shiftless and intemperate" who were unwilling to work were categorized as "Unworthy, Not Entitled to Relief."[25] In this group were "those who prefer to live on alms," those with "confirmed intemperance," and the "vicious who seem permanently so."[26] Volunteers who agreed to visit such individuals had to be of hardy stock and often of rough experience; the best were often ex-alcoholics or ex-convicts.

How would agencies know the categories into which applicants fell? Background checks helped, but "work tests" were a key self-sorting device, and one that also allowed dispensing aid while retaining dignity. By 1890 Gurteen's recommendations were accepted throughout the United States: when an able-bodied man in almost any city asked an agency for relief, he often was asked to chop wood for two hours or to whitewash a building. A needy woman generally was given a seat in the "sewing room" (often near a child care room) and asked to work on garments that would be donated to the helpless poor or sent through the Red Cross to families suffering from the effects of hurricanes or tornadoes. In 1890 woodyards next to homeless shelters were as common as liquor stores were in 1990, and the impact was far more exhilarating: charity managers could see whether applicants were willing to work, and the applicants could earn their keep.

The work test, along with teaching good habits and keeping away those who did not really need help, also enabled charities to teach the lesson that those who were being helped could help others. The wood was often given to such as widows among the helpless poor. At the Chicago Relief and Aid Society woodyard in 1891, 872 men reportedly chopped wood and, while receiving 6,337 tickets for meals and lodging, did so much that 2,396 tickets could be given to invalids and others unable to work. In Baltimore, the Friendly Inn was exact: free room and board to those unable to work, but for the able "sawing and splitting four sticks entitles to a meal, ten sticks to a lodging." (At the inn, 24,901 meals were worked for in 1890 and 6,084 given without work.) Categorization, Jacob Riis wrote repeatedly, was essential: the way to fight "real suffering in the homes of the poor" was to hang tough on "enforcing Paul's plan of starving the drones into the paths of self-support: no work, nothing to eat."

Many organizations kept careful records of their categorizations. At Boston's Associated Charities, 895 volunteers visited 2,094 families requesting relief (the typical goal was one volunteer for two families). The visitors found that 18 percent of all applicants were "worthy of continuous relief" because of old age, incurable illness, orphan status, and so on; 23 percent were "worthy of temporary relief" because of accidents, illness, or short-term trouble; 33 percent were able to work (a few were out of work not by their own choice, and others were the "shiftless or intemperate where reform may be hoped for") and were sent to employment bureaus which had jobs aplenty; the remaining 26 percent were "unworthy" of support because they had property or relatives to fall back on, or because work tests and investigation had indicated that they were without "desire to change."

With Associated Charities help and pressure, 817 clients found and accepted jobs that year and 278 refused them ("98 refusals with good reason, 170 without"). In addition, the Associated Charities gave loans to 81 persons (the repayment rate was 75 percent), legal aid to 62 persons, and medical help to 304, and it persuaded 53 relatives to offer aid. Volunteers helped 185 families to save money and pushed 144 alcoholic breadwinners into making attempts at temperance (27 were not intoxicated during the year, and 118 had "less frequent" periods of intoxication). Finally, nearly six hundred children were helped directly by volunteers who found adoptive families or guardians for orphans, influenced truants to attend school more often, or placed them in day nurseries or industrial schools.[27]

The New Orleans Charity Organization Society also emphasized "personal investigation of every case, not alone to prevent imposture, but to learn the necessities of every case and how to meet them."[28] It had a sewing room for women and a woodyard for men, "where heads of families can earn household supplies, and the homeless food and lodging"; in the process, the willingness of applicants to work would be checked, and assistance given "in a way that does not pauperize."[29] Some 1,328 investigations in a typical year at the New Orleans COS led to 926 individuals being classified as worthy of help, 276 as "unworthy," and 126 as doubtful. In the "worthy" category, 271 individuals were unemployed but willing to work, 252 had jobs but wanted additional work, 205 were ill, 64 were old, and 48 women who had been abandoned by their husbands. Among the "unworthy" were 41 drunkards and professional beggars unwilling to change their conduct, 143 "shiftless," and 72 not in true need.[30]

Categorization and self-categorization were accompanied by *discernment*, which grew out of the benign suspicion that came naturally to charity workers who had grown up reading the Bible. Aware from their theology of the deviousness of the human heart, nineteenth-century charity workers were not surprised when some among the poor "preferred their condition and even tried to take advantage of it."[31] The St. Louis Provident Association noted that "duplication of alms is pursued with cunning and attended most invariably with deceit and falsehood."[32] One magazine reported that a "woman who obtained relief several times on the ground that she had been deserted by her husband, was one day surprised at her home with the husband in the bedroom. She had pretended that the man was her boarder." The husband turned out to have a regular income.[33] Jacob Riis noted that some claims of illness were real, but other times a background check revealed "the 'sickness' to stand for laziness, and the destitution to be the family's stock in trade."[34]

Only discernment on the part of charity workers who knew their aid-seekers intimately could prevent fraud. Baltimore charity manager Mary Richmond wrote that her hardest task was the teaching of volunteers "whose kindly but condescending attitude has quite blinded them to the everyday facts of the neighborhood life."[35] To be effective, volunteers had to leave behind "a conventional attitude toward the poor, seeing them through the comfortable haze of our own excellent intentions, and content to know that we wish them well, without being at any great pains to know them as they really are."[36] Volunteers had to learn that "well-meant interference, unaccompanied by personal knowledge of all the circumstances, often does more harm than good and becomes a temptation rather than a help."[37]

Discernment by volunteers, and organizational barriers against fraud, were important not only to prevent waste but to preserve morale among those who *were* working hard to remain independent. One charity worker noted, "nothing is more demoralizing to the struggling poor than successes of the indolent or vicious."[38] The St. Louis solution was to require volunteers to abide by set rules of giving:

> To give relief only after personal investigation of each case....
>
> To give necessary articles and only what is immediately necessary....
>
> To give what is least susceptible of abuse.
>
> To give only in small quantities in proportion to immediate need; and less than might be procured by labor, except in cases of sickness.
>
> To give assistance at the right moment; not to prolong it beyond duration of the necessity which calls for it....
>
> To require of each beneficiary abstinence from intoxicating liquors....
>
> To discontinue relieving all who manifest a purpose to depend on alms rather than their own exertions for support.[39]

Doles without discernment not only subsidized the "unscrupulous and undeserving" but became a "chief hindrance to spontaneous, free generosity": they contributed to "the grave uncertainty in many minds whether with all their kind intentions they are likely to do more good than harm...."[40] Only when "personal sympathy" could "work with safety, confidence, and liberty," would compassion be unleashed.[41] The New Orleans COS tried to impress on its volunteers maxims of discernment by printing on the back cover of its annual reports statements such as, "Intelligent giving and intelligent withholding are alike true charity," and "If drink has made a man poor, money will feed not him, but his drunkenness."[42]

It was also important for every individual approached by a beggar to be discerning—and teaching *that* proved to be a very difficult task! *Charities Review* once asked the designer of an innovative program whether its success satisfied "the 'gusher' who desires to give every evening beggar 25 cents." S. O. Preston responded, "No, nothing satisfies the 'gusher'; he will persist in giving his (or someone else's) money to the plausible beggar as often as he appears." The magazine was filled with criticism of "that miscalled charity which soothes its conscience with indiscriminate giving." Gurteen called giving money to alcoholics "positively immoral" and argued that if givers could "foresee all the misery which their so-called charity is entailing in the future," they would "forgo the flutter of satisfaction which always follows a well-intentioned deed."[43] New Haven minister H. L. Wayland criticized the "well-meaning, tender-hearted, sweet-voiced criminals who insist upon indulging in indiscriminate charity."[44]

The drive to stop foolish "compassion" continued throughout the 1880s and 1890s. *Charities Review* quoted Ralph Waldo Emerson's famous self-criticism: "I sometimes succumb and give the dollar, but it is a wicked dollar, which by and by I shall have the manhood to withhold." Sociological analyses of the "floating population of all large modern cities" showed the homeless including some "strangers seeking work" and needing temporary help, but a larger number of "victims of intemperance and vice"—not all that different from today, with studies showing a majority of the homeless in major cities suffering from alcohol or drug abuse.[45] *Charities Review* criticized "that miscalled charity which soothes its conscience with indiscriminate giving," and proposed that individuals and groups restrict "material relief to those cases in which such relief would be given by the true friend." True friendship was not encouraging "lazy imposture," for "such mercy is not mercy: it is pure selfishness."[46] Instead, true friendship meant helping to deliver a person from slavery to a bottle, a needle, or his own laziness.

Affiliation and bonding, categorization and discernment—when the process was working well, the next key element was long-term *employment* of all able-bodied household heads. *Charities Review* stressed the importance of work and proclaimed that "Labor is the life of society, and the beggar who will not work is a social cannibal feeding on that life,"[47] and Indiana officials declared that "Nothing creates pauperism so rapidly as the giving of relief to [able-bodied] persons without requiring them to earn what they receive by some kind of honest labor."[48] Such emphasis on work would have been savage had jobs not been available; but, except during short-lived times of "business panic," they were. (In 1892 charity experts from several major cities were asked whether honest and sober men would spend more than a short time out of work: they all said such a situation was "rare" or "very exceptional."[49]) Such emphasis also would have been unfair if alternatives to begging did not exist during short-lived periods of unemployment; but, as seen, private charities in every major city provided work for food and lodging.[50]

Most of the able-bodied poor accepted the work obligation, partly because of biblical teaching and partly because they had little choice.[51] S. O. Preston in New Haven reported that fewer than one out of a hundred refused to work in the woodyard or sewing room, perhaps because "there is no other institution in this city where lodging can be secured except by cash payments for same."[52] Had there been alternatives, bad charity might have driven out good, for charity leaders argued that it took only a short time for slothful habits to develop.[53] After several years of easy-going charity in Oregon, N. R. Walpole of Portland "found among the unemployed a reluctance to work, and regarded compulsory work as the only solution of the problem."[54] Take a hard line, charity leaders demanded, or problems would worsen: New York charity leader Josephine Lowell wrote, "the problem before those who would be charitable, is not how to deal with a given number of poor; it is how to help those who are poor, without adding to their numbers and constantly increasing the evils they seek to cure."[55]

Jacob Riis agreed; when some New York groups appeared to be weakening, Riis foresaw a tribe of "frauds, professional beggars . . . tight ening its grip on society as the years pass, until society shall summon up pluck to say with Paul, 'if a man will not work neither shall he eat,' and stick to it."[56] Riis, like other Christians a century ago, kept alluding to the apostolic teaching. Jewish leaders, meanwhile, were stressing that poverty was not a desirable status within Judaism, and that a person unwilling to work could not justify his conduct even by citing a desire to study the Bible; they quoted a Talmudic saying, "All study of the Torah that is not accompanied by work must in the end be futile and become the cause of sin."[57] Within the Talmudic tradition, avoiding dependency was so important that even work on the Sabbath was preferable to accepting alms: Rabbi Jochanan said, "Make thy Sabbath a weekday and do not be reduced to need the help of human beings."[58] All charity leaders argued that even poor-paying jobs provided a start on the road from poverty; since travel down that road required solid work habits, true friendship meant challenging bad habits and encouraging a person to build new, productive ones.

Along with employment came the emphasis on *freedom*— defined by immigrants (such as my grandparents) not as the opportunity to do anything with anyone at any time, but as the opportunity to work and worship without governmental restriction. Job freedom was the opportunity to drive a wagon without paying bribes, to cut hair without having to go to barbers' college, and to get a foot on the lowest rung of the ladder, even if wages there were low. Freedom was the opportunity for a family to escape dire poverty by having a father work long hours and a mother sew garments at home. This freedom did not make for an instant victory against poverty at a time when 200,000 persons were packed into one Manhattan square mile. Snapshots of abject poverty could show horrible living conditions, but those who persevered starred in a motion picture of upward mobility.

It was clear to most that government subsidy could not provide the kind of freedom that was important. In 1894 Amos G. Warner's mammoth study *American Charities* compiled what had been learned about governmental charity in the course of the nineteenth century:

1. It is necessarily more impersonal and mechanical than private charity or individual action....
2. There is some tendency to claim public relief as a right, and for the indolent and incapable to throw themselves flat upon it. This feeling will always assert itself whenever it is given an opportunity to do so....
3. In public charities, officialism is even more pronounced than under private management. The degradation of character of the man on a salary set to the work of relieving the poor is one of the most discouraging things in connection with relief-work....
4. It is possible to do so much relief-work that, while one set of persons is relieved, another will be taxed across the pauper line ... the burden of supporting the State tends to diffuse itself along the lines of the least resistance; consequently, money which is raised for the

> relief of the poor may come out of pockets that can ill
> spare it....
>
> 5. ...The blight of partisan politics and gratuitously awk-
>   ward administration often falls upon the work....
>   Charitable institutions are spoils of an insignificant
>   character, thrown frequently to the less deserving
>   among the henchmen of the successful political
>   bosses.[59]

Warner provided details of brutal treatment of patients, embezzle-
ment, and other corrupt practices in the state welfare programs of
Wisconsin, Michigan, Pennsylvania, Indiana, Illinois, and New York.[60]

The goal of charity workers, therefore, was not to press for governmental programs, but to show poor people how to move up while resist-
ing enslavement to the charity of governmental or private masters.
Charity leaders and preachers frequently spoke of freedom and showed
how dependency was merely slavery with a smiling mask. Minister
Joseph Crooker noted that "it is very easy to make our well-meant charity a curse to our fellow-men."[61] Social worker Frederic Almy argued
that "alms are like drugs, and are as dangerous," for often "they create
an appetite which is more harmful than the pain which they relieve."[62]
Governmental welfare was "the least desirable form of relief," according
to Mary Richmond, because it "comes from what is regarded as a practically inexhaustible source, and people who once receive it are likely to
regard it as a right, as a permanent pension, implying no obligation on
their part."[63] But if charity organizations were to do better, they had to
make sure the poor understood that "dirt and slovenliness are no claim
to help; that energy and resource are qualities which the helper or helpers will gladly meet half-way."[64] Freedom could be grasped only when
individuals took responsibility.

Affiliation and Bonding, Categorization and Discernment, Employment and Freedom...and the seventh seal on the social covenant of the late nineteenth century was the relationship of *God* to all these things. "True philanthropy must take into account spiritual as well as physical needs," one charity magazine proposed.[65] Poverty will be dramatically reduced if "the victims of appetite and lust and idleness... revere the precepts of the Bible and form habits of industry, frugality, and self-restraint," Pennsylvania state charity commissioners declared.[66] The frequent conclusion was that demoralized men and women needed much greater help than "the dole of organized charities."[67]

There were some differences between Christians and Jews about that help. The biblically orthodox Christians of the late nineteenth century worshipped a God who came to earth and showed in life and death the literal meaning of compassion—*suffering with*. Christians believed that they—creatures made after God's image—were called to *suffer with* also, in gratitude for the suffering done for them, and in obedience to biblical principles. (The goal of such suffering, of course, was to promote those principles, and not to grease a slide into sin.) But Jewish teaching stressed the pursuit of righteousness through the doing of good deeds, particularly those showing loving-kindness (*gemilut chasadim*). The difference was significant, but both approaches led to abundant volunteering.

Similarities in theistic understanding led both Christians and Jews to emphasize the importance of personal charity, rather than a clockwork deistic approach. The Good Samaritan in Christ's story bandaged the victim's wounds, put him on a donkey, took him to an inn, and nursed him there. The Talmud also portrayed personal service as "much greater than charity," defined as money-giving.[68] Christians and Jews also had many similarities in understanding because they both read an Old Testament that repeatedly depicted compassion not as an isolated noun, but as the culmination of a process. Repeatedly in Judges and other books, the Bible told how when Israelites had sinned they were to repent and turn away from their sin; only then, as a rule, would God show compassion. Late nineteenth-century Americans who read the Bible regularly did not see God as a sugardaddy who merely felt sorry for people in distress. They saw God showing compassion while demanding change, and they tried to do the same. Groups such as the Industrial Christian Alliance noted that they used "religious methods"—reminding the poor that God made them and had high expectations for them—to "restore the fallen and helpless to self-respect and self-support."

In addition, Christians had the expectation that the Holy Spirit could and would rapidly transform the consciences of all those whom God had called. Those who believed in poverty-fighting through salvation were delighted and surprised to read in the *New York Herald* of how "the woman known as Bluebird up to a year ago was one of the worst drunkards in the Lower East Side.... Scores of times she had been in the police courts." Then she talked with an evangelist and agreed to go to the Door of Hope rescue home. She was converted and the *Herald* reporter told what happened:

> I went to 63 Park Street, the Five Points Mission Hall. A big crowd of ragged, bloated and generally disreputable looking men and women were seeking admission.... A very pleasant looking young woman dressed neatly in black and having a bunch of flowers at her waist... spoke to them of love and hope. The crowds kept coming until the break of

day. No one would ever think that the neatly attired young lady speaking so appealingly had once been the terror of the slums, always alert to get in the first blow.[69]

Some one hundred of Bluebird's former gang associates changed their lives over the next several years as, in the words of the *New York Times*, she was "transformed into one of the most earnest and eloquent female evangelists who ever worked among the human derelicts in dark alleys and dives" and "threw her whole soul in the work of evangelism among her former associates."[70] Most of those hundred changes were permanent, a follow-up years later concluded.

Affiliation, Bonding, Categorization, Discernment, Employment, Freedom—and, in the end, God's grace. But the question still remains: Did the late nineteenth-century war on poverty work, and what use are its lessons to us?

In 1890 Jacob Riis combined realism and optimism. New York's "poverty, its slums, and its suffering are the result of unprecedented growth with the consequent disorder and crowding," he wrote, and added,

> If the structure shows signs of being top-heavy, evidences are not wanting—they are multiplying day by day—that patient toilers are at work among the underpinnings. The Day Nurseries, the numberless Kindergartens and charitable schools in the poor quarters, the Fresh Air Funds, the thousand and one charities that in one way or another reach the homes and the lives of the poor with sweetening touch, are proof that if much is yet to be done... hearts and hands will be found to do it in ever-increasing measure.[71]

The good news Riis declared was that through many charitable efforts "the poor and the well-to-do have been brought closer together, in an every-day companionship that cannot but be productive of the best results, to the one who gives no less than to the one who receives."[72] Riis concluded that, "black as the cloud is it has a silver lining, bright with promise. New York is to-day a hundredfold cleaner, better, purer, city than it was even ten years ago.... If we labor on with courage and patience, [these efforts] will bear fruit sixty and a hundred fold."[73]

CHAPTER SEVEN

And Why Not Do More?

Much was accomplished—but much remained to be accomplished. New York Police Commissioner Thomas
Byrnes estimated that forty thousand prostitutes worked
the city in 1890. A survey in 1894 found 6,576 New York slum families
living in tenement "inside" rooms—rooms without windows facing
out but only on air-shafts, which many tenants used as garbage
chutes. These rancid-smelling rooms were deathtraps for small children and the elderly during summer heat waves.[1] When New York's
Health Commission tested 3,970 milk samples in 1902 it found that
2,095, or 53 percent, were adulterated.[2] In the 1890s, the per capita
consumption of alcohol in the United States was about seventeen
gallons per year; Jacob Riis counted 111 Protestant churches below
14th Street in New York and 4,065 saloons, many so bad that dogs
could not stand the atmosphere and fled into the street.

Riis saw all this, wished that more were being done, proposed
private construction of model apartment buildings, and recommended
action against adulterated food—but, throughout, he remained convinced that an impoverished person was perched precariously halfway

up the ladder, capable of being helped toward independence or pushed (often by those with good intentions) into the pit of pauperism. "It is money scattered without judgment—not poverty—that makes the pauper," Riis wrote.[3] Although he did not oppose all governmental welfare, he did not want payment to be a right, since he wanted the subsidized to feel guilty. "The stigma which fortunately attaches to *public* relief," Riis argued, prevents creation of an "incentive to parents to place their children upon the public for support."[4] He wrote that material distribution to the able-bodied, whether by the state or private charities, led to "degrading and pauperizing" rather than "self-respect and self-dependence."[5] He praised the Charity Organization Society and "kindred organizations along the same line" for showing "what can be done by well-directed effort."

Others argued, especially concerning Manhattan, that overcrowding made desperate conditions hard to fight, and that solutions would come only when people moved to outlying areas or other, less-crowded cities. And yet, the city continued to attract those who, in the words of Frederick Law Olmstead, wished to drink of the "juices of life" that it supplied. "If I were offered a deed of the best farm," he quoted one poor city dweller saying, "on the condition of going back to the country to live, I would not take it. I would rather face starvation in town."[6] United Hebrew Charities leaders in 1900 noted the general reluctance to leave New York although Manhattan's island status and location made continued overcrowding likely:

> By its geographical position the city of New York has peculiar limitations with respect to population, which may not be overstepped without a serious menace to the community. As a matter of fact, we have long since passed the

boundaries of normal housing, and we are beginning to reap the harvest of poverty and crime and immorality which are the natural concomitants of such abnormal congregation.[7]

Staying even was about as much as could be done under such situations, the United Hebrew Charities concluded.

One of the other outstanding reporters of his time, Ray Stannard Baker, came to a different conclusion. He saw that charity workers were having an impact, and wrote of the McAuley Mission, "Whenever I went downtown to see this work I always came away hopeful...."[8] Yet, Baker also argued that "one comes away from such a mission filled with a conviction as deep as his soul that in some way the whole spectacle of horror and misery is grotesquely and irretrievably wrong."[9] Baker was right that the misery was wrong, but, like other Social Universalists, he was particularly upset that many who came to the mission went away without undergoing dramatic change. Nineteenth-century charity, as Reverend Dodge had observed at the McAuley memorial service, was based on hand-picking, one by one, but Baker demanded a fruit-grabbing machine that could motor throughout the orchard.

Baker's concerns, evident in his magazine articles and in his correspondence maintained at the Library of Congress, were thoughtful. He summarized them in a plaintive outcry in *The Spiritual Unrest*:

Why should there be any Bowery... in an age which calls itself civilized? Why should not a civilized nation provide a better school of training than the Bowery for bold and original boys like Jerry McAuley?[10]

Baker spoke of the saloons and other "potent agencies for tearing down and ruining men and women...." He described the waste, apparent even among those who did change: "A man cannot be a drunkard or a thief, and come out in most cases, although converted, and be the same, strong, sure, serviceable man or woman he or she would have been without passing through such horrors."[11] Baker even titled one of his *American Magazine* articles, "Lift Men from the Gutter? or, Remove the Gutter? Which?"[12]

For those nineteenth-century leaders with a biblical view of man's nature, the question was not either/or. Their goal was to remove as many sections of the gutter as possible, so that no child would be forced to grow up in it. Through temperance movements and other activities they also worked to clean up sections. And yet, they were grimly aware that some men and women would seek out those portions of the gutter that remained, or build new sections themselves, and sometimes drag their children or friends into them—"the poor you always have with you." Social Darwinists at that point would give up, but those who took to heart the story of the prodigal son would not. There would always be the need for reclamation projects.

The consolation, for those going through reclamation, was that the time of torment was not wasted. Baker, assuming an essential goodness in man, saw no need for a visit to the pit, but McAuley and others understood that for some persons the learning process could not be skipped; for some, it was necessary to hit bottom before they were ready to head up.[13] As Edward T. Devine, secretary of the New York Charity Organization Society, reported to the National Conference of Charities and Correction in 1897,

> The question which we try through investigation to answer
> [is,] Are these applicants of ours ready to work out with

us... some plan which will result in their rescue from dependency...? If such elements are entirely lacking—no basis of good character, no probability of final success—then we do not assume the responsibility of asking societies or churches or private persons to help, and may even, if our advice is asked, urge them to refrain from blind interference with natural educational agencies....[14]

The COS goal was not "that poor families should suffer, but that charity should accomplish its purpose."[15] Mission workers also steeled themselves to bid farewell to those on the street who would not accept the challenge to change. Some who left never came back—but as one volunteer wrote, "the prodigals commonly returned confessing their weakness and laboring earnestly to prove their penitence."[16]

The question, nevertheless, continued to ring out: Why not do more? For many people dire poverty was only a short-term curse—but why did they have to suffer at all? Yes, charity and challenge aided individuals to escape from poverty, and yes, economic growth led to upward mobility, but was it fair that many citizens advanced slowly, and some not at all? A reporter for the *New York World* described his entrance into a tenement:

Push open the grimy door. Faugh! The air is fetid. There is a confused murmur of voices, the shrill cries of children, the shouts of quarrelling women, the gutteral oaths of drunken men, the jargon of many languages. The narrow stairway is crowded with children; some clothed and some almost naked.... The furniture of the room consisted of a dilapidated chair...and a pile of blankets and rags in a corner that constituted the family bed.[17]

Even if many were helped, how could this condition be tolerated?

The pressure became general. A charity leader who told "the story of one little girl," a child abuse victim helped to blossom, seemed on the defensive for describing the rescue of only one individual. Indiana's John Holliday asked his audience, "Who of you, who have a daughter of your own, will not thank God that an instrumentality exists that could save even one from shame and death?"[18] And members of the audience would ask why much more could not be done, and soon? And if charity leaders responded that the one-by-one help offered by volunteers was a slow but sure way of helping some and not making life worse for others, they were blamed for failing to alter the lives of masses in their preoccupation with individuals.

Underlying this demand for mass transformation was the belief that man was naturally good and productive unless an oppressive system got in the way. In contrast to the Social Calvinists and the Social Darwinists, those who believed this could be called "Social Universalists." Ignoring the experience of the 1860s and 1870s, and harkening back to the commune spirit of the 1840s and the Greeleyite message of that era, their faith was clear: the only reason some people did not work was that they were kept from working, and the only reason some lied about their needs was that they were forced to lie. Social Universalists at the end of the nineteenth century thrilled to the classic statement of their case in Edward Bellamy's best-selling Looking Backward, 2000–1887. In the novel Bellamy's protagonist, Julian West, goes to sleep in 1887 and awakes by a fluke in the year 2000. West, impressed by the equal division of abundant wealth in what has become an American socialist paradise, asks, "By what title does the individual claim his particular share? What is the basis of his allotment?" The wise denizen of the future, Dr. Lette, replies, "His title is his humanity. The basis of his claim is the fact that he is a man."[19]

Social Universalism, with its combination of theological liberalism and political socialism, gained great support among the intellectual and literary elite. In Boston, the Society of Christian Socialists included authors William Dean Howells and Hamlin Garland, ideologues Laurence Gronlund and Daniel De Leon, and a variety of ministers.[20] Professor Richard Ely founded the American Economic Association with the goal of disseminating universalistic ideas, including his own belief in "the exercise of philanthropy" as "the duty of government."[21] As Ely urged economists and theologians to unite behind the "philanthropy of governments, either local, state, or national," he won converts to his faith that only "coercive philanthropy" could "establish among us true cities of God."[22] Liberal theologian George Herron went one step further, claiming "that the public ownership of the sources and means of production is the sole answer to the social question, and the sole basis of spiritual liberty."[23] Books praising the ideas of Social Universalism—including Ely's *Social Aspects of Christianity*, William G. Fremantle's *The World as the Subject of Redemption*, and George Herron's *The Christian Society* and *Between Caesar and Jesus*—began to pour off the presses.

These books had in common a high-minded earnestness, a desire to help, and a willingness to do more, as long as the "more" could be universalistic and unconditional. Their theology, labeled with public relations brilliance the "social gospel," emphasized God's love but not God's holiness, and thus urged charity without challenge. Their gospel declared that the work test was cruel, because a person who has faced a "crushing load of misfortunes" should not be faulted if he does not choose to work: "We ask ourselves whether we should have done any better if we had always lived in one room with six other people." Herron, Ely, and others argued that challenge was not necessary because individuals who needed to change would do so as soon as they were placed in a pleasant environment so that their true, benevolent natures could come out. Their gospel declared that the homeless of the time primarily needed housing, not affiliation: in 1893 magazine editor B. O. Flower envisioned governmental construction of "great buildings, each covering a square block and from six to eight stories high."

The materialist tendencies of the "social gospel" led some new philanthropists to exhibit embarrassment and annoyance with the evangelical emphases of the older programs. Why did the Magdalen Benevolent Society have to use "Christian principles" in its "work among fallen women"? Why did leaders of the New York Christian Home for Intemperate Men (Madison Avenue at 86th Street) think it vital to embrace "distinctly Christian" principles of "physical, moral, and spiritual restoration" in order to help inebriates and opium addicts? The social gospel-oriented *Encyclopedia of Social Reform* suggested that such emphases were wrongheaded, for university-educated people now knew that "social wrongs" caused individual problems that would readily disappear as the poor were placed in a better material environment.

The goal and the vehicle were given their clearest treatment in Fremantle's *The World as the Subject of Redemption*, labeled by Ely "one of the most useful books in recent times.... It indicates the whole scope and purpose of philanthropy."[24] Fremantle approved of collective organizations as ways of breaking down individual "selfishness." He was particularly impressed by the potential of civil government to reorder society and make men "better." Government, Fremantle wrote, has the power "of life and death over our persons. Hence it calls forth a worship more complete than any other." Government alone, Fremantle asserted, "can embrace all the wants of its members and afford them the universal instruction and elevation which they need."[25]

The worship of power had rarely been stated so explicitly by a church leader, but Fremantle was not done: "When we think of [the Nation] as becoming, as it must do more and more, the object of mental regard, of admiration, of love, even of worship (for in it preeminently God dwells) we shall recognize to the fullest extent its religious character and functions."[26] The Nation was the new Church, and as such was to take on the church's traditional functions of charity:

> We find the Nation alone fully organized, sovereign, independent, universal, capable of giving full expression to the Christian principle. We ought, therefore, to regard the Nation as the Church, its rulers as ministers of Christ, its whole body as a Christian brotherhood, its public assemblies as amongst the highest modes of universal Christian fellowship, its dealing with material interests as Sacraments, its progressive development, especially in raising the weak, as the fullest service rendered on earth to God, the nearest thing as yet within our reach to the kingdom of heaven.[27]

Fremantle ended with a call for the establishment of "supreme power" by those with "a clear intellectual perception" of the need and functions of such power. Although the task was mighty and the means difficult, he wrote, "The good thus aimed at, both temporal and spiritual, is so great that we cannot despair of attaining it."[28]

Clearly, for Fremantle, government in many respects had replaced God: government was to be honored and prayed to, and government was expected to produce manna. This substitution led to an interesting parallelism. Throughout the late nineteenth century universalistic doctrines of salvation gained strength in Christianity as previously dominant Calvinistic beliefs were jettisoned. Calvinists had little difficulty with the idea that not all persons would be saved, that some were destined for Hell; to accuse God of unfairness, they said, would be (quoting the apostle Paul) like the clay pot talking back to its maker. But those who were universalistically-inclined did talk back, and then preached that all would be saved spiritually. What, then, of the temporal dimension? Was it fair that some should suffer materially? If government on this earth was the agent of God, should it not save all?

The desire was clear. But was such an approach practical? If affiliation, bonding, and the rest were important, and if the experience of several centuries indicated the inability of government to address such concerns properly, was there any experience that could suggest otherwise? As it turned out, there was: the experience of the missions, charity organizations, and national evangelical groups had showed social universalists how to operate at the neighborhood, city, and national levels.

On the neighborhood level, the imitation of missions (but without their emphasis on Christian conversion) was evident in the launching of a "settlement house" flotilla in the 1890s, with Jane Addams' Hull-House, begun in 1889, as the flagship. Historian Robert Bremner has pointed out that there was nothing particularly new in the settlement house concept:

> Missions contributed the idea of lighthouses in the slums to help the poor find their ways to better lives; institutional churches suggested the community-center program which the settlements adopted; and charitable organizations promoted interest in voluntary service as the noblest form of philanthropy. Even the idea of "settling" in the slums was not entirely new.[29]

But there was one big difference: Hull-House, describing itself in a Chicago charity handbook, proclaimed with some huffiness, "There are no religious affiliations."[30] Out went the hymns and testimonies and in came political action. Those who came to live in the settlements were often good-hearted people with a desire to be compassionate in the true, *suffering with* sense of the word—but they wanted to save the world, not the individual.

While ideas of affiliation and bonding did remain to some extent, the stress on collective action was apparent. Jane Addams, in her first autobiography in 1910, reminisced that "one of the first lessons we learned at Hull-House was that private beneficence is totally inadequate."[31] The downgrading of biblical caution was equally important, but was usually treated as outgrowing fear rather than adopting a different worldview. Jane Addams told the National Conference of Charities and Correction in 1897, "I have not the great fear of pauperizing people which many of you seem to have. We have all accepted bread from someone, at least until we were fourteen."[32] Deletion of the idea of a sinful nature and delight in Utopian hopes worked hand-in-hand, for if handouts no longer were corrupting, mass transformation down a broad highway of material distribution became not only possible but preferable.

The settlement house movement's emphasis on volunteer residency was excellent, but its stress on societal transformation rather than personal change turned some of the settlement clients into means to an end. Robbins Gilman, who helped to develop the Northeast Neighborhood House in Minneapolis, argued that "the living among people, the maintenance of a home in the midst of the neighborhood… gives the settlement that strategic hold on the affections and confidence of its neighbors, that no other community organization has secured."[33]

Catheryne Cooke Gilman stressed the three "R's of settlement work: 'residency, research, and reform.' "[34] Volunteers, she said, were to live in and "know intimately" the neighborhood so they could lead the fight against "unemployment, bad housing, unsanitary conditions, ill health, civic neglect, vice, delinquency, and crime."[35]

The settlement house movement, through its emphasis on the material over the spiritual and the political over the personal, became the inspiration of governmental social work programs of the 1930s and community action programs of the 1960s. Some historians have argued that "the real novelty" of the settlement house movement "lay in the buoyant spirit, the fresh outlook, and the new attitudes its leaders introduced into philanthropic work."[36] The "new attitudes," of course, often were nothing more than the recycled ideology of the Greeleyite communes two generations before—the "dream," as Jane Addams put it, "that men shall cease to waste strength in competition and shall come to pool their powers of production."[37] When Mary Richmond of the Baltimore COS was invited by Jane Addams to some settlement house discussions in 1899 that included a note of realism, she

> was not a little amused to find that many of the settlement
> workers were put on the defensive and forced to see what
> we charity workers are often forced to see; namely, that it
> is impossible for the world to stop until everything starts
> over and starts right.... [38]

Mary Richmond was impressed by the "earnestness of all the meetings."[39]

Such earnestness was apparent because Greeleyite attitudes *were* new for the "cultivated young people" who, as Addams wrote, were attracted to settlement work because they had "no recognized outlet for their active faculties."[40] Like their predecessors in the 1840s and their successors in the 1960s, many settlement workers of the 1890 to 1920 era grew up in households where the need to move away from past verities was preached, but little alternative was offered. As Addams wrote,

> They hear constantly of the great social maladjustment, but no way is provided for them to change it, and their uselessness hangs about them heavily.... These young people have had advantages of college, of European travel, and of economic study, but they are sustaining this shock of inaction. [They] feel a fatal want of harmony between their theory and their lives, a lack of coordination between thought and action.[41]

Would there be a new way to be useful, to help rescue not only individual sufferers but to do away with "the great social maladjustment"? That would become a key question of twentieth-century government and economics.

On citywide levels, lessons emerged from both the failures and successes of late nineteenth-century charity coordination efforts. Failures first: the technology of the time had long made it hard for small points of light to benefit from information about applicants that other twinkling stars had. In New York, charity leaders from the 1860s worked to set up a central charity office where, in Charles Brace's words,

> lists of names and addresses of those assisted could be kept
> for examination, and frequent comparisons could be made

by the agents of these societies or by individuals interested. One society, formed for a distinct object, and finding a case needing quite a distinct mode of relief or assistance, could here at once ascertain where to transfer the case....[42]

A short-lived New York Bureau of Charities in 1873 did attempt to "secure a system of registration of the persons receiving aid from the societies, and to arrange for such intercommunication of the officers as will prevent imposition."[43] But "intercommunication" without telephones, photocopying machines, or faxes was cumbersome, and the effort fizzled.[44] A similar Boston effort, which began with the high hopes of a card for each applicant, cards for members of the same family clipped together, hand-copied cards sent to volunteers that would be matched up with particular applicants, and other copies sent to relevant agencies, suffered death by a thousand paper clips and pen nibs.

Organizational innovation provided a partial solution to technological gaps. Although no one put it in exactly these terms, the coordination systems of the 1870s were designed largely on a grid pattern, with small groups asked to reach out and touch other small groups. But in the 1890s, the ninety-two Charity Organization Societies in large cities around the country became paperwork hubs. In Baltimore, for example, thousands of individuals and most Baltimore charitable institutions agreed to forward to the COS all requests for aid, and the COS in turn became responsible for giving all applicants "work tests," providing home studies, and keeping records. The smaller agencies in essence became—for purposes of communication—spokes on the wheel, and the paper flow became more manageable.

A second problem, however, soon emerged: Some antipoverty programs, particularly those started by newspapers seeking a reputation for "compassion," refused to do any categorization or accept the categorization of others.[45] Such funds—those sponsored by newspapers included the *New York World* Bread Fund, the *New York Herald* Free Clothing Fund, and the *New York Tribune* Coal and Food Fund—simply passed out material quickly and indiscriminately, and then applauded themselves.[46] COS backer Stanton Coit complained in 1894 that

> the results of years of work by the Charity Organization Society may be swept away in one season of unusual distress by sentimentalists and by newspaper advertising schemes for relieving the poor.[47]

Bad charity drove out good charity.

What could be done? By the mid–1890s some observers were drawing two lessons from the quest for coordination. First, they believed that coordinated efforts could work if one organization could become the hub. Second, some were beginning to suggest that a central organization, based on the most scientific methods of poverty-fighting, might need to have the power to dominate charity distribution and push others to comply with them. Coit argued that only government "can limit the relief of each agency to a given district, so that there shall be no waste or overlapping[.]" Only government, he wrote, "can gather, week by week, full and accurate statistics of the condition of the unemployed[.]" Only government, he stressed, "can compel every agency to follow careful methods to avoid fraud[.]"[48] He concluded, "Scientific philanthropists will some day learn that charity organization is a distinctive municipal function."

Such a view downgraded the frequent nineteenth-century conclusions that government was unable to foster the spirit of affiliation,
bonding, and so on; but the organizational advantages, in Coit's eyes,
loomed larger. Ironically, the charities' emphasis on coordination and
districting was pointing the way toward governmental takeover of their
functions. This might have remained very much a minority view but
for another growing problem of the 1890s: sectarian warfare over funding of orphanages and other social programs.

In the nineteenth century, as noted earlier, many religion-based
orphanages received assistance from public funds, on an equal access
basis, with a certain amount allocated per child. Protestants often followed the Brace plan of emphasizing placement of children in private
homes; Catholics, more heavily urbanized than their Protestant counterparts, did not have as many farm families to fall back on.[49] By the
1880s Catholic leaders, concerned that some children whose parents
had been Catholic were being sent to Protestant homes, urged the use
of orphanages as a "ways and means of preventing Protestant inroads
on the faith."[50] Some Protestant agencies, not wanting Catholic orphanages to receive government subsidy, began campaigning against any
payment of public funds to private institutions. Those Protestants who
pushed for state education as a way of stopping Catholic parochial
schools also demanded that the state care for orphans and others
through state-run agencies (which, they believed, they could control).

In time, government officials would be only too happy to
comply—particularly because the orphanage trends of the late nineteenth century illuminated another tension that contributed to increased governmental influence over the long haul. Charles Brace had
said repeatedly that what was truly important in caring for orphans
was affiliation and bonding, which worked best over a family dinner

table, even if the food was plain, the table a plank, the chairs boxes, and the dining room part of a shack. The "family is a thousand times better charity than all our machinery," Brace insisted, as he complained that some orphanage supporters seemed more interested in "the condition of the buildings." Brace generalized beyond orphans to others in need, and argued that the physical surroundings are "nothing compared with the improvement in character and mind of the persons aided, and this is generally best effected by simple rooms, simple machinery...."[51]

And yet, while the superficial emphasis on material was "the great danger for all charities," it was also the most likely outcome if contributions of money became more important than contributions of time. Brace forecast trouble in the age of mass charity that he could see coming, for "the majority of people are most moved by hearing that so many thousand pairs of shoes, so many articles of clothing, or so many loaves of bread are given to the needy and suffering by some benevolent agency."[52] This trend lent impetus to additional governmental power, for the state could not save families but it could build edifices. Was housing a problem? The *Proceedings* of the National Conference of Charities and Correction (which in 1917 changed its name to the National Conference of Social Work) began to include lectures on how poor housing caused crime and how governmental housing projects would help.[53] The trend was clear: Any time the charitable emphasis moved from the person to the mass and from souls to stones, government became the popular engine of progress.

The 1890s did not lack those who remembered the lessons of the past. Robert Ellis Thompson of the University of Pennsylvania argued in 1891 that "the state, as the institute of rights, can give nothing to any man without conceding that it is his right to have it. Therefore, the state is the worst possible dispenser of alms."[54] Thompson noted the message that state welfare sent: "Every dollar it spends on the relief of the poor, is an admission that they have the right to be supported at the public expense, whether their need be due to idleness and improvidence, or to a blameless failure to succeed in life."[55] Thompson concluded:

> State relief of the poor cannot but be indiscriminate and degrading. The state, at its best, has a wooden uniformity in its operations.... It must treat all on the basis of equality, without much regard to merit, motives, or equity.[56]

Others in the 1890s recalled the experience of ancient Rome, medieval times, American colonial days, and nineteenth-century England.

And yet—so much needed to be done, and organizations were showing that much could be done on not just a neighborhood or city-wide level but a nationwide basis as well. National evangelical organizations such as the Young Men's Christian Association (YMCA), the Young Women's Christian Association (YWCA), and the Salvation Army were showing that it was possible to be large *and* effective. From its start just before the Civil War, the Young Men's Christian Association movement grew until by 1900 there were 1,429 local YMCAs with about 250,000 members. Those numbers are particularly significant because at the turn of the century the YMCA was still as much a center for spiritual as for physical workouts. YMCAs proclaimed their intention to battle poverty by promoting "the welfare of the whole man—body, soul and spirit." They raised funds for buildings that contained not only gyms but auditoriums for evangelistic meetings.[57] Several million men annually participated in YMCA-sponsored evangelistic meetings, and a YMCA vote was available only to members of evangelical churches. (Others could join to use the facilities, but had no say in the decision-making.)

As these activities continued, YMCAs also tried to serve material needs. YMCA buildings around the country housed 338 employment bureaus through which thirteen thousand jobs per year were found. The YMCA's Bowery branch provided nearly 35,000 lodgings a year and served over 100,000 meals. The Baltimore YMCA had six branches with about three thousand members who could use gymnasia, baths, and reading rooms.[58] Over time, the YMCAs specialized in the body and began to ignore soul and spirit.

Meanwhile, the seventy-five local groups and 78,000 members of the Young Women's Christian Association at the turn of the century maintained thirty-seven boarding houses (with room for 2,800 women) and eleven vacation houses. The YWCA nationally provided some 200,000 transient accommodations at a cost ranging from 25 cents to one dollar. Each YWCA had its own activities: the New York branch featured a library of 27,000 volumes and a circulating music library, along with frequent prayer meetings, while the Brooklyn YWCA offered courses in sewing, dressmaking, millinery, cooking, nursing, embroidery, art, German, and French.

The Salvation Army, operating often at a lower social level, had the most dramatic story. In 1900 the Salvation Army had seven hundred corps and outposts, with 2,600 officers and employees and twenty thousand volunteers; its employment bureaus were placing about 4,800 persons per month.[59] The army sponsored 141 social relief institutions, including 52 shelters for men and women, 8 labor bureaus, 14 rescue homes for fallen women, and 2 children's homes. Learning from Gurteen and Lowell, army officers set up industrial depots and wood-yards in some of the most destitute urban areas.[60] The able-bodied who

came to Salvation Army centers were required to work, often at woodyards. Some of them even became self-supporting; in 1895 the profits
of a well-run woodyard in Patterson, New Jersey—
more than $3,000—were distributed among those unable to work.[61]
Other woodyards ran at a loss but were such a valuable tool in assessing
willingness to work and avoiding the pauperization pressure that they
were continued for many years.

Salvation Army leaders had a wonderful record of innovation in
those years. They developed another type of woodyard approach in
1896, when an officer in Manhattan began walking the streets with a
pushcart asking for broken items that homeless men could repair at the
army shelter.[62] The idea caught on, and soon "salvage brigades" with
horses and wagons walked the streets of Chicago, Boston, Brooklyn,
and other cities.[63] Salvation Army buildings soon became combination
shelters, workshops, warehouses, and stores. Five hundred men lived
and worked in one Chicago building in 1898, repairing castoff items
that could be sold to the poor at low prices with funds used to pay for
their food and temporary lodging. The goal at such shelters was not to
provide permanent housing but to press for spiritual change while
building good work habits.[64] By 1900 Salvation Army leaders in the
United States were claiming fifty thousand or more conversions a year;
a spin-off group, Volunteers of America, claimed thousands more.[65]

Social Universalists who watched the success of the YMCA,
YWCA, and Salvation Army argued that government (without the
conversion emphasis, of course) could develop similar activities on
an all-encompassing basis. Wasn't charity following the consolidation
path of industry, where great corporations with hired management
were amazing the world with their efficient production? Might the
next step be a governmental Prosperity Army that would be in charge

of most charity, and similar to the "trust of trusts" that was predicted in industry?

Such expansive thinking largely ignored, of course, the understanding that the key to poverty-fighting was, in the words of Christian social worker Richard Holz, "a renewal of character and a change of the inner man, which can be brought only by the grace and power of our Lord Jesus Christ."[66] It ignored the religious and ethnic ties that underscored the efforts of Jewish organizations and other groups that worked hardest to aid members of their own community. It ignored the faith expressed by workers at one mission: "The Lord has made a job for every saved drunkard, as soon as He sees it safe for him to have it."[67]

Could the steamship travel without its furnace? The beliefs of the Salvation Army at that time showed how the need for spiritual change ran the entire organization. "Souls! Souls! Souls!" the Salvation Army's magazine *War Cry* insisted.[68] The cry was echoed in the army's New York "Garet, Dive, and Tenement Brigade," which began work in 1889 with "the Saviour-like work of visiting, helping, and reclaiming the lost,"[69] as well as by Salvation Army founder William Booth's son Ballington, who scoffed at schemes for reform apart from character change and argued that an educated devil was only a devil made more resourceful.[70] "Hard work and simple religious truth" were the answer to poverty, he said, and his troops slapped together employment bureaus and chapel services.[71]

Could government workers provide, as did the Salvation Army, "daily work in the homes of the people, watching over the sick and dying, and loving service in trying hours...?"[72] Could regulations bring out the "self-sacrifice not short of heroism which [the Salvation Army] has evoked in hundreds?"[73] The *War Cry* noted that "when

Christ said... 'Neither do I condemn thee,' He also added, 'Go and sin no more.' "[74] Could a pluralistic government pinpoint sin and oppose it? Those who treasured governmental programs saw the success of groups like the Salvation Army but failed to grasp the spiritual basis, and then asked, over and over again, "And why not do more?" As a new century arrived, the Utopians began to be heard, and followed.

CHAPTER EIGHT

Excitement of a New Century

A new spirit was evident as the twentieth century began. There was so much to do! The problems were so great! Cautionary tales about the easy slide from poverty into pauperism seemed unimportant in a new era. Instead of looking backward, magazines in January 1900 hailed a new beginning:

> Let all the clocks of time in loud accord
> Intone the hour that marks the century's end
> Let all the eager earth on tip-toe stand
> And watch the sunburst of a cycle new...
> Your eyes behold the white light of a day,
> Whose sheen in glory's mantle shall enwrap
> The world, and golden years enfold in an
> Unbroken round of sweet and happy peace.[1]

A popular minister of the period, the Reverend Dr. R. M. Newton, proclaimed in the pages of the nation's most-read newspaper, the *New York Journal*, that a "new and absolutely unprecedented dominion over Nature provides man with the physical means for preparing a new earth, in which there shall be health and wealth, peace and plenty and prosperity."[2] Every problem of "social misery and wrong" will be solved, Newton proclaimed, by those with "a genuine and earnest and passionate desire for the betterment of mankind."[3]

Statement after statement put forth the view that much was achieved during the nineteenth century and much more could be achieved in the twentieth, by taking recent trends to their logical extension. Since scientific progress during the nineteenth century was spectacular, social progress during the twentieth could be just as enthralling: "With their mastery of nature the men of the twentieth century will learn how to master themselves. They will solve the social problem."[4] Since charitable organizations had grown substantially, it was time to cover every problem by making government the greatest charitable organization of them all. "Perhaps the most remarkable of all the characteristic developments of the nineteenth century has been the growth of human sympathy," the *New York Journal* stated: "The feeling that every man is really his brother's keeper has become stronger than ever before."[5]

Overall, the mood was unrelentingly upbeat: we "welcome the golden time that is coming."[6] No longer should those concerned with "compassion" speak of the difficulties of change; instead, hope prevailed:

> *Faith is not dead, tho' priest and creed may pass,*
> *For thought has leavened the whole unthinking mass.*
> *And man looks now to find the God within.*
> *We shall talk more of love, and less of sin.*[7]

Hopes were so high that the *Christian Oracle* magazine changed its name in 1899 to the *Christian Century*, and explained, "We believe that the coming century is to witness greater triumphs in Christianity than any previous century has ever witnessed, and that it is to be more truly Christian than any of its predecessors."[8] Short essays on "Why the World is Becoming Better" displayed the same optimism. One contributor, H. O. Breeden, stated, "Statistics prove that the actual volume of righteousness compared with the population is greater than ever before and growing. The sentiments of justice, liberty and love are stronger and more universal."[9] Breeden was particularly impressed by "the wonderful development of humanitarian and charitable agencies for the alleviation of suffering and the promotion and permanent enthronement of righteousness."

Repeatedly, *Christian Century* editorialists argued that understandings developed in the past were no longer relevant:

A great breaking up, a spring thaw, is going on in the religious world....Our "old faiths" must be viewed in "new lights."... We cannot pin our faith to Calvin or Luther, Wesley or Campbell. Much less can we pin our faith to old forms. The living, loving Christ alone is sufficient.[10]

Sometimes, the political agenda was specific. Reverend Newton, for example, concluded that "the task of the new century is to socialize the magnificent forces which the closing century has handed over to man."[11] Governmental welfare programs, he proposed, should "become the outer form of the altruistic spirit—the unselfish, loving, just nature of the new man." Writer after writer lauded what church groups had accomplished in the charitable realm, but stated that churches now were confronted "by a problem infinitely bigger than they can handle—a problem so big indeed that no institution short of society itself can hope to cope with it."[12] Overall, the *Christian Century* told its readers, "There can be no foundation for any other feeling than one of profound and enthusiastic optimism."[13]

Early twentieth-century reformers wanted to start fresh—and the first aspect of the fresh start was theological. Readers of the *Christian Century* were told that only "an ignorant age can safely venture to be dogmatic," and that "a new knowledge has come to humanity which has opened secrets of nature and history."[14] Studies in human evolution and social processes were said to provide understanding that required reinterpretation of the Bible, since God was now most visible "in the great common places of life, in nature, in the long evolutionary process."[15] Biblical statements could not be taken literally.[16]

In particular, the new social understanding attacked the biblical concept of a sinful human nature. Man's basic nature was not corrupt, but good; there were sins but not sin, evil acts but not evil. Problems arose from social conditions rather than inherent moral corruption. The *Encyclopedia of Social Reform* stated that "almost all social thinkers are now agreed that the social evils of the day arise in large part from social wrongs."[17] Frank Dekker Watson, director of the Pennsylvania School for Social Service and professor of sociology and social work at Haverford College, concluded that "no person who is interested in social progress can long be content to raise here and there an individual."[18] Nor was there any need to be content with such a limited objective; since actions were determined by environmental factors, a bad environment caused men and women to engage in activities which eventually left them shuffling off to a mission. A good environment would save all.[19] Compassion meant accepting wrongful activity and postponing any pressure to change until the person was in a good environment.[20]

In short, the Greeleyite idea that all should by natural right have a piece of the pie, whether or not they contributed to its making, was gaining vast intellectual and theological support. Just as it was considered unfair within the new, liberal theology that anyone should go to Hell—if there were something called sin, God was considered responsible for it—so it was unfair that anyone should physically suffer in this life. The universalistic theology that all must be saved, regardless of their belief and action, was matched by a universalistic sociology that all must receive provision.

More changes in thinking followed. If the key goal was provision of material aid but not personal change in the individual receiving aid, programs could be measured by the amount of material transferred; nonquantifiable considerations that complicated the evaluation could be dropped. Just as Social Universalists believed God would be unjust were He to leave any souls unsaved, so they criticized the new god—centralized government, as Fremantle has argued—for acting unjustly should any bodies remain unfed.

Soon, the "crowding out" idea—the nineteenth-century concern that private charity would diminish if the state took over—was turned upside down. In the new era in which the state was seen to have essential responsibility, some thinkers began to call for less private charity; they argued that private charitable efforts might let government off the hook. Watson in 1922 described the common understanding developed during the previous two decades:

> It became evident in many communities that so long as private agencies, including charity organization societies, continued to care for those families eligible for a pension, it would be easy for the state to evade the responsibility.[21]

Watson praised one Philadelphia group for announcing that it would no longer help widows—for, only when private groups went on strike, would "public funds ever be wholly adequate for the legitimate demands made upon them."[22] Increasingly, some saw the existence of charitable organizations as a token of governmental weakness rather than a sign of social strength—and as a slippage in universalism.

Since, furthermore, theological liberals assumed that individuals freed from material pressures would also be freed from the sinful tendencies assumedly growing out of those pressures, the focus increasingly was on material needs. Hall Caine, a well-known novelist of the period and author of *The Christian*, described in the *Chicago Tribune* the extent to which material comfort was believed to drive moral progress:

> The world is constantly growing better and happier.... There can hardly be any doubt about this [when one sees] the changes which the century has brought about in the people's health, education, and comfort.... People are better housed, and for that reason, among others, their morality has improved.[23]

The primary cause of immorality was not sin, but lack of housing projects. Caine called for "state control of great trusts," and Social Gospel leader Walter Rauschenbush said straightforwardly, "God is against capitalism."[24] Clearly, not all or even most church members subscribed to this new thinking, but many of the most articulate and influential parts of American Protestantism hugged the Left and became thoroughly modern millenialists.[25]

Journalistic powers, particularly the Hearst and Scripps-McRae newspaper chains, conducted national editorial campaigns to promote governmental welfare programs. Hearst ordered his editors to "make a great and continuous noise to attract readers; denounce crooked wealth and promise better conditions for the poor to keep readers. INCREASE CIRCULATION."[26] Hearst's "ostentatious sympathy with the 'underdog' " led him to call for guaranteed incomes.[27] One Hearst reporter wrote that his job was "to enlighten and uplift humanity. Unequaled newspaper enterprise, combined with a far-reaching philanthropy, was to reform [the United States] under the banner of William R. Hearst...."[28] But liberal Herbert Croly compared Hearst to Robespierre, writing that Hearst's ambition was to bring about a "socialistic millennium."[29] Congressman John A. Sullivan called Hearst the Nero of American politics for his attempts to incite class conflict.[30]

Overall, the points of light from the late nineteenth-century's war on poverty, and those from the settlement house movement as well, seemed to be flickering and even insignificant when viewed from a universalistic plateau.[31] Writers and clerics who saw Utopia around the corner were not satisfied with prodigal sons coming home one by one. The journalistic push and the theological pull led to attempts to build a national welfare system.

The attempt's first major political success came in January 1909, when two hundred prominent men and women met at the White House Conference on the Care of Dependent Children and proposed programs to help the two classically needy groups, widows and impoverished children. The presidential call for a conference in itself represented a departure from White House positions held since 1854, when Franklin Pierce vetoed the expenditure of federal funds for mental hospitals. President Theodore Roosevelt, in contrast, patted the nose poking into the tent by telling charity professionals that relief was essential, and that he did not oppose governmental welfare: "How the relief shall come, public, private, or by a mixture of both, in what way, you are competent to say and I am not."[32]

First came proposals for what were called "widows' pensions" but were actually "mothers' pensions." The difference was crucial. Josephine Lowell always wanted widows-only help, since she believed that helping abandoned women would lead to more abandonment. But the White House Conference proposed aid to "children of reasonably efficient and deserving mothers who are without the support of the normal breadwinner."[33] Groups that stressed affiliation and bonding rather than government programs objected. Otis Bannard, head of New York's Charity Organization Society, called mothers' pensions "an entering wedge towards state socialism," with "relief to the able-bodied" not far behind.[34] Bannard's colleague Edward Devine called governmental support of abandoned women "an insidious attack upon the family" and an encouragement to abandonment.[35] Mothers' pensions, Devine added, were "inimical to the welfare of children and injurious to the character of parents."[36]

But none of these reservations made any difference when newspapers were filled with gripping accounts of particularly worthy families living in poverty that could be helped by the proposed programs. The effective writing of New York *Evening World* columnist Sophie Loeb led to the rise of the Widowed Mothers' Fund Association. As Frank Bruno recounted,

> Sophie Irene Loeb was the dominant personality. The influence of this association spread beyond the borders of the city [and] made a clean sweep of the country....Such well-defined movements do not just happen.[37]

This one happened because of major media backing and the work of deeply committed journalists. After some hard lobbying, breakthroughs came with the passage of mothers' pension bills in Missouri and Illinois. The New York state legislature passed its law in 1915, and the bandwagon, with press support, was rolling: one article published that year was entitled the "Wildfire Spread of Mothers' Pensions."[38] Loeb herself became president of the board that administered New York's law, and then president of the Child Welfare Committee of America.

By 1919 mothers' pensions were available in thirty-nine states.[39] Critics of the bills generally were able to insert legislative language requiring a recipient to be "a proper person, physically, mentally and morally fit to bring up her children."[40] Evidence of extramarital relations could mean rejection.[41] Nevertheless, although Michigan was the only state to specify that unmarried or divorced mothers were eligible, most states did not restrict eligible recipients to widows alone. Over the years coverage was extended to women whose husbands for whatever reason were unable to support their families. By 1930 only four states provided no assistance, and state funds were going to over 200,000 children whose fathers were dead, disabled, or absent from home because of divorce, desertion, or imprisonment.

As the mothers' pension movement blossomed, so did another outgrowth of the 1909 conference, the drive to establish a "federal children's bureau." Theodore Roosevelt called for one, but stressed its limited function: the bureau was not to act by itself, but was to gather information so that others might act. "In the absence of such information as should be supplied by the Federal Government many abuses have gone unchecked," he said: "[P]ublic sentiment with its great corrective power, can only be aroused by full knowledge of the facts."[42] Again, a coalition of many social and civic organizations, liberal church groups, new welfare professionals, and journalists, went to work. Again, the fight was hard; it took a series of hearings and five days of bitter floor debate for the bill to pass the Senate in 1912, and another two months of discussion for the bill to pass the House and be signed into law by President Howard Taft. The precedent was established; the federal government, which before had taken on only limited functions in public health and education, now was involved in broad questions of welfare.

The U.S. Children's Bureau quickly became a factory that churned out plans for extension of governmental involvement. Bureau head Julia Lathrop, who entered government after working alongside Jane Addams at Hull House, provided strong leadership. Over the next decade she fought for federal grants to states that set up maternal and child health services in accordance with children's bureau specifications. Some doctors attacked her campaign for "state medicine" and pointed to precedents being set, but the Maternity and Infancy Act, also known as the Sheppard-Towner Act, became law in 1921; it provided for the first direct federal child welfare expenditures.[43] Sheppard-Towner's practical importance should not be exaggerated; yet, although appropriations under it were small, the act represented the advancement of an idea that would receive greater backing in the Social Security Act of 1935 and other New Deal programs.

Furthermore, as the mothers' pension and child welfare programs put down roots, governmental outdoor relief, which late nineteenth-century reformers had fought against so hard, made a comeback. From 1911 to 1925 governmental outdoor relief payments in sixteen of the largest cities increased from $1.6 million to $14.7 million.[44] Evidence of the change was also evident in smaller cities across the country, including Kansas City, Denver, Dallas, and Grand Rapids. And it was a statewide phenomena in most areas; the Indiana State Board of Charities reported an increase in outdoor relief from $266,000 in 1910 to $841,000 in 1925.[45]

Private agencies also stepped up their soup kitchen efforts even though there was no evident increase in need. In New Haven, as governmental outdoor relief expenditures increased from $16,000 in 1910 to $112,000 in 1925, the city's private charities marched right alongside, increasing their expenditures from $50,000 to $178,000 (in constant 1913 dollars).[46] One philanthropy-watcher reported in 1922 that the "opposition to public outdoor relief...in charity organization circles" had disappeared.[47] In addition, the National Federation of Settlements campaigned throughout the 1920s for the construction of government housing projects in the form of large-scale, multiple-dwelling units surrounded by parks:

> Hundreds of millions of dollars ought to be devoted to this purpose, by means of which fine, well-planned communities could be developed...affording the finest environment for the development of a physically, mentally and morally sound citizenship.[48]

Given the theological changes and social demands, such calls for state-provided housing and income support seemed inevitable. So strong was the drive for governmental action that a federal Department of Public Welfare almost came into existence in 1921. Warren Harding, known as a conservative, proposed one during his 1920 campaign for the presidency; following the election he refined the proposal by outlining a department that would include a Division of Education, a Division of Public Health, a Division of Social Service, and a Division of Veterans' Service Administration. The new department, a Harding spokesman said, would see to "the essential things that are necessary to make the best American citizens from the physical standpoint."[49] The department would ensure "the proper education of teachers," and its social service director would "say what is necessary and also what is right."[50]

But the bill that would have established the department never made it out of committee. Hearings revealed opposition from congressmen concerned about cost and from educators who wanted a separate Department of Education, while Samuel Gompers and other leaders of organized labor worried that a new department would cut away some of the power of the recently established Department of Labor. As Gompers wrote, "The enemies of organized labor would like to ruin the labor department by dismembering it under the guise of creating a department of welfare."[51] The idea died during the political wrangling, but its initial proposal and support showed that the concept of active federal involvement in many areas of welfare was putting down deep roots.

Furthermore, the growing call for and incidence of governmental action accompanied a new stress on professionalism in social work. New York's Charity Organization Society had established a Summer School of Philanthropy in 1898, but the program lasted only six weeks and was designed to help volunteers, not supplant them.[52] The school's program, however, soon expanded to fill an academic year, and then two; it eventually became the Columbia University Graduate School of Social Work.[53] Mary Richmond began to worry that professionals were being "exalted...at the expense of the volunteer."[54] She wondered if "it is assumed that only officials should be permitted to be charitable." She also complained about a certain opinionated and self-righteous attitude in some of the trained social workers [who saw the world as a stage] upon which we professional workers are to exercise our talents, while the volunteers do nothing but furnish the gate receipts and an open-mouthed admiration of our performances.[55]

In 1911 Frederic Almy of the Buffalo COS remarked, sardonically but seriously, that "social workers like doctors [soon] will have to pass an examination before they are allowed to practice upon the lives of the poor."[56]

By 1920, a clear theological understanding was shared by most of the professional social workers, according to Owen Lovejoy, president of the National Conference of Social Work. "Conventional creeds seem to find little place in the mental equipment of many of us," he acknowledged, "and people who appear to be rendering the highest kind of social service are often accused of being irreligious."[57] Lovejoy noted that most social workers did not wish "to 'defend' the Bible, the Church, the flag or the Constitution." Social workers, he generalized, detested "the intolerance of the Puritans, the odor of sanctity about those imperial forms that bend so willingly under the profitable white man's burden...."[58] The typical social worker's goal, according to Lovejoy, was to have "sympathetic consideration" of all attitudes and beliefs in order to be "of service to humanity."[59]

Lovejoy, in essence, argued that a new social work religion was growing, with new definitions to words previously quite adequately understood. For example, Lovejoy defined "the communion of saints" as "the fellowship of people who are devoted to something, the fellowship of the devoted … ,'" without specifying the God of the Bible as the object of devotion.[60] He defined the "invisible church" as that "bond of union among congenial spirits which under whatever name is bound to work itself out in those cooperative activities of the human race," and the "apostolic succession" as all who are "keen in the service of humanity."[61]

The new religion had its practical applications. In the previous century, Lovejoy said, social work volunteers endeavored

> tenderly to ameliorate evil social conditions, to lighten the burdens of poverty, to reduce the volume of ignorance, combat the ravages of disease and otherwise labor diligently to assuage the flood of human sorrow and wretchedness.[62]

But those were all palliatives, according to Lovejoy, offered by "those who look upon a kingdom of right relations as an impossibility in this life." In the new era, Lovejoy argued, social workers and their allies were "social engineers" capable of creating "a divine order on earth as it is in heaven."[63] Modern social workers, he argued, were "dissatisfied with programs limited to a treatment of social effects," for "the idea of simply making the earth a place that will be humanely endurable and stopping there [is] an intolerable belittling of the innate qualities in man."[64]

This idea of innate qualities brought Lovejoy to the crux of the "irreconcilable difference in social faith" between the old and the new social work leaders.[65] Those of the past

> cling[ed] to a belief in the sacrifice of another in order that the wrath of God may be cooled, and He may find it

possible, without violating eternal justice, to forgive those
who have broken his law.[66]

But the new wave was made up of "adventurous souls who do not
hesitate to call in question this ancient idea" of "spiritual cannibal-
ism."[67] The new faith, in Lovejoy's words, emphasized "human improvableness.... All that is best in the achievement of the race is an
evolution of this very principle of human improvableness."[68]

In conclusion, Lovejoy and his new social work corps looked to
"the divinity in every man" and yearned for "a day when humanity
itself may become a harmonious social organism...."[69] The modern
social worker's faith, Lovejoy insisted, was and should be "a positive,
though perhaps unanalyzed, confidence in the essential divinity of
every man."[70] Three years later, conservative theologian J. Gresham
Machen analyzed the views of leaders such as Lovejoy. Modern theological liberalism, Machen wrote,

> has lost all sense of the gulf that separates the creature from
> the Creator; its doctrine of man follows naturally from its
> doctrine of God.... According to the Bible, man is a sinner
> under the just condemnation of God; according to modern
> liberalism, there is really no such thing as sin.[71]

Machen concluded that the chief characteristic of such belief was "a
supreme confidence in human goodness." God was not needed.[72]

This faith in Man danced throughout Lovejoy's speech of 1920. It
shone in 1924, when a Rockefeller Foundation study concluded that
economic assistance to families without fathers set in motion "a
healthy succession of redemptive forces [that] began to work *of their*

own accord."[73] And it inspirited the social work leaders who argued that only a radical reconstruction of the nation's economy would provide long-term help to the poor. At the National Conference of Social Work in 1924, Mary van Kleeck, director of the Division of Industrial Studies of the Russell Sage Foundation, proposed paving the road to social advance with "industrial democracy." Former social worker Roger Baldwin, who became better known as director of the American Civil Liberties Union, called similarly for a "cooperative commonwealth" that would abolish "economic classes, poverty, privilege."[74] To accomplish that he proposed that social workers band to form a Labour Party (as in Britain) that could bring about government control of natural resources and public utilities. Social workers, Baldwin argued, should be advocates rather than referees: "If social workers are to be participants in the essential struggle for larger human freedom in this generation, they can achieve it only by identification with the cause of labor."[75]

Van Kleeck and Baldwin were among the radicals, but many of their presuppositions were similar to those of "the average modern social worker," described by Reinhold Niebuhr in 1931 as

> very often of the type in whom traditional religion no longer awakens interest.... [H]e is probably engaged in social work precisely because that vocation is to him the most logical means of expressing his sense of mission to mankind, which has been aroused by the religion of his youth.[76]

Niebuhr saw danger in this transfer of vocation, for he argued that social work could be "saved from sentimentality only by the shrewder insights" of a faith that recognized the "selfishness of human life."

Liberal Christianity, which Niebuhr called "the most sentimental religion of our day," was not that kind of faith, and he was worried.[77]

So were others—for as professionals began to dominate the realm of compassion, volunteers began to depart. It is not clear whether the supply first slackened, or whether professionals worked to decrease the demand. Some cities showed simultaneous movement. In Chicago, Kathleen McCarthy noted,

> Even as the city's stewards withdrew from the decision-making arena, professionals conspired to further diminish their role, setting restrictions on gifts and reshaping the prerogatives of boards.[78]

Agencies began to report a dearth of volunteers, while at the same time narrowing the field for those who did volunteer. At the United Charities of Chicago by 1915, "interested laymen were as likely to be consigned to a desk job as they were to be assigned to a family."[79] When board members at one charity organization wanted more involvement, its president announced, "our staff is so well organized that there is very little for our Board Members to do...."[80]

Boards did retain one major function: "Under the exacting gaze of a freshly certified professional elite, boards were remodeled into fund-raising bodies...."[81] The growth of economic segregation and mediated compassion made it easy for many of the better-off to

> measure community needs through abstractions: publicity, lectures, the photographs in annual reports. Communications innovations, like professionalization, separated the twentieth-century donor from the object of his largesse. [Donors]

could exercise the obligations of stewardship at a safe remove
from the problems they were helping to solve.[82]

Annual reports, instead of being technical documents presenting financial information, became key middlemen: "Bonding" was reduced to donors receiving photographs of grateful clients. Discernment was unlikely when supporters merely received glib accounts that attempted to hit sentimental notes as they foot-peddled praise and self-satisfaction.[83]

By the 1920s, a University of Chicago sociologist who interviewed nearby suburban residents found them complacent in their isolation and hardly likely to venture into poor areas. One woman, explaining her unwillingness to visit the slums, said, "They're too dirty and besides its too dangerous. I can't see how anyone could get a kick out of doing that. Merely the idea of it is nauseating to me."[84] Initially, the willingness to give money grew as the desire to give time decreased. In 1929 the *Literary Digest* noted that rich citizens, "[l]ike some of Shakespeare's characters...have developed a habit of flinging purses at the least provocation and crying: 'Spend this for me!'"[85] One wealthy Chicagoan, when asked why her peers were not involved in person-to-person activity, said, "Organizations look after everything, and they give to them, so why think about it?"[86]

The picture was brighter in some areas. Chains such as the Florence Crittenton homes and the "Doors of Hope" emphasized help to "fallen women" and still maintained strong principles of bonding. Millionnaire Charles Crittenton's work in urban slums began after his daughter Florence died in 1882. Once, when he asked two prostitutes to leave the trade, he realized there was no good place for them to find help—and he decided to start one.[87] The Florence

Mission opened in 1883 and provided a home to an annual average of 250 girls and young women over the next decade.[88] By 1930 there were forty-five Crittenton homes that afforded both spiritual challenge and the training of character necessary to instill habits that would lead to employment.[89]

The "Doors of Hope" had similar roots in the late nineteenth century. Mrs. Emma Whittemore, converted to Christianity at Jerry McAuley's Water Street mission in 1875, had felt particularly moved to help women trying to escape prostitution, and others who were pregnant but unmarried. The number of her homes for needy women jumped from one in 1890 to sixty-one in 1903; by the time of her death in 1931 the Door of Hope Union had nearly one hundred member homes.[90] The homes provided housing, food, clothing, medical care, spiritual challenge, and training in skills such as sewing, dressmaking, and cooking.

In several other ways the older emphasis on affiliation, bonding, and additional aspects of *suffering with* also showed its staying power—but almost always in those organizations where the old theology held sway. The more secularized settlement houses, by comparison, tended to lose their initial stress on personal contact. By the early 1930s, settlement house workers often saw themselves "as professional men and women, rendering a specific service desired by the neighborhood, however paid for, rather than as 'neighbors' or 'social explorers.'"[91] Many refused to live in slum areas; one irritated defender of personal involvement, Albert J. Kennedy, complained that "the antagonism which certain young staff workers feel to residence is based partly on their thinking of themselves...."[92] Many began to emphasize large-scale social and political change rather than personal involvement, which they saw as old-fashioned; in Kennedy's words, "the revolt is against that grain of sentimentalism."

What all this also led to was a sense that private charity was irrelevant. But the change was not inevitable. In 1933 the form of the
old, and a considerable part of the function, remained. Thirteen different Protestant religious bodies had a vast array of social service
organizations; 600 Catholic child-care institutions housed over
80,000 children; and 60 Jewish institutions cared for 4,000 dependent
children.[93] Men who might otherwise have been homeless could stay
at one of the 614 city YMCAs (dormitory accommodations for
62,000), the 89 Salvation Army barracks (sleeping 7,000), the 75
Goodwill Industries dormitories (with room for 3,000), and more.[94]
Sections of the *Social Work Year Book* for 1933 contained impressive
statistics concerning "Catholic Social Work," "Jewish Social Work,"
"Mormon Social Work," "Protestant Social Work," and more.

But the question was: How were these programs really different
from governmental programs? Were they based on a different
world-view, a different sense of the nature of man? Did they see
spiritual change as the key to material change, or had they adopted
the belief that the sum of man is what he eats and where he lives?
The general sense was that many religious programs had effectively
been secularized, and with it the excitement of sacrificing to keep
them going was gone. There seemed to be no reason, except "conservative stinginess," to oppose the establishment of a new, massive
governmental system. There seemed to be little reason to take seriously long-standing concerns about federal activities "crowding
out" local volunteer effort—the soul of those efforts had already
been crowded out by the new philosophy of "loaves and shoes."[95]

This is not to say that private agencies were without problems of
supply in the early 1930s. They had their own short-term exigencies,
as the better-off also were affected by economic pressures, and as

groups devoted to personal interaction had trouble adjusting to masses at the door. Sadly, just as the Depression increased demand—from 1929 to 1932—at least four hundred of the nation's private welfare agencies went under. But the problems of supply were also the result of a long-term trend toward impersonal contribution. Philanthropy had become "as cold as the payment of taxes," journalist Alan Herrick noted: "Indeed the objectives of the two are often the same."[96]

In short, the movement away from personal action was easy when problems seemed overwhelming, and when Community Chest emphasis on cash already provided "the ultimate in bureaucracy—an anonymous public supporting anonymous machinery supporting anonymous clients."[97] Radical change was accepted because the ground had long been prepared. The New Deal battles to come were won on the playing fields of theologically liberal seminaries and in the meeting rooms of private charities.

CHAPTER NINE

Selling New Deals in Old Wineskins

O ne of the current historical myths concerns American attitudes during the Depression: how rapidly these attitudes changed; how "forward-looking" they became as economic pressures mounted; and how conclusively the old order of the late nineteenth century passed away. There is some surface truth to this legend, for legislation in 1933 was fast and rhetoric was fiery. But in a deeper sense, the 1930s showed how wise the old charity leaders had been in their concern about "pauperization."

Without doubt, the Depression was far, far worse than previous economic dislocations. During every decade since the 1850s some workers had suffered in the aftermath of "business panics," but the layoffs usually were short-lived. Charity experts had noted that most unemployed men of earlier eras were jobless because of personal problems needing individual rather than collective care. But after 1929, both liberals and conservatives remarked upon the "new unemployment." The breadth and longevity of the economic emergency was unprecedented, with a surge in legitimate need for help far exceeding that of any previous recession.

The statistical basis for claims of "new conditions" was clear. Four out of five applicants to New York's Social Service Exchange in January 1930 were individuals who had never before requested relief.[1] A *Fortune* survey of one thousand relief recipients later in the decade showed that more than two-thirds had held their longest job for more than five years, and that one-fifth had held the same job for twenty years or more before hard times hit.[2] *Fortune* called this "an employment record that argues a good deal for the steady-going habits of those who were thrown out of work by depression."[3] The magazine's survey of Depression effects showed fewer than one of ten losing their job because of their own fault, or even through personal failure in their own businesses.

Overall, unemployment rose from 1.6 million in 1929 to a high of 12.8 million (25 percent of the labor force) early in 1933; many more were semiemployed. The ripple effect was greater than in years past or to come, because "broken families or lone persons" represented only about 17 percent of the relief population.[4] Since most men on urban relief rolls came from "a relatively experienced group of workers," unemployment often brought not only material problems but the particular psychological and spiritual difficulties of those who had earned solid positions and now had lost them through no fault of their own.[5] As fruitless job-hunting went on month after month, and observers noted fear among the unemployed, "fear driving them into a state of semi-collapse, cracking nerves; an overpowering fear of the future [as they watched] their children grow thinner and thinner."[6]

There was, nevertheless, a remarkable unwillingness to go "on the dole." Government welfare and shame still were a horse and carriage in the popular mind. Researchers into popular attitudes found an accountant turned ditch-digger saying, "I'd rather stay out in that ditch

the rest of my life than take one cent of direct relief."[7] Later, Studs Terkel
in *Hard Times* quoted Ben Isaacs making a typical statement:

> Shame? You tellin' me? I would go stand on that relief line,
> I would look this way and that way and see if there's nobody
> around that knows me. I would bend my head low so no-
> body would recognize me. The only scar it left on me is my
> pride, my pride.[8]

Such beliefs were scientifically recorded by E. W. Bakke, who wrote
the definitive study of 1930s' attitudes toward unemployment and welfare; he often heard comments such as, "I'd rather be dead and buried"
than take relief.[9] Bakke's research showed that unemployed workers
often tried seven alternatives, sequentially, before applying for government aid. They gathered up their accrued benefit rights, applied for
commercial credit, or dipped into the savings of immediate family
members. When necessary, they moved onto further steps. Members
of the family not normally expected to earn money would go to work,
and new loans on property would be assumed. When more aid was
needed, they would turn to members of the extended family for loans
(which might turn into gifts) and then to friends, again for loans or
gifts. Only when all those steps were taken would they look to government, with the hope of getting work relief.[10]

Going through these steps took time. When Bakke interviewed
two thousand heads of families in New Haven in 1933, he found 988 to
be unemployed. Two years later, when he reinterviewed those who
were still unemployed, he found that only one-fourth of them had
sought relief, and many of those had taken a long time to do so.[11] In
going through those steps, individuals and families were also following

the law. In 1937 two-thirds of the states had provisions requiring that, before relief could be given, relatives with "sufficient ability" were to be called upon to support poor persons, and were subject to prosecution if they refused.[12] They also were following a cultural sense of honor built over the decades.

The political impact of these beliefs was that whenever the New Deal emphasized straight subsidy of those who could work, animosity toward it grew. On the other hand, "temporary" programs would be acceptable, since the economic emergency was seen as a plague that eventually would run its course. New York's prototypical relief program of the 1930s was labeled the Temporary Emergency Relief Administration, thus showing through a double-emphasis that subsidies would be short-lived.[13] Franklin Roosevelt's nationalization of the idea was called the Federal Emergency Relief Administration (FERA), and other programs were similarly viewed, or at least sold, as brief necessities. A half-century after the New Deal, Kentucky journalist John Pearce recalled, "I don't think it ever occurred to any of us" that the New Deal legacy would be "a welfare system that today supports millions who have neither prospect nor intention of earning their own living."[14]

Some leaders within the Roosevelt administration also retained the older values and saw programs only as "temporary." Bureau of the Budget Director Lewis Douglas, for example, warned emphatically that "thousands would settle into government-made jobs" if programs were long lasting, and the result would be long-term economic collapse. Douglas argued that any program given time to sink roots "might become so great that it might be impossible to end it." U.S. Surgeon General Thomas Parran, for his part, told a Senate committee that "self-reliance, the satisfaction of work, the joy of acquisition, the sense of equality, the opportunity of leading a normal family life" were vital to good health. He noted that

our destitute citizens [must have] an opportunity of a livelihood earned by individual effort. I emphasize useful work;
no other type fills the mental needs [or repairs] losses to
human character and mental health....[15]

Parran supported temporary programs that provided real work, but
not permanent entitlements. Roosevelt himself acknowledged the
danger of welfare programs becoming "a habit with the country," and
pledged to avoid it.[16]

Respecting the cultural mandates, most New Deal programs for those
free to work were based not on ideas of entitlement but on provision of jobs.
Roosevelt attacked government handouts in language—"a narcotic"—with
which Josephine Lowell would have been comfortable. In November 1933
Roosevelt stated, "When any man or woman goes on a dole something
happens to them mentally and the quicker they are taken off the dole the
better it is for them the rest of their lives."[17] And early in 1935 Roosevelt
added, "We must preserve not only the bodies of the unemployed from
destitution but also their self-respect, their self-reliance and courage and
determination...."[18] Later that year he noted that

in this business of relief we are dealing with properly
self-respecting Americans to whom a mere dole outrages
every instinct of individual independence. Most Americans
want to give something for what they get. That something, in
this case honest work, is the saving barrier between them and
moral disintegration. We propose to build that barrier high.[19]

Whether such rhetoric was protective coloring is still debated by historians, but the New Deal was sold as a reshuffle of the same old cards,
not production of a new pack.

Many social workers, however, desired permanent programs, not emergency gap-fillers.[20] The bad news to millions was an opportunity for social workers generally, and particularly for those who long had yearned for the advent of social universalism. "The great depression of the 1930s revolutionized social work," Frank Bruno wrote. "Instead of being the Cinderella that must be satisfied with the leavings, social work was placed by the depression among the primary functions of government."[21] The revolution did not come spontaneously. In August 1931, for example, the Rockefeller Foundation gave the American Association of Public Welfare Officials a grant of $40,000 for activities that included a program to "educate public opinion regarding the fundamental importance of welfare work in present-day government."[22] Other groups also began proselytizing; the Milford Conference of the American Association of Social Workers (AASW) concluded that "the future of social work is bound up with the coming of a sounder social order."[23] This meant that "the members of this profession have not only the obligation to work for justice... but the professional duty to make real the conditions under which their service can be given."[24]

Soon, some of the more circumlocutious euphemisms were dropped. The AASW Committee on Federal Action on Unemployment concluded in April 1933 that "National Economic Objectives for Social Work" should include social and economic planning through which all who desired it would be entitled to governmental support.[25] Alongside this, individual competition and incentives for personal gain would be curbed. In February 1934 the AASW Conference on Governmental Objectives for Social Work adopted a program which stated that social problems arise out of "our faulty distribution of wealth."[26] Mary van Kleeck, now dubbed a "high priestess" of social welfare, praised Soviet planning and presented at both conferences papers that insisted on "A Planned Economy as a National Economic Objective for Social Work."[27]

The National Conference of Social Work came fully up-to-date at its May 1934 annual meeting, held in Kansas City. Some 1,500 social workers crowded a room designed for one-third that number to hear the high priestess discuss "Our Illusions Concerning Government."[28] The conference awarded Van Kleeck a prize for her work that proposed "a socialized, planned economy for the raising of standards of living...."[29] Her demand for a national income maintenance program (as part of a "collective, worker-controlled society") was cheered.[30] Gertrude Springer of *The Survey*, published largely for social workers by Van Kleeck's Russell Sage Foundation, described the reaction:

> Never in a long experience of conferences has this observer witnessed such a prolonged ovation as followed....
> To her wearied and discouraged colleagues in social work she brought a new hope and dream when they had ceased to hope and dream.[31]

Springer's report was public relations puffery—many social workers did not embrace the Russell Sage agenda—but a new framing of the social work issues was evident.

That became obvious when the conference handed another prize to Eduard Lindeman for his paper on "Basic Unities in Social Work." In it he argued that social workers should "build a new society" based on "redistribution of national wealth...nationalization of utilities, currency, credits and marginal lands," and "elevation of a large proportion of housing to the status of public utility."[32] Some of Lindeman's proposals were still partly sheathed—"Circumscribed control over private property in relation to a national plan.... Functionalization of government without abandoning entirely the representative system"—but the intent of his verbal swordplay was evident. "There have always been radical sideshows," *The Survey* exulted, "but this year the radicals had the big tent and the conservatives were in the sideshows."[33] And in those spots the groups would remain.

What was missing in all this, of course, was any suggestion of affiliation, bonding, and the rest. Talk now was of the mass, of the "industrial armies" Bellamy hoped would come in the twentieth century when he wrote *Looking Backward* at the end of the nineteenth. The movement among social workers had its parallels in other areas, too. Editor William Allen White, recalling in 1934 Bellamy's novel, observed that "out of his vision for the young men of yesterday we elders of today dream our dreams."[34] The *Christian Century*, key voice of liberal Protestantism, called for government to curtail "the unhindered individualism of profit-seeking production."[35] Noting that the Soviet Union had a five-year plan, that nationalists in India were proposing a ten-year plan, and that Great Britain was preparing a plan of its own, the *Christian Century* asked plaintively, "Why is not America considering a two-year plan, or a five-year plan, or a ten-year plan, or some sort of definite economic plan of her own?"[36]

Harry Hopkins and others with social work backgrounds who entered the Roosevelt administration gained great influence. Henry Morgenthau, Jr., Adolf A. Berle, Jr., Frances Perkins, Grace Abbott, Paul Kellogg, and Lindeman were among the settlement veterans in Washington. Many others close to Roosevelt, such as Herbert Lehman, Gerard Swope, Charles A. Beard, and Sidney Hillman, also had worked at Hull-House, Henry Street, or both.[37] But these leaders had one foot in the radical currents of social work discussion and another foot in the mainstream of American thought—which, though swirling amidst Depression agitation, was not ready for revolution. "Our task is to project a conception of society which is sufficiently revolutionary on the one hand to eliminate accumulated evils," Lindeman told the National Conference of Social Work, "and at the same time sufficiently indigenous to our cultural tradition to insure workability."[38]

To gain popular support, it was vital to present new programs not as radical innovations but as either temporary expedients or simple expansions of past programs. Donald Richberg presented governmental redistribution as civil religion:

> It may not be written in the Constitution, but it is written in the religion of America, that the wealth of America is held in trust for the people of America. And it is written in the Constitution that the power to tax the wealth of America to provide for the common defense and general welfare lies in the Congress of the United States.[39]

Government programs acknowledged the dangers of pauperization and emphasized work rather than handout.

The New Deal also sold itself by emphasizing the traditional goal of helping widows and orphans (with perhaps some wiggle room for deserving women with disabled husbands). Backers portrayed the "Aid to Dependent Children" provisions of the Social Security Act of 1935 as merely an expansion of the mothers' pension programs established by most states during the 1910s. The provision did not provoke controversy at the time of passage, and only a few sentences had to be spoken in its praise in the House of Representatives:

Death through the loss of the breadwinner has broken
many a home. For centuries the widows, orphans and dependent children have cried aloud for help and assistance
in their tragic periods of economic insecurity.[40]

The program's emphasis on making it possible for bereaved mothers
to stay home with their children—and out of the labor market, thus
leaving open a job for a male breadwinner—seemed incontestable.[41]

The Works Progress Administration, popularly known as the WPA
(and, by its critics, as "We Piddle Around") also tried to fit within
traditional values, in its case by focusing on employment. The U.S.
Conference of Mayors resolved that the mayors would "never consent
to the abandonment of the work principle.... The dole, based upon
idleness and groceries, has no place in our American scheme of society."[42] And Harry Hopkins argued, in words Gurteen would have liked,
that relief for the able-bodied without work "pauperizes."[43] When the
FERA field staff in 1934 reported that a "gimme" attitude was developing, as people began to feel "that the government actually owes" them
a relief payment, "[a]nd they want more," the search for an alternative
intensified.[44]

Underlying the urgency of the task was not only economics but
sociology. Disintegrating family relationships, reported more frequently as the strain of unemployment increased, were the most
dangerous aspect of social collapse.[45] Doles sapped male familial
leadership, as both husbands and wives began to perceive government as a more secure provider than the unemployed breadwinner.
A perception of not only economics but the damage to underlying
relationships figured prominently in the FERA conclusion con-
veyed to Roosevelt in 1934:

> Direct relief has little to commend it. While at the present time
> it may happen to be the cheapest way of meeting the problem,
> in the end…it probably will prove the most expensive.…[46]

And so the WPA became the alternative of choice.

Evidence for labeling the WPA both benefit and boondoggle
abounds. It had all the problems of a big bureaucracy; for example,

> in New York City there were 100 warehouses full of work
> material but no inventory of what was in which, even
> though relief administrators used 21 tons of paper a year
> and employed 16 clerks who did nothing but make dupli-
> cate copies of forms that had been lost.[47]

The inefficiency of some WPA projects was legend, and the difficulty
in firing someone who lazed around was matched only by the reluctance of supervisors to do so in the midst of a depression. Critics soon
were calling the WPA "We Pay for All" and asking, "Why is a WPA
worker like King Solomon?" Answer: "Because he takes his pick and
goes to bed."[48]

Nevertheless, the WPA did offer challenge to some, and its goal
was to provide income without chloroforming America's work
ethic—and in doing so, to preserve families by keeping desperate men
from wandering off. As Harry Hopkins wrote in 1936,

> Direct relief might do to tide over a few months or a
> year, or even longer. But millions had already been out
> of a job for several years. In addition to want, the unem-
> ployed were confronting a still further destructive force,

that of worklessness.... [T]he unemployed themselves
[were] protesting against the indignity of public charity.... They were accustomed to making a return for their
livelihood...from which they chiefly drew their
self-respect. The family of a man working on a Works
Progress Administration project looks down its nose at
neighbors who take their relief straight.[49]

One WPA release contended that "the ultimate injustice" was "to inflict
upon the unemployed person the contempt that we feel for a para-
site...."[50] An administration pamphlet quoted a recipient as saying,

Now I can look my children straight in the eyes.... [When]
the kids in the house find that you contribute nothing toward their support, very soon they begin to lose respect for
you. It's different now. I'm the bread-winner of the house
and everybody respects me.[51]

One study of 137 WPA workers found marital relations improving as
wives once again viewed their husbands as protectors.[52] A handbook
developed for WPA workers stated, "Work keeps us from going nuts."[53]

Furthermore, although some WPA programs soon did nothing
but dig and fill up of holes, the goal, and sometimes the reality, was
productive work. By 1940 WPA records showed half a million new
miles of rural roads and 45,000 miles of paved roads in urban areas.
WPA workers also built 4,400 school grandstands, 18,000 miles of
storm and sanitary sewers, and 200 aviation landing fields, improved
about 350 additional landing fields, sealed over 200,000 abandoned
mine openings, sewed over 200 million garments for individuals on

relief, and renovated 67 million books for school and public libraries.[54] Simultaneously, WPA administrators argued that unproductive work programs not only wasted time and money but hurt recipient workers as well, since they would tend to consider themselves worthless.

In 1942, the WPA itself was ended as war needs reduced unemployment virtually to zero—but its memory lived on. For some, the memory was of waste and complicated bureaucratic wage scales. (The Emergency Relief Appropriation Act of 1935 mandated that three and-a-half-million persons previously on the lists for direct relief were to receive a "security wage," defined as more than straight relief and less than private sector work, so that workers would have the incentive to move into private employment.) For others, the legend of a Bellamy industrial army had come partially to life and made "tangible the spirit of compassionate generosity which the citizens of the nation were beginning to feel," as if the previous century of compassionate activity had not existed.[55] And for some hard-working individuals who were desperate through no fault of their own, the memory was of family survival. But whatever the memory, the fact was that the WPA did not attempt to change American values toward work and dependency; it consciously worked within them.

Others, however, had a deeper agenda in mind. Even though the New Deal pace slowed once the crisis of the 1930s was over and events abroad absorbed national attention, ideas of future steps continued to bounce around. At the end of the 1930s and during the war three subtle changes pointed America toward a universalistic welfare system that would not stress work and worthiness as did the New Deal programs, at least in theory.

First, as emphasis on collective action grew, many observers noted a decreased sense of personal responsibility. In 1938 J. Donald Adams, a *New York Times* editor, summarized the movement when he wrote in *The Atlantic* that

> personal conscience in the United States has fallen to a new low in our history as a nation. It has been largely lost to our sight in all the din and dither that have been raised about that other moral concept, the social conscience, which, we are constantly reminded, has a nobler and more widely embracing function. And, the more we hear of the one, the less we hear of the other. The personal conscience has been steadily submerged; the very foundation upon which any broader conception of individual responsibility towards society must rest is being washed away....

Adams concluded:

> There is a distinct flavor of cant about much of the talk concerning social conscience. The phrase slips readily from the tongue; it offers a large and easy generalization, and substitutes a vague beneficence for definite individual responsibility.[56]

McGuffey's century-old warning about the tendencies of "Mr. Fantom" seemed applicable.

Second, as emphasis on personal responsibility decreased, many social observers breathed a sigh of relief, for they saw no possibility of successful personal contact with the urban needy. Journalist Herrick wrote that "in the cities the boundary line between actual need and complacent fraud is so hazy that only clairvoyance can distinguish it. Charity rackets flourish."[57]

Herrick wrote that many givers turned to Community Chest programs but disliked them because

> Chest work is cold, impersonal, and institutionalized. Perhaps no adequate defense can be made against this charge. The fault, however, lies with the changing character of society, not with the agencies.[58]

Impersonal giving seemed inevitable.

Third, many social work leaders, heavily influenced by leftist ideas, argued that an emphasis on individuals was a "trivial and reactionary" practice that "imposes on the individual the cruel burden of adapting himself to a psychotic society, and, insofar as it succeeds, constitutes a brake on social action."[59] A typical journal article of 1935, Ellery Reed's "Efforts of Social Workers toward Social Reorganization," noted proudly that

> trained social workers in the relief field are helping fundamentally to bring about a new social order [through] the reorientation of clients from the still prevalent viewpoints of "rugged individualism" to the newer social philosophy dictated by the interdependent, complex society of today.

If that "traditional ideology" could be defeated, Reed argued, nothing would stand in the way of "the growth of large and vigorous radical parties."[60]

Overt Marxism was opposed by some; Grace Marcus, assistant executive secretary of the American Association of Social Workers, attacked those who "retreated from any acknowledgement of personal factors in maladjustment into economic dogmas that caricature Marxian theory."[61] But liberal doctrines that upheld the idea of income as entitlement, and showed little interest in stressing work or in noting the danger of pauperization, became the conventional wisdom among social workers and their allies.

In 1937, for example, Edith Abbott, president of the National Conference of Social Work, declared that relief should not be "means tested."[62] That same year, Dorothy C. Kahn of the Pennsylvania School of Social Work (and former president of the American Association of Social Workers) told a group of colleagues that their work was hindered by

> the widely held belief that those who work, with the excep-
> tion of an increasing group of so-called natural dependents,
> are the only ones who have a right to maintenance.[63]

The responsibility of social workers was clear: "Social workers must try to modify the social attitudes.... We must remove the organic connection between work and maintenance."[64]

Two years later, in a National Conference of Social Work paper significantly titled "Democratic Principles in Public Assistance," Kahn criticized the

> belief that under ordinary conditions people are in need
> through some fault of their own, a belief rooted in our culture,
> fostered by religious injunctions, nourished by education...a

significant indication of the outmoded doctrines influencing our social structure.[65]

The following year Edith Abbott's paper, "Relief—No Man's Land and Its Reclamation," called for the extension and nationalization of aid to those unemployed for any reason. By 1943 one participant in National Conference of Social Work proceedings could report that "there was no debate on the merits of Federal participation."[66]

During the next two decades a host of studies purported to show that welfare stipends *did not* harm individuals by undermining independence and self-respect, and that the federal government should be the nationwide dispenser of cash. One of the first of these was an 835-page study of the WPA and welfare programs by Russell Sage Foundation official Donald Howard, published by the foundation in 1943. The Russell Sage study proposed not only increased governmental activity generally, but a much larger federal role specifically. Turning the long-standing argument against centralization on its head, Howard argued that

the federal government is in a peculiarly favorable position to meet emergencies promptly, wherever and whenever they may arise. State action, by contrast, requires not one but 48 separate and independent series of actions and as many legislative campaigns. Action by local authorities entails still further delays....[67]

Similarly, Howard saw advantages, where others had stressed hazards, in the federal government's "freedom from inflexible constitutional or debt limitations...."[68]

Howard was in the mainstream of new social work thinking; he went on to become president of the American Association of Social Workers and dean of the UCLA School of Social Welfare. His enthusiasm over centralization, which "makes it easier for observers and interest groups that are really concerned for efficient administration to keep a watchful eye on it," reflected and contributed to academic trends.[69] So did his lack of concern about the "crowding out" effect of federal activity on local action: "this would be all to the good," he wrote.[70] Like many of his colleagues, Howard wanted relief to be depersonalized and a structure of "rights" established, so that "no person would have the discretionary power to deny to any eligible applicant the aid to which he is entitled." Like Grace Abbott, Howard opposed background checks and instead proposed that benefits "be paid upon a worker's declaration that he was without work and that his family was of a given size, without recourse to humiliating investigations either of his own needs and resources or of those of close relatives."[71]

The Russell Sage study even cast doubt on the conclusions reached only a few years before concerning the advantage of jobs over doles: Howard praised "direct assistance administered in accordance with up-to-date standards of adequacy and decency."[72] Howard's priorities were not always clear, however. On the one hand, he clearly wished to establish a rationale for releasing abandoned mothers of dependent children from work obligations; he hoped "to render acceptance of public assistance less of an ordeal by assuring recipients that the care they give their children, for example, is an important return to the community for the relief they are given."[73] On the other hand, Howard complained that "persons without dependents are frequently among the last to be granted relief, and the group most likely to be denied aid when relief funds run low. Such discrimination has no basis in law...."[74]

Overall, the goal seemed to be to extend relief in every direction at once. Howard expressed support for researchers who stated that "by and large, the effect of federal control is to keep to a minimum administrative abuses, inefficiency, and political control which tend to shake public confidence."[75] In the 1940s, such an apologetic apparently could be delivered with a straight face.

The Russell Sage study concluded with a yearning to establish a nationalized welfare system. Howard saw that it could not be done quickly, since, regretfully,

> established mores are undoubtedly too deeply embedded in the American spirit for the present to permit adequate relief to employable persons without requiring work in return. Thus, to make the giving of relief contingent upon recipients' willingness to perform some kind of work may be regarded as a price that—public opinion and attitudes being what they are—must be paid for adequate and decent relief to employable persons.[76]

But there was hope: "Fortunately for those who need public assistance," Howard wrote, "the mores do change."[77] He observed that "traditional attitudes toward 'getting something for nothing' are already undergoing change, and in the future will be further modified." His concluding words of optimism were, "it may not forever be necessary to think of direct assistance as 'demoralizing,'" or to make sure that aid recipients work in order to "preserv[e] their own personal integrity."[78]

And yet, the process of changing public consciousness was slow. Throughout the 1940s and 1950s there seemed little popular enthusiasm for social universalistic claims of entitlement. "Detroit Cracks

Down on Relief Chiselers" was the title of a typical article from 1949 in the magazine perhaps most identified with the American middle class, *The Saturday Evening Post.* Author Rufus Jarman had no quarrel with categorized payments "to persons in specific groups of the population who lack resources of their own to meet their essential needs," but he attacked "shameless cheats who claim charity they don't need."[79] Jarman also waxed sarcastic about "social-science theorists [who] hold that forcing a welfare client to answer unpleasant questions may produce a 'traumatic experience'"; he supported investigation of claimants to make sure they fell into the established categories of need and had no other means by which to purchase basic necessities.[80]

Gallup Polls throughout the 1950s showed majorities of Americans in favor of restrictive welfare rules, and journalists reported a "wave of resentment" against those who claimed entitlements.[81] Such popular sentiment and press coverage made politicians very reluctant to approve new programs or sizeable expansion of older ones during the late 1940s and 1950s. Housing legislation in 1949 had set in motion slum clearance ("urban renewal," which became known as "Negro removal") and a reduction in the stock of low-cost urban housing. The Social Security Act of 1950 provided benefits for an additional 10 million persons. But political compromises were such that, throughout the 1950s, increases in federal social services spending were gradual. Most eligible individuals did not rush in to take advantage of new programs; for a time, those with pride turned down a free ride. On the state level, legislators such as Michigan State Senator Colin Smith vowed to fight the "social-science theorists" who favor a "philosophy that is debasing freedom by disorganizing self-discipline and social discipline."[82]

Yet clearly the New Deal had established the organizational basis for social revolution. In 1956 Marion B. Folsom, secretary of the Department of Health, Education, and Welfare, noted that social workers had "helped strengthen in America the voice of compassion, of duty, of social justice, of vision."[83] The social revolution, however, was still to come.

CHAPTER TEN

Revolution—and Its Heartbreak

In the early 1960s, even after a generation of softening up, many of the old values were retained both by welfare workers and recipients. In Philadelphia, half of all applications for relief were rejected. In New York City, welfare workers were still told that withholding assistance was often as important as giving relief; they still tried to reach relatives and proposed that the family assume financial obligation. Applicants for welfare were still supposed to verify their eligibility by providing marriage and birth certificates, and information about past employment, income, and savings.[1] In many areas unwed mothers who wanted relief promised not to "have any male callers coming to my home or meeting me elsewhere under improper conditions." They also pledged not to "knowingly contribute or be a contributing factor" to shaming their children by their conduct.[2]

Before the push for a Great Society began, recipients themselves often viewed welfare as a necessary wrong, but not a right. Two gatekeepers—the welfare office and the applicant's own conscience— scrutinized each applicant. A sense of shame was relied upon to make people reluctant to accept "the dole" unless absolutely necessary; for those without shame, welfare officials were to ask hard questions and investigate claims. In black communities, according to the Reverend Buster Soaries,

> when folks strayed, they were embarrassed. They were never glorified for wayward behavior. If a person was walking down the street drunk and swearing, his whole family would be embarrassed. If a child got pregnant out of wedlock, they would send that child somewhere where folk didn't know her until she came back. The virtues that were preached were industry and thrift and patience, what we might call today the Protestant work ethic. This was normative in our community....[3]

With dependency considered dishonorable, government- and self-imposed restrictions meant that, as late as the mid–1960s, only about half of those eligible for welfare payments were receiving them, and many of the enrolled were taking only part of the maximum allowance.[4]

The result of community moral pressure and an official refusal to make dependency easy meant, as columnist Walter Williams remembered recently, that residents of North Philadelphia's Richard Allen housing project during the 1950s were "poor in the pocket book [but rich] in spirit and morality." In the housing project, Williams wrote,

> My sister and I were "latchkey" kids, but no sweat, latchkey had not yet become an excuse. Mom's rules were, "Come in from school, get a snack, do your homework, and don't leave the house." None of us could remember

an instance of a kid using foul language in addressing, or within earshot of, a parent, teacher or any adult.[5]

Adults were expected to work and children were expected to read, Williams noted, for the 1950s' decade was before "we stopped holding people accountable for their behavior and began assigning blame to society." Those who started to deviate received neighborly pressure to get back into line.

But, in the 1960s, attitudes changed. Suddenly it became better to accept welfare than to take in laundry. Michael Harrington, author of the popular book *The Other America*, complained that some who were out of work for a long time "would take low-paying jobs" and "accept humiliation rather than go on the public dole."[6] Until the 1960s, the public dole was humiliation, but thereafter young men were told that shining shoes was demeaning, and that accepting government subsidy meant a person "could at least keep his dignity."[7] This, then, was the key change of the 1960s—not so much new benefit programs as a change in consciousness concerning established ones, with government officials approving and even advocating not only larger payouts but a war on shame. Underlying the change were the theologically liberal tendencies within social work (and related fields) that had been criticized by Niebuhr a generation earlier, and which were becoming more evident than ever.

Typical of the new theology was a monograph from Columbia University's New York School of Social Work that called government welfare, rather than any spiritual commitment, the "ultimate instrument of social conscience in the modern world."[8] Authors Elizabeth Wickenden and Winifred Bell—the former soon to become chief lobbyist for the National Social Welfare

Assembly—buttressed their faith with several carefully chosen texts from scriptures old and modern, the Bible and the United Nations Declaration of the Rights of the Child. Their report opposed any emphasis on personal responsibility for economic problems: there should be no penalty for able-bodied and mentally competent individuals who, for whatever reason, were unable "to hold a job, to spend their money sensibly... or otherwise rise to the challenges of social responsibility." Personality flaws, the report suggested, had social origins, and in any event "social justice" required an end to scrutiny of behavior, since "the origin of economic or social need is far less important than the fact of its existence."[9]

Wickenden and Bell's clenched-teeth attack on opposition to entitlements—a desire to restrict subsidy was not just wrong but "patently absurd and self-defeating"—showed a new orthodoxy at work.[10] They saw *no* valid reason for categorizing individuals as "deserving" or "not deserving": "Arguments against the perpetuation of a categorical system of assistance entitlement are compelling on all counts." They chastised attempts to restrict support to groups such as widows and orphans: "Assistance has become less a 'right' to which certain groups have earned special entitlement than an obligation on society." And they opposed regulations designed to involve relatives in providing support, arguing that any such rules "force responsibility beyond the current economic and cultural pattern... and undermine assistance standards."[11] Vestiges of past practice were to be fought as the drive for universal "economic and social security" continued.[12] All groups, whether state or private, were to unite in a push for *more*:

> Public welfare agencies should encourage a continuing experimentation and expansion of new services, whether

under their own auspices, those of other public agencies, or voluntary arrangements.[13]

And all roads led to Washington: "A positive obligation rests upon the federal government to provide national leadership."[14]

Underlying the new demand for action was a ripened combination of philosophical materialism, economic relativism, and progressive sentiment. The Ford Foundation spent $100 million on programs to alleviate "urban problems and conditions" during the 1953–1962 decade, and had ready experimental programs (such as "Model Cities") that could be picked up by the federal government as soon as the mood turned expansive. One ditty summarized well the Ford Foundation's nature:

Take a dozen Quakers—be sure they're sweet and pink—
Add one discussion program to make the people think;
Brown a liberal education in television grease
And roll in economics seasoned well with peace....
Garnish with compassion—just a touch will do—
And serve in deep humility your philanthropic stew.[15]

Deep humility was soon submerged in massive confidence. Foundation official Paul N. Ylvisaker explained in January 1963 that a city should be viewed as a "social production system" in the same way that "AT&T, for example, has long viewed it as a communications system." Ylvisaker argued that "certain parts of the urban social system can be perfected by rational means and specific devices."[16]

The rationalistic materialism of which Ylvisaker sang was also evident in a Ford Foundation-sponsored study, produced by the

University of Michigan Survey Research Center study, that purportedly showed how "the elimination of poverty is well within the means of federal, state, and local governments."[17] The report, assuming that a material fix could wipe out poverty, argued that poverty could be abolished

> simply by a stroke of the pen. To raise every individual and family in the nation now below a subsistence income to the subsistence level would cost but $10 billion a year. That is less than two percent of the gross national product. It is less than ten percent of tax revenues.[18]

If money could change ways of thinking, then Michael Harrington was accurate when he wrote that "only one agency in America is capable of eradicating both the slum and slum psychology from this land: the Federal Government."[19] If cash was indeed king, then a 1964 *Economic Report of the President* was correct to state that "the conquest of poverty is well within our power."[20] James Tobin, a member of President John Kennedy's Council of Economic Advisers, calculated that the percentage of families with annual incomes under $3,000 (in 1965 dollars) declined from 51 percent in 1936 to 30 percent in 1950 to 20 percent in 1960 and 17 percent in 1965; additional governmental transfer programs, he suggested, could push that percentage all the way to zero, and realize a dream of the centuries.[21]

Church groups generally might have been expected to counter such materialistic emphases, but, in fact, the mainline National Council of Churches became one of the leading sellers of entitlement. In a great reversal from church positions of the nineteenth century, council reverends argued not only that all the poor had a right to handouts, but that the better-off should be ashamed if they did not provide them. The NCC suggested in the early 1960s and was arguing by mid-decade that poverty was still with us because of "the influence of unrestricted economic individualism."[22] The council demanded that the federal government provide "leadership" in the creation of "adequate mechanisms for income distribution and income maintenance in an affluent society."[23] The NCC brushed off the biblical statement that the poor would always be with us, since it arose in the past when the "primitive status of human technology and the scarcity of developed resources" existed. Since then, however, technological breakthroughs have allowed for "adequate levels of living for all."[24] The Christian emphasis, according to the council, should not be on "personal attitudes" but on societal defects that "seem to lock some people into perpetual poverty."[25]

Not all agreed. The National Association of Evangelicals' magazine, *United Evangelical Action*, was skeptical in 1962:

> In striving for total economic security for all men as the supreme goal, the churches may get something like the desired results through the help of friends, agencies, and the patronage of the state, only to discover that one day they are more in debt to them than to Christ, and have lost not only their momentum, but also their unique reason for being in existence.[26]

Christianity Today editor Carl Henry proposed that making justice a subset of compassion "not only destroys the biblical view of God on the one hand, but also produces the welfare state on the other."[27] A *Christianity Today* article observed that

faith in God puts courage, compassion, and determination
into the hearts of men. These are the qualities that conquer
poverty and solve other social problems. It is the business
of the Church to mobilize spiritual power. By doing so, it
can solve our perplexing social and economic ills.... [28]

But such voices had only minor influence at the time.

The mainline theological message of the 1960s among both
Christians and Jews which prevailed was that poverty was socially
caused and could thus be socially eliminated. When the Institute for
Religious and Social Studies of the Jewish Theological Seminary of
America sponsored a lecture series in late 1963 and 1964, mention of
either God or the need for spiritual change was markedly absent. The
message of the series, as summarized by the editor of the published
lectures, was that "the age-old plague" of poverty would end as soon
as "proper direction" and "imaginative planning" bore down on it.[29]
"We have reached the stage where old concepts of charity and almsgiving no longer apply," the editor continued: "There will always be the
need for the spirit of generosity and neighborly benevolence, but it will
act on a higher and happier level."[30] That happier level was governmental action, based on "a five-year or a ten-year or a fifty-year plan... to
end this abject poverty. To aid in this endeavor is a high responsibility
of our spiritual leaders."[31]

That introduction, written in July 1964, began on a breath-catching
note: "As this book goes to press, the newspapers of the United States
daily record progress in plans for a nationwide 'war on poverty.'..."[32]
While liberal theologians planned tours of the celestial city, Lyndon
Johnson already was declaring his intention to create "a Great Society:
a society of success without squalor, beauty without barrenness, works

of genius without the wretchedness of poverty."[33] Johnson envisioned a replay of the New Deal, but this time from a position of economic strength rather than one of desperate economic weakness. He called the "fight against poverty" an "investment" in the great tradition of the 1930s: "in the future, as in the past, this investment will return its cost many fold to our entire economy." As in the 1930s, a president argued that federal redistribution programs were actually a way to facilitate work; in Johnson's words, "We are not content to accept the endless growth of relief rolls or welfare rolls."[34] Again, presidential appointees—such as Sargent Shriver, director of the Office of Economic Opportunity (OEO)—snapped that they were "not at all interested in running a handout program or a 'something-for-nothing' program."[35]

As it turned out, Johnson would die discontent, and Shriver would soon be very interested in what he had disdained. But excitement reigned in 1964 and 1965, and Lyndon Johnson's legislative triumphs—the Economic Opportunity Act, food stamp legislation, Medicare, Medicaid, public works programs, and so on—were immense. The speed of passage, unrivaled since the New Deal, showed a disregard for real-life effects and was more remarkable in that it was not prompted by the mood of crisis so evident in 1933. The Great Society legislation was truly a triumph of faith, the social gospel walking on earth: Joseph Kershaw, chief economist with the Office of Economic Opportunity, argued that a guaranteed income is "the next great social advance.... It's inevitable, it's got to come."[36]

Driven by such faith, the White House mood was—in the words of Johnson biographer Doris Goodwin—"Pass the bill now, worry about its effects and implementation later."[37] Johnson's advice for officials concerned with implementation was minimal but memorable: he told

Shriver, "I just want you to make sure that no crooks, communists or cocksuckers get into this [community action] program."[38] But even those programs that kept out the triple c's often were wracked by waste and mismanagement. As the nineteenth-century charity leaders well knew, bureaucratic programs tended to produce social folly at the margin. In Detroit, the War on Poverty meant that some auto workers could earn more by joining job-training programs than by staying at their posts. In Johnson, Rhode Island, it meant that seventy-three parents of children in a poverty program owned more property—fifty-eight homes and 113 cars—than the typical nonpoor residents.[39]

Reports on such inequities were embarrassing—but the underlying assumptions, although rarely analyzed, proved more dangerous. Materialist thinking was dominant: as one administration official put it, "The way to eliminate poverty is to give the poor people enough money so that they won't be poor anymore."[40] Columnist Stewart Alsop wrote that for $12 to $15 billion a year (2 percent of the gross national product at that time) "poverty could be abolished in the United States," as if a change in material circumstances would inevitably alter attitudes that, left unchanged, would create new poverty.[41]

This sanguinity allowed people to ignore the key contribution of the War on Poverty: the deliberate attempt to uncouple welfare from shame by changing attitudes of both welfare recipients and the better-off. It was hard work. As late as 1966 studies showed that welfare recipients generally hated the thought of being on welfare, and as a rule accepted the obligation of welfare departments to investigate their behavior. One 1966 study quoted a welfare recipient as saying,

I think the welfare department is too soft, too lenient. They don't make investigations to see how the welfare money is being spent. If the workers went to the houses more often, they would be able to tell if the people are cheating.⁴²

But, in the end, Great Society legislation, not so much by extending benefits as by funding advocates to change that consciousness, helped sever welfare from shame in the minds of many dole-holders.

The key governmental units in the uncoupling process were one thousand "neighborhood service centers" funded by the Office of Economic Opportunity and devoted to disseminating the belief that welfare payments were tokens of freedom that should be seized with a bulldog grip. The centers were a mainstay of what the *New York Times* called "a new philosophy of social welfare," one that "seeks to establish the status of welfare benefits as rights, based on the notion that everyone is entitled to a share of the common wealth."⁴³ The goal was material goods for all, without regard to the causes of destitution. The service centers immediately began to jack up the number of welfare individuals and families. During the first year after the first service center in Baltimore opened, for example, the AFDC caseload in its area increased by 37 percent, compared to citywide AFDC growth of 9 percent during the same period.⁴⁴

Such activities were hailed by those committed to Social Universalism—in particular, by two professors at Columbia University's School of Social Work, Frances Fox Piven and Richard Cloward. They praised New York's OEO-funded Stanton Street center because

> the center staff became skilled in fighting the welfare depart-
> ment.... They argued and cajoled; they bluffed and threat-
> ened.... "When I go to welfare," one Stanton Street staff

member declared, "I don't wait around for the stall. If I don't get treated with respect, I start hollering for the supervisor, and then I threaten legal action." Another said of the welfare department: "Any way you cut it, they are the enemy."[45]

Welfare departments, with their philosophical legs already cut from under them and propped up only by paper, crumpled under such frontal assaults.

Significantly, not only governmental groups were transformed by the new hubris of thought and action. Piven and Cloward reported jubilantly that

> the federal government used financial inducements to re-direct and coordinate the activities of a vast segment of the private social welfare field, the legal profession, religious institutions, civil rights groups, and unaffiliated activists into a far-flung attack on the public welfare system (and on other municipal institutions).[46]

Three-fourths of OEO's community action programs were operated by settlement houses, family service agencies, and other traditional private social agencies, as well as by newly created ghetto organizations. Some of the older groups at one time had embraced principles of mutual obligation, but under OEO prodding they prepared handbooks, which instructed welfare recipients to take as much as they could get without any obligation on their part. ACLU chapters also became active in this war against shame.

Crucially, the new idea of welfare had support from the top. OEO director Shriver told a meeting of social workers in 1965, "I said to

Congress that if our activities did not stir up a community, then Congress should investigate it."[47] The following year Shriver proudly told a Yale Law School crowd that the Economic Opportunity Act established "a new grievance procedure between the poor and the rest of society."[48] Soon poetic (or at least doggerel) justice arrived: Shriver's home outside Washington was surrounded one evening before Christmas by sarcastic carolers who boomed out,

> Hark the Herald Angels sing/ Glory to the newborn king/....Shriver go to LBJ/ Tell him what the poor folk say./ Charity begins at home./ We want gigs to call our own.

And then:

> O come all ye poor folk,/ Soulful and together/ Come ye, O come ye to Shriver's house./ Come and behold him, politicians' puppet./ O come and let us move him,/ O come and sock it to him...[49]

Other War on Poverty leaders who had expected to be praised for their "compassionate" antipoverty work received their own share of jeers.

But other immediate effects were more tragic than comic. The resolution at the 1966 U.S. Conference of Mayors that had accused Sargent Shriver of "fostering class warfare" proved prescient.[50] When reality inevitably fell short of over-the-rainbow promises of "abolishing poverty," anger flared. The poverty program was "almost worse than nothing at all," said Detroit Mayor Jerome Cavanaugh as he looked over his "riot-scarred" city in 1967. "We've raised expectations and haven't been able to deliver."[51] Another frustrated planner noted "a trail of broken promises" and then said, "No wonder everybody got mad and rioted."[52] Soon, *Time* was reporting that "the world's wealthiest nation seems caught in a paradoxical trap: the more the U.S. spends on the poor, the greater the need seems to be to spend more still."[53] This new "paradox," of course, was exactly what Josephine Lowell and others in the late nineteenth century had predicted.

Piven, Cloward, and company were not satisfied with perpetual paradox, however. Like Saul Alinsky and other organizers, they had a larger vision of radical upheaval. They argued that few individuals would break out of poverty: "Most of the people whom we now call very poor are not going to participate in occupational roles, at least not in this generation."[54] The good news was that activism among the permanently unemployed could "exacerbate strains among Negro and white working-class and middle-class elements in the urban Democratic coalition."[55] Publicizing the plight of poor families would "create a crisis, a crisis that could lead to some kind of reform of traditional means of distributing income in the country."[56] Out of the chaos that ensued would come socialism and, for the poor, a guaranteed income.[57] The old Greeley/Bellamy dream would come striding out from among the clouds of hatred.

Piven and Cloward needed an organization and a spokesperson. "Searching for a man to put muscle into their plan, they found George Wiley," *Look* magazine reported. But their man was not a puppet. Wiley, a chemistry professor who had left Syracuse University to work for the Congress for Racial Equality, was looking for a new opportunity.[58] From the brains of that organization emerged the National Welfare Rights Organization, with its "Boston model" for mobilizing the poor. The Boston model emphasized "continuous personal contact" between organizers and women on welfare, with the goal of convincing welfare recipients that the fault lay in the stars ("systemic pathologies") rather than themselves. If their propagandizing was effective, "shame" would leave the consciousness of welfare recipients and be replaced by a conviction that "the system was the 'enemy.'"[59]

The NWRO proved successful in its immediate objectives. In its first four years an estimated 100,000 welfare recipients were organized and trained to demand payments, not ask for them. Observers at organizing meetings were struck by how welfare mothers came to them with a sense that welfare should be avoided, but "Wiley's constant repetition of the word *rights* got through to the women."[60] *Time* quoted welfare mother and leader Mrs. Johnnie Tillmon as saying that the organization's goal was "everybody get what's coming to them. Everybody is entitled...."[61] Another mother recalled that she "had grown up being told by my mother and others that welfare was terrible," but now she was proud of her status.[62] Under the flag of universal entitlement, potential welfare recipients came to meetings "tightly controlled by the organizers to ensure the desired results." There they learned how to carry out "collective confrontation with the welfare authorities."[63]

And while the training continued, the radicals worked to gain support for NWRO from other black organizations. They largely failed. NWRO attracted minuscule support from black churches where scriptural injunctions about work were still taken seriously; Wiley admitted that efforts "to pull the black churches in...had not been successful."[64] Some established black organizations were also committed to the older values, at least initially. Piven wrote that

> we met with Whitney Young, director of the Urban League, and he gave us a long speech about how it was more important to get one black woman into a job as an

airline stewardess than it was to get fifty poor families onto welfare.[65]

Others wanted to remove the welfare stigma that sometimes, and unfairly, became attached to those thrown into dependence through no fault of their own—but they did not want to eliminate categorization entirely. Martin Luther King had told Washington marchers in 1963, "I have a dream that one day my four little children will live in a country where they will not be judged by the color of their skin, but by the content of their character." Through the mid-1960s, many of the black poor fought not for a universalistic absence of judgment, but for a categorization based on character rather than color.

The radicals were more successful in gaining support from mainline church organizations. Liberal Protestant churches contributed 47 percent of the NWRO budget in 1967, and the Inter-Faith Church Organization (IFCO), a creation of the National Council of Churches, added much of the rest. In the four years from 1968 through 1971, IFCO gave $500,000 to NWRO, along with "emergency grants when Wiley was in desperate need of money to pay long overdue bills."[66] NWRO's single largest denominational contributor from 1970 to 1973 was the United Church of Christ, and in particular the church's Board for Homeland Ministries. The denomination's Welfare Priority Team (WPT) gave 65 percent ($142,500) of its operational budget to NWRO from 1970 through 1973 and employed NWRO representatives as consultants.[67] United Methodists gave up to $35,000 a year, and United Presbyterians $25,000 during each of the first few NWRO years.

The NWRO was welcomed with open wallets because it was seen as a vehicle of liberation for the poor; as Harvey Cox of the Harvard Divinity School wrote, the liberal Protestant leadership was determined to become "a supporter and strengthener" of groups seen as beacons of such liberation.[68] The National Council of Churches even went on the record in 1968 with a proposal for "a guaranteed income" for everyone, regardless of conduct.[69] On the other hand, the U.S. Catholic Conference stayed aloof, although some local Catholic churches did support NWRO activities in their areas.[70] Largely white evangelical, fundamentalist, and Reformed churches—the theological conservatives among the Protestants—responded as negatively as did their brethren among the black churches. Nelson Bell predicted in *Christianity Today* that poverty's politicization would create a

> grave danger...its alleviation will become motivated by other than compassion, and its victims will be pawns in a sociological experiment that can cost billions in waste and bureaucratic management while it destroys initiative and breeds dependence on others.[71]

Francis Schaeffer warned that Christians should avoid giving more power to the "monolithic monster of a bloated state" and instead emphasize the "compassionate use of accumulated wealth."[72]

Media reaction was generally positive. *Time* tried to sell to the American people the "relative poverty" faith—that even though the welfare families had the essentials, in all fairness they ought to have the same perquisites as the affluent. *Time* acknowledged that

> unlike the destitute of others times and places, [the American poor] are not usually distinguishable by any of the traditional tell-tales of want: hunger-distended bellies or filthy rags...the tawdry tenements of Chicago's South Side are forested with TV antennas.... In the Los Angeles district of Watts, California's most notorious Slough of

Despond, the orderly rows of one-story stucco houses reflect the sun in gay pastels.[73]

But, nevertheless, they still took a social universalistic position, suggesting that programs stressing "individual achievement and mobility" were wrong in "a society with both the conscience and creative resources to hold out for all its people the actuality of the American dream."[74]

The NWRO also found itself receiving support from federal, state, and local welfare administrations—the very institutions it was attacking! The federal Department of Health, Education and Welfare, and some of its state and local counterparts, were quick to establish NWRO—without benefit of vote—as the bargaining agent for the welfare poor. Johnson administration officials even signed a contract with NWRO to give it $435,000 over a one-year period. (With the change of administrations in 1969 only $106,000 ended up in NWRO hands.)[75] NWRO received $36,500 from the National Association of Social Workers, even though some members of the organization were the victims of sit-ins by the welfarists, but this was not surprising, for the organization already was supporting "income as a matter of right."[76]

NWRO movement historian Guida West has stated that, "paradoxically, allies for NWRO were found not only among liberals in the private sector but also within the federal government—the major target of the welfare rights movement."[77] Paradoxes such as this one, or the "paradox" of more welfare heightening tensions rather than defusing them, were real only as long as the older consciousness of mutual obligation held firm. When the goal of social welfare became not challenge but lubrication, then those demanding more and those who wanted to hand out more (but regretted being hamstrung by legislatures and taxpayers) were on the same team. OEO's Legal Services division clearly perceived the situation that way. Not only did Legal Services groups provide office space to NWRO, but over 1,800 mostly young, mostly energetic lawyers fought test cases for NWRO causes, brought class action suits before sympathetic judges, and became "lead actors in bringing about a new welfare era."[78]

Soon, with all the legal horsepower revved up, rules that allowed categorization and discernment—tasks that governmental officials were not likely to handle well even without enormous pressure—were no more. Rules that welfare officials, without extensive hearings, could declare a person employable and require him to take a job, were struck down. Rules that women receiving AFDC could not have a "man in the house" were struck down.[79] Rules that recipients suspected of fraud had to answer questions or else face possible loss of subsidy, were struck down. A welfare official who demanded recipients to present information that might reduce their grants was seen as violating their Fifth Amendment rights.[80] And welfare benefits were seen as a new form of property, deserving the same legal protection as earned or inherited property received. This thinking, first presented by Charles A. Reich in a *Yale Law Journal* article in 1964, found a home in some lower court cases, and the Supreme Court itself ruled in 1970 that welfare recipients had a constitutional right to trial-like hearings before their benefits could be terminated.[81] (Reich was famous by then as the author of the best-selling musing, *The Greening of America*, but he made his first mark by aiding in the greening of the welfare system.)

By the late 1960s, legal activists in a variety of venues were learning that change could proceed fastest when legislatures were circumvented. Legal Services became "the most successful instrument of social change," and leftist economist Robert Lekachman in 1973 said that if he could choose "one strategy" from the War on Poverty to preserve "it would be Legal Services...."[82] Indeed, the Legal Services activity represented a new dimension to legal aid for the poor. The traditional mode was typified by the New York Legal Aid Society's statement back in 1903 that it hoped not only to win cases but to "exert upon its clients a strong educational influence."[83] The goal early in the century was to look at the facts of the case and not assume injustice; to sue if necessary, but to strive for an understanding of mutual obligation. By the mid–1960s, however, the goal was *more*. The law became a handmaiden of income transfer, and a way of battering anyone who stood in the way. "Justice" equalled income redistribution, and government officials soon worked alongside protesters.

Since the American welfare system had relied to some extent on self-restraint and investigation, it had few defenses before the entitlement attack. OEO neighborhood legal attorneys taught welfare recipients to request more hearings, each of which required five to eight hours of work from a hearing officer. Most local officials learned to give in so they could avoid such time-consuming activities. "In this new climate, many intake workers, the 'gate-keepers' of the system, have tended to make more liberal decisions," backers of the new order reported jubilantly.[84] Those officials who were slow to acquiesce faced frequent demonstrations. Sit-ins and sleep-ins *at* welfare departments made the lives of administrators difficult. *Look* magazine reported in 1968 the pattern that had emerged: "Welfare officials tend to cave in, if possible, before reporters arrive, and quick victories rouse the timid to fight."[85] The result was a welfare population explosion: "Acceptances rose sharply in the middle and late 1960s, and client protests were undoubtedly one cause."[86]

Statistics suggest the scope of that explosion. During the 1950s AFDC rolls rose by 110,000 families, or 17 percent—but during the

1960s the increase was 107 percent, or 800,000 families.[87] About three-fourths of that increase occurred from 1965 to 1968 alone, during a time of general prosperity and diminishing unemployment. Slicing the numbers a different way, the overall AFDC population increased from 4.3 million in 1965 to 10.8 million in 1974.[88] Administrators were astounded by the sudden leap. Year after year officials muttered that the increase "can't go on, it can't go on, but it does." By 1970, applicants and subsidies reached "levels that would have been unimaginable two or three years ago."[89]

Instant explanations for that explosion varied: some spoke of continued migration of the black poor from the South and others noted the deterioration of black family structure. All of these had an impact, but studies showed that, surprisingly, the size of the pool of eligible people did not change much during those years. The major change was that a much higher percentage of those who were eligible suddenly decided to take advantage of welfare benefits.[90] An increase in formal benefit levels and a simplification of the process of signing up probably had some impact, but officials observed that a prime reason for the surge was "a changing outlook among many poor and the near poor." They had been taught by organizers that welfare is "nothing to be ashamed of."[91]

Welfare officials who tried to retain old procedures were lambasted for their lack of "compassion." When George Miller, director of the Nevada Department of Welfare, announced early in 1971 that "21 percent of the people receiving aid [in Nevada] had been terminated for cheating," poverty lawyers filed lawsuits in the federal courts, and political and press advocates of more welfare orchestrated hearings and forums with sad testimony by poor women.[92] Soon, celebrities such as Sammy Davis, Jr., and Jane Fonda journeyed to Nevada and made publicized protests. Two months later, a federal district court judge ordered that everyone who had been terminated, or whose benefits had been reduced, should be reinstated. The Great Society's War Against Shame was a success.

Yet, as the smoke cleared in 1971, *Time* magazine writers looked at the price tag in cash, and others looked at the price tag in lives. Both groups noted that Great Society compassion "satisfies no one: under the system it is unblessed both to give and to receive."[93]

CHAPTER ELEVEN

Questions of the 1970s and 1980s

At a reunion of Johnson administration officials in Austin, Texas, a quarter century after the War on Poverty fired its first cannonade, the mood was akin to Wordsworth's enthusiasm following the French revolution: "Bliss was it in that dawn to be alive..."[1] Sargent Shriver exulted that the Reagan years had not really damaged Great Society programs, most of which were "still in existence, all helping millions of Americans today" *New York Times* columnist Tom Wicker described the sumptuous affair and proposed that it is time to stop moaning and instead drink a toast to "vision and aspiration, confidence and compassion."

Vision, aspiration, and confidence were all there. But was there compassion? In the 1970s, sociologists and economists such as Sar Levitan were correct to point out that the basic economic needs of all people who involved themselves in the welfare system—and it was very easy to do so—were being met. Levitan wrote in 1977 that "if poverty is defined as a lack of basic needs, it's almost been eliminated."[2] Robert Haveman, a fellow of the Institute for Research on Poverty at the University of Wisconsin, similarly noted that "the day of income poverty as a major public issue would appear to be past.... A minimum level of economic well-being has by and large been assured for all citizens."[3] But was a minimum level of challenge assured? Were affiliation, bonding, and other aspects of *suffering with* encouraged or discouraged?[4]

By 1980, it was clear that the entitlement revolution had created several big losers. One was social mobility. In the 1940s, sociologist William Whyte saw poverty-fighters working "to stimulate social mobility, to hold out middle-class standards and middle-class rewards to lower-class people."[5] But this goal was discarded in the 1960s and 1970s, as radicals attacked "bourgeois values," and as "rising politicization and new consciousness" among welfare recipients led many to "identify themselves as nonconformists."[6] The result was stasis. Lyndon Johnson's economic advisors warned in 1964 that the poverty rate, in the *absence* of federal action, could be as high as 13 percent by 1980. After sixteen years of multibillion-dollar programs, the poverty rate at the end of that year was—13 percent.[7]

Lack of mobility was not caused by lack of opportunity—the dramatic successes of immigrants from Asia and Cuba during recent decades show that. Those who adopted the traditional work-hard-and-rise pattern by staying out of the welfare system usually succeeded in rising—but native-born Americans who took advantage of the proferred liberality stayed put. Some welfare recipients even gave up jobs and educational opportunities in order to remain in the poor but secure spot that welfare payments afforded them.[8] Increasingly, the hard but heroic sagas of effort in previous generations were replaced by a dull history of "nothing ventured, nothing gained."

Another big loser was the remnant of private, challenging organizations. The McAuley Mission in New York had held on through all the years and governmental social programs, but when the Great Society kicked in, mission superintendent Earl Vautin noted that

> rescue missions are seen as just another welfare program.... The men who come to us confuse us with the welfare department. A man feels the mission ... is not really doing its job unless he gets what he thinks he is supposed to get. Now this is the attitude of the "client" and not the attitude of a man seeking love and friendship and spiritual help. The early mission did not have this to contend with—this feeling that "the world owes me a living."[9]

Vautin said he explained to "those who come that, if they want to improve their lives, they must be prepared to take the first step."[10] Those who received food and lodging were expected to do simple chores such as making beds, cleaning floors, or helping in the kitchen—but many homeless men told Vautin that other "helping places" required nothing.

One journalist, Arthur Bonner, wrote that during the three-week period of extensive counseling following arrival at the McAuley Mission,

> a man is not allowed to sit back and drift. In interviews with the counselors ... whatever excuses a man has used to paper over his troubles are held up to him for what they are. Eventually, a man is expected to face the truth about himself. Often, when the probing comes too close to his real trouble, the man walks out to return to the Bowery or is never seen again.

The attrition rate is high. The mission could easily keep a man longer by putting less of an emphasis on religion or by relaxing some of its other rules. It could also serve a far larger number of men by limiting itself to transients and serving free food to all comers several times a day. This could be justified as elemental Christian charity. It would result in impressive statistics regarding the number of men served and perhaps make it easier to raise funds. But few, if any, men would be rehabilitated either socially or spiritually.[11]

The McAuley Mission continued its one-by-one approach, but the War on Poverty demanded massive body counts.

A third big loser in the entitlement revolution was marriage. Prior to the 1960s, marriage was both a social and an economic contract; viewed in economic terms, it was a compassionate antipoverty device that offered adults affiliation and challenge as it provided two parents for raising children. So strong was support for marriage that—before the revolution of the 1960s—an unmarried woman who became pregnant usually would get married; 85 percent of teenaged mothers in the 1950s were married by the time their babies were born. Those who did not want to be married had a second acceptable option: placing a child for adoption. Fewer than one of every ten pregnant women chose single parenthood, for they feared social ostracism and lacked institutional and financial support.[12] Marriage under pressure certainly was not optimal, but it did not leave a woman alone. Placing a child for adoption also was difficult, but one result of the marriage/adoption emphasis was that children had fathers living with them during their early years.

In the 1960s, however, as governmental obligations to single mothers increased, marital obligations decreased. As no-fault divorce laws spread, women knew that husbands were allowed to be unfaithful without suffering much economic penalty. Sociologist Jack Douglass noted,

> Almost all women have enough economic common sense to realize that the marriage contract has been tremendously devalued by the legal changes. Since any potential husband can fly free of his family at the first impulse, women have far fewer incentives to get married, even when they are pregnant.[13]

Women also knew that the government was required to be faithful, within its capacities. The reduction of social and financial barriers to single-parenting made it seem logical to raise a child alone, even though the children of never-wed mothers often grew up not only materially poor—three out of five were in poverty—but emotionally impoverished as well. Their mother's husband, in essence, was the federal government. They did not know what it was like to have a father who could love them and discipline them.

Programs described as "compassionate" were thus actually the opposite, since they made affiliation less likely. To gain a full share of government-funded social services, pregnant teens had to be on their own, without support from either family or the child's father. While there was no clear evidence that government entitlements led women to become pregnant, they did influence heavily the choice of whether to choose parenting or adoption, whether to marry or not, and whether to live at home or in an apartment. Studies showed that adolescents were aware of opportunities for financial support and "did not consider the expense of raising a child as a barrier" to setting out on their own.[14] To a teenager the monthly stipends looked like a great deal—but they were available only if bonds were broken. For example, a single mother could receive AFDC (Aid to Families of Dependent Children) payments only if she had her own apartment.

Overall, cultural changes that glorified unrestrained sexuality, minimized the importance of marriage, and accepted single-parenting and easy divorce, were a tremendous blow to the poor. Christopher Jencks in *The New Republic* noted that some educated women were able to go it alone, but "for less privileged couples, the demise of traditional norms about marriage and divorce posed more serious problems."[15] Jencks added that, as a result, boyfriends had felt "freer to walk out after they [had] conceive[d] a child," and that the breakdown of social pressure to "marry, to live together, and to support children" had led to increased economic vulnerability for children.

There were many more losers in the entitlement revolution, but even a quick look at the losses in social mobility, mission challenge, and marriage leaves a sad feeling about the hopes of the 1960s. It is sad that the 1960s' pincer movement of social revolution and economic disincentive, designed to liberate all from material pressures, claimed its greatest number of victims among the children of the poor. And it is tragic that shame in fathering children and not supporting them disappeared in some urban neighborhoods, and that one defense of such action was that the children would not starve, thanks to a governmental daddy.[16] Charity leaders of the late nineteenth century had predicted that entitlement would produce more abandonment—but the realization of nightmares walking was still a shock.

Although some have danced on the graves, it is sad that one by one the dreams of the 1960s died during the 1970s. The National Welfare

Rights Organization began its fatal decline when internal battles pushed out George Wiley, who left in 1973 to organize the Movement for Economic Justice. (Wiley died in a boating accident later that year.) As Guida West has recorded, "the gathering momentum of the women's liberation movement in the 1970s" led to new priorities within the mainline denominations: the "top priority issue" for social action shifted from "welfare" in 1972 to "women's rights" in 1975. Many of the welfare recipients were women, of course, but "programs with greater appeal to the middle class" gained more attention.[17] Once the mainline denominations changed their emphases, the NWRO folded; in March 1975, the organization declared bankruptcy.

Dreams died quickly among some social workers who had been in the forefront of change. Soon, they were reporting compassion fatigue, and in the early 1970s *Time* noted that

> one young caseworker, speaking for thousands like her in urban areas, says: "The paper work is just amazing. There are copies and copies of everything, dozens of forms to fill out.... You want to issue some furniture because the family needs it desperately. But you can't get anyone to sign the authorization. All we have time to do is move paper. I have yet to solve any social problems."[18]

The stories were the same year after year, with new idealists replacing burn-out victims. Recently Nathaniel Dunford "fulfilled a longstanding dream by quitting a job at the *New York Times* to take a position at half the pay as a caseworker with New York City's Child Welfare Administration."[19] Dunford described what happened in a column published by his former employer:

I lasted two months.... Paperwork ruled the office; social
work was secondary. I got more forms and documents on
my first day than I had seen in seven years at *The Times*....
Cases would usually arrive in the morning, faxed from a
central office.... They would be shifted from desk to desk,
getting "attachments"—more forms for the caseworker to
fill out. They would eventually reach our supervisor, to sit
for a few more hours and a few more "attachments." Nothing
was allowed to interfere with the lunch break. Meanwhile,
in various parts of the city, the children and the sympathetic
adults trying to help them were left to fume....

The tragedy of American compassion is evident in Dunford's lament
that he "had a calling; it was that simple. I wanted to help."

Dreams died as compassion fatigue deepened among many who
had at least practiced the "compassion" of the checkbook. Five hundred
different categorical social service programs under federal auspices
became safety nets for the better-off, allowing them to ignore problems
without the sting of conscience. Individual giving as a proportion of
personal income dropped 13 percent between 1960 and 1976.[20] The
proportion of philanthropic giving devoted to social welfare declined
from 15 percent to 6 percent.[21] By the mid–1970s governments spent
about ten times as much on social services as nonprofit agencies, and
the nonprofit agencies themselves received half of their revenues from
governments.[22]

Dreams died among the American public generally. From the early
1960s to the early 1970s public opinion polls registered a consistent
decline in the numbers of Americans who saw poverty and welfare as
among the most important problems facing the United States. Some

media leaders remained true believers. *Time* explained to its readers that "the reality of the new poverty lies in its contrast to U.S. affluence.... Even if this poverty is not like any earlier poverty or the poverty of the rest of the world, it is worth declaring a war on."[23] But a 1976 Harris survey showed almost nine of ten respondents agreeing that "too many people on welfare cheat by getting money they are not entitled to."[24] Almost two-thirds agreed that the "criteria for getting on welfare are not tough enough."[25] Neoconservatives joined with conservatives in proposing that welfare should not pay more than work. Nathan Glazer in *The Public Interest* in 1975 cited the case of a savvy welfare mother who understood her entitlements well enough to achieve an income equivalent of $20,000 per year (1975 dollars), which was then more than three-fourths of the families in the United States earned.[26]

Dreams especially died among many poor individuals themselves. They saw that mass pauperism was accepted and pressure to leave welfare was very slight. Sometimes, those (formerly known as the "worthy poor") who were willing to put off immediate gratification and sacrifice leisure time in order to remain independent, were called chumps rather than champs. Poor individuals who retained older values complained. A *Christian Science Monitor* interviewee noted that many of her pauperized associates remained poor because they were "satisfied" on welfare: "If they'd rebel against it, they'd get out of it."[27] A *Los Angeles Times* survey of poor Americans found more than 40 percent believed that welfare benefits made them more dependent.[28] Many argued that recipients should be required to move toward independence, but the growth of welfare as a right made it logically impossible for newly defined compassion to be conditional.

As the entitlement revolution created more and more negative results, some academics and journalists redoubled their defenses of it, but others searched for the guilty parties. It was easy to blame bureaucracy for opportunities lost. *Time's* summary of one set of problems would have come as no surprise to the late nineteenth-century charity-watchers: "Rarely is bureaucracy flexible enough to encompass complex human situations."[29] The professionalization heralded as savior early in the century was often haunting those it was designed to help. "With 125 cases it's hard to remember that they're all human beings," a California caseworker said. "Sometimes they're just a number."[30] One television film about the mother of basketball star Isiah Thomas captured the mood on the receiving end of a bureaucratized system: Mary Thomas, confronting a governmental caseworker who treated her as a number, said, "I'm a real person. If you remember that next time we'll have a better conversation."[31]

Bureaucracy was clearly a major problem, but would less paperwork have made the welfare system work? No, because behind the harried bureaucracy stood a "poverty wall" that reduced incentive and contributed to the creation of "a new caste, the 'Dependent Americans.'"[32] Increased welfare benefits of the 1960s led to a very high marginal tax rate for those on welfare. As one congressional subcommittee reported in 1974,

> When a recipient participates in more than one benefit program, as most do ... [the marginal rate] could climb to 85 percent. It does not seem reasonable to expect persons to work for a net gain of only 15 cents per extra dollar, especially at possibly unpleasant work.[33]

The marginal tax wall, high as it was, could still have been climbed had shame pushed potential welfare recipients to stay off or get off the rolls as long as possible, or had families in urban areas not been in a process of disintegration. But when ideas of work and family were devalued, economic disincentives became dominant. Poor individuals who filled out questionnaires still said "yes" to the statement, "I want to work," but performance in starting jobs showed that few persevered as long as newly respectable alternatives were available.[34]

Year after year proposals to tinker with the bureaucracy and reduce the marginal tax wall caused mild stirs in Washington, but even the best proposals mirrored Hercules's early attempts to kill the nine-headed monster Hydra; each time he hacked off one head, he found two growing in its place. Not until Hercules and his servant Iolaus burned off eight of the nine heads, then cut off the immortal head and buried it under a rock, was the monster finally slain. Few poverty analysts concentrated on that central head, the substitution of depersonalized dependence for true compassion. Horace Greeley and Edward Bellamy had envisioned every person having "an equal share" of all resources and goods, that share to be distributed by a central authority regardless of individual performance; on the basis of that vision "we elders of today dream our dreams," New Deal advocates had reported. After the 1960s those dreams were walking vigorously, and walking all over other dreams.

Year after year, as changes seemed to increase rather than decrease poverty, some politicians made attempts to smooth over the problem through rhetoric. Early in the 1970s, books such as *A People of Compassion: The Concerns of Edward Kennedy* (a collection of his speeches set in type as blank verse) were innovative. For example, Kennedy's speech "To Respond to Truth" began, "The irresistible force of youth is still irresistible." It came to a crescendo in its discussion of student interests and abilities:

We have found not only that the students
Were thoughtful and informed,
but also that we needed them,
because they could help us,
and we could help them.[35]

Kennedy also had advice for older individuals:

Men in public life to be true to themselves
must be more candid with whomever they speak,
regardless of the political consequences.
Our ministers, our priests and our rabbis,
must be more relevant
in social sermons with their flocks....[36]

Kennedy used and reused the word "compassion" throughout the 1970s and 1980s: "The work of compassion must continue," and so on.[37]

Other, more prosaic works throughout this period similarly attempted to push Americans over the top, toward acceptance of Social Universalism. Books with titles like *The Philosophy of Compassion*, *The Veins of Compassion*, *The Power of Compassion*, *The Beauty of Compassion*, *Truth and Compassion*, *A Spirituality Named Compassion*, and *Tear-Catchers: Developing the Gift of Compassion*, generally argued that we must be compassionate not just to widows, orphans, and other victims, but to all, even if they had victimized themselves and continued to do so. Some of the books purported to ground themselves in the Bible, and others were based in Buddhism, but their typical theme was that compassion was "a vision that dissolves division" and teaches us to be "seeing the unity in things."[38] For that reason, we must oppose any attempt to distinguish between those "deserving" welfare support and those undeserving of it, because any such attempt "legitimates inequality on the basis that it is deserved or merited."[39]

The political agenda in this use of compassion was evident. Sar Levitan declared:

> Only through greater reliance upon programs that offer the promise of opportunity as envisioned in the Great Society is the nation likely to reject policies of negativism and retrenchment for a more compassionate response to poverty in America.[40]

Later, Leslie Dunbar of the Ford Foundation would argue that the federal government should control all welfare and provide free housing, fuel, and health insurance.[41] Underlying many of the political ideas, as in the 1960s, was a theology. In 1982 the National Council of Churches' "Commission on Stewardship" distributed a book that called for "the extrication of stewardship from its almost indelible association with economic capitalism."[42] Author Douglas Hall demanded "a new look at the socialist alternative" and a "search for new forms of community—including a 'New Economic Order' that can more adequately reflect our faith's concern for justice, equality, and mercy."[43]

By the 1980s wise observers were noting abundant misuse of the word "compassion." Clifford Orwin pointed out that "[o]ur century has hardly seen a demagogue, however bloody and monstrous his designs, who has not known how to rally compassion and mine its potential for sympathetic moral indignation."[44] John Agresto in 1982 stated that "compassion these days…has become hidden behind something far lower and simpler, behind mere sentimentality."[45] Alan Bloom wrote about "conspicuous compassion" designed to bring about "nihilism with a happy ending," and George Will complained in 1989 about "the reflexive rhetoric of perfunctory compassion."[46] Mickey Kaus in *The New Republic* noted that Americans were now supposed to have

> compassion for the unmotivated delinquent who would rather smoke PCP than work. Compassion makes few distinctions—we're all in Cuomo's "family"—which is why a politics based on mass-produced compassion leads naturally to the indiscriminate dispensing of cash in a sort of all-purpose socialized United Way campaign.

Kaus, concluding that "compassion has become the all-purpose Democratic password," proposed that "the word should be banned from Democratic speeches."[47]

Despite such warnings, a bull market in "compassion" raged throughout the 1980s, particularly as the issue of "homelessness" became popular. When Speaker of the House Tip O'Neill favored more spending on "the homeless," columnist Mary McGrory wrote that his "compassion was the size of his frame."[48] O'Neill's successor Jim Wright also was praised in the *Washington Post* for his legislative compassion concerning the homeless. So was Mayor Marion Barry, who said that he and his friends would be "very vigorous in our efforts to be compassionate."[49] Throughout the decade the *Washington Post* continued to employ the word "compassionate" as a euphemism for "more-heavily-funded." As columnist Hobart Rowan declared in a standard usage, "We need a compassionate social program that pays more than lip service to adjustment, retraining and education...."[50] University of Georgia Professor Dwight Lee concluded, "The notion that compassion toward the poor requires favoring expansion of government transfer programs has achieved the status of revealed truth."[51]

Meanwhile, disagreement in the ranks of those who emphasized Christian revealed truth continued. In 1985 Larry Burkett, a popular evangelical writer on economic issues, called "indiscriminate giving" of government welfare the cause of "permanent dependence and poverty."[52] In 1986 Calvinist poverty-fighter George Grant charged "centralized government welfare" with "splintering families, crushing incentive, decimating pride, and fouling productivity."[53] On the other hand, evangelicals who were universalistically inclined saw government care as essential. William Diehl wrote that

> even if all Christians had the commitment to care for the poor, how could I or my congregation possibly know where *all* the unmet needs were, and how could we be *certain* that there would be an *equitable* distribution of our benevolence? Some *overall* agency is needed for such a task, and it is *obviously* civil government.[54] [my emphasis]

Diehl's belief that government could and would cover all the bases equitably showed a faith in things unseen. Similarly, Ron Sider's *Rich Christians in an Age of Hunger* survived heavy barrages and found readers throughout the 1980s; Sider proposed simple living but accepted conventional ideas of poverty-fighting through collective action rather than individual challenge.[55]

Sadly, the evangelical orchestra was producing cacophony just as new harmonies were desperately needed. The *New York Times* profiled the frustration of "mainline" ministers in inner-city churches: "Most have been influenced by Liberation Theology, [which] fuses Christian and Marxist utopianism," but "churchgoers mostly prefer Bible-thumping harangues and emotional services provided by indigenous evangelical, Pentecostal and charismatic churches."[56] One black United Church of Christ pastor, the Rev. A. Thomas Board, explained that the material support sent to inner-city churches

> assuag[es] the guilt of the white Christians in the suburbs who support them. Neither the congregations nor the ministers understand that black folks don't want to go to a mission every Sunday where they pick up food stamps and surplus cheese. Black folks want to know that their church is a place where they can meet Jesus.[57]

The article concluded, "Members of the struggling mainline churches… want to attract new members but admit that they have little understanding of the culture of their new neighbors." Ironically, a century ago the mainline churches had also been a place "to meet Jesus."

By 1989 some journalists tended to be justifiably cynical about "compassionate" gestures. The *Los Angeles Times* pick-axed politicians who "wander through the city's needy neighborhoods, usually in an election year and usually trailing cameras to film their expressions of compassion."[58] Many conservatives were appropriately sarcastic. *The American Spectator* asked, concerning Senator Orrin Hatch's cosponsorship of the ABC child care bill, "Do readers have other evidence of Sen. Hatch's growing sensitivity, compassion, etc.?" The magazine also gave a spot in its "Readers' Enemies List" to "Anyone who uses the word 'compassion' when talking about foreign policy."[59] But such assaults seemed to do little good: the *Washington Post* continued to stress the importance of remaining "unshaken in liberalism's belief in governmental compassion for the weak and poor."[60]

As the 1980s came to an end, the word "compassion" was being used more loosely than ever before. In one month in five major newspapers, the word was used three hundred times, largely as a synonym for "leniency." Chicago lawyers asked a judge to be "compassionate" when sentencing a sheriff's deputy for selling cocaine.[61] California lawyers asked a jury to have compassion for an accused murderer by letting him off.[62] Baseball star Steve Garvey asked for compassion when he exercised his passion through informal bigamy or trigamy.[63] Defense witnesses for televangelist Jim Bakker tried to help out by labeling him "a compassionate preacher."[64]

At times the word was even more blurred. Critics used "compassion" as a synonym for "I like it." A music reviewer in Chicago complained that an LP record was filled with "make-out ballads" for "the wine-and-cheese crowd," but was saved by "the mix of spiky aggression and compassion."[65] A California musical group received praise for its attempt to "communicate" the idea of compassion in a "non-cognitive way."[66] Movie critics were equally vague: an actor was perfect for a role because "he's got the strength, the compassion."[67] Some politicians were no better; the last refuge in a drowning campaign often were words like Jim Courter's in New Jersey: "I'd like to be considered as a person who is compassionate."[68]

It is important to keep in mind the problems of welfare bureaucracy and the disincentives of tax structures. But behind these problems stands the idea that true compassion is outmoded or impossible. The ruins of Shakespeare's Globe Theatre recently were excavated; what remained of the theater had been covered over by a parking lot. The ruins of true compassion are in the same predicament, and it is time for the excavation project to begin.

We might start with a bit of historical lexicography. The Oxford English Dictionary gives, as the original definition of compassion, "suffering together with another, participation in suffering." The emphasis, as the word itself shows—"com," with, and "passion," from the Latin *pati*, to suffer—is on personal involvement with the needy, suffering with them, not just giving to them. Noah Webster, in the 1834 edition of his *American Dictionary of the English Language*, similarly defined compassion as "a suffering with another; painful sympathy...."[69] But in the twentieth century, a second definition of compassion has become common: "The feeling, or emotion, when a person is moved by the suffering or distress of another, and by the desire to relieve it...."[70] Currently, in *Webster's Third International Dictionary*, compassion is defined as a "deep feeling for and understanding of misery or suffering and the concomitant desire to promote its alleviation."[71] There is a world of policy differences between those two definitions: One demands personal action, the other a "feeling" that requires a willingness to send a check.

Words carry a political charge, as Orwell pointed out so well in his essay on "Politics and the English Language." Words shape our ideas, and the shifting definition of compassion has so shaped our understanding that the *New York Times*, usually a stickler for precise language, prints oxymoronic phrases such as "compassionate observer." The corruption is general: the *Washington Post* refers to "personal compassion," as if compassion did not have to be personal.[72] The corruption of our language, the related corruption of our thought, and the sadly abundant evidence of the past several decades, suggest that the road to effective antipoverty work in America cannot be paved with more well-intended legislation. Instead, we need to look at ourselves and our society more honestly. We celebrate America as a compassion-ate, caring society. But most of us are actually stingy—not because we refuse to spend more government money (we're actually doing quite well there, thank you), but because we no longer offer the poor our time and a challenge. Our willingness to do so shows whether we care for hearts, minds, and souls, or just bodies—and, as a society, we fail the test.

Just as we need to recapture an earlier meaning of compassion, so we need to grasp again a broader understanding of what it means to be stingy. Historically, that has not meant a mere unwillingness to part with money. In 1770, a man could be called "liberal in promises, and stingy in performances." In 1878, a minister sarcastically noted that "Christ is put off with a stingy hour or two on the Sunday." And in 1885, an irritated lover complained, "Who is she, to be so stingy of her smiles?"[73] In other words, we are likely to be stingy of whatever is most valuable to us: perhaps money, but often time and smiles. The priest and the Levite who passed by the beaten traveler in chapter ten of Luke's gospel probably tithed, but they were stingy—only the Good Samaritan was not. A professor who gives high grades to mediocre papers, so that students will go away happy and he need not explain how they erred, is stingy. Parents who give their children Nintendos or Turbographic 16s but do not walk with them by the roadside and play games with them on the dining room table are stingy.

We need to be honest in our self-criticism. It is easy for conserva-tives to criticize government, especially since the increase of govern-mental cash flow contributed greatly to our current problem. But at this point, the corruption is general, not just governmental. A stingy temperament slowly and somewhat insidiously has taken over our entire society, including the many points of light.[74] We need real change in our language, thought, and action; offering the small change in our pockets is insufficient. Real change does not mean just running out and offering time to the local Point of Light, unless we are sure that the Point actually offers light. We need to go beyond the bumper-sticker messages—Give!!!—of philanthropic trade associations. Their implication is egalitarian: the direction of the giving is not spelled out; it is the thought that counts, not the result. We are not to think too long, however, since what could be called Nike philanthropy demands that we "Just Do It." Cotton Mather's exhortation "that you may not abuse your charity by misapplying it" has long been buried.

The danger in arguing that Something is not necessarily better than Nothing, is that caution in action can lead to Nothing. That is not the intention of this book. To show that a thoughtful Something is both essential and attainable, the next chapter will take the two most difficult problems of contemporary poverty—abandoned women and children, and homelessness—and show how a different view of compassion can make a major difference in lives.

CHAPTER TWELVE

Putting Compassion into Practice

N owhere has the movement away from true compassion, and its emphasis on affiliation and bonding, been more evident (and more tragic) than in the area of unmarried pregnancy. Christopher Jencks has argued that

> even when almost every "respectable" adult thought unwed parenthood, desertion, and divorce immoral, it was hard to keep families together in poor communities. Now that the mass media, the schools, and even the churches have begun to treat single parenthood as a regrettable but inescapable part of modern life, we can hardly expect the respectable poor to carry on the struggle against illegitimacy and desertion with their old fervor. They still deplore such behavior, but they cannot make it morally taboo. Once the two-parent norm loses its moral sanctity, the selfish considerations that always pulled poor parents apart often become overwhelming.[1]

Logically, government antipoverty programs should help the respectable poor in their struggle by working *against* the establishment of
separate households by single mothers, yet, as one study showed, "the
provision of public assistance facilitated movement to independent
household headship, particularly when increased benefits were provided to women for establishing a separate household."[2]

Behind the illogic stood a combination of new ideology and old
selfishness. During the 1960s, from the social top down, educated
women who were most influenced by feminist ideology advocated
avoidance of all entangling alliances. From the social bottom up, men
eagerly read the new playbook and slithered like halfbacks through the
gaping holes of the old moral line. Twenty years ago, when there were
"only" 300,000 illegitimate births, there may have still been time to
reverse the trend. *Time* magazine's refusal to criticize what "the wom-
en's movement with its emphasis on self-sufficiency has stimulated,"
was typical.[3] By the time a backlash against feminism developed in the
late 1970s, patterns of single-parenthood were well established, and
other alternatives seemed to be part of ancient history.

The growth of single-parenting accompanied societal and governmental acceptance (and even encouragement) of premarital and extramarital pregnancy, through the passage of laws and regulations that
made divorce easy and adoption hard. Programs that declared themselves "compassionate" were often the opposite, because most tended
to emphasize individual autonomy. Even those organizations that
struggled to inculcate moral values accepted the notion that neither
marriage nor reliance on family, church, or traditional voluntary
organizations—which might be dominated by "patriarchal values"—
should or could be encouraged. "About the only thing you can rely on
is your personal feeling about what makes sense for you," one resource
directory declared.[4]

Instead of emphasizing affiliation and bonding, many programs stressed bread alone. *Time* praised social agencies that offered "help with the economic troubles that plague nearly every unmarried mother," and reported that Blue Cross was paying maternity benefits for single women and that public schools now had special facilities for pregnant girls.[5] As the number of single mothers grew, programs to help them generally, and pregnant teens particularly, mushroomed; program planners said they were responding to a crisis, but chickens and eggs seemed to be racing each other.[6] Agencies sometimes even competed with each other to attract clients and receive more support.[7]

Governmental and private agencies began by stressing the economic problems of single mothers and fatherless children. Those problems clearly grew out of a breakdown of affiliation: children almost always are poor because they do not have fathers living with and supporting them.[8] But even when enough money was available, the young mother who accepted governmental incentives to set up her own household often was left with nothing except an apartment in which she could sit, separated from real help. When a woman was isolated and sometimes estranged from family, church, and other groups, no one in the next room could relieve her or give her good, immediately applicable child care information. It soon became apparent that economic concerns were only part of the overall danger. Planned Parenthood researchers in North Carolina noted that "adolescent girls reared without fathers are much more likely to be sexually active" than girls raised in two-parent families.[9] Studies showed too that children raised without fathers were more likely to be victims and accomplices of crime, including child abuse.[10] Researchers such as David Gil, author of *Violence Against Children*, slowly began to find "an association between physical abuse of children and deviance from normative family structure...."[11]

Furthermore, fixation on the supposed autonomy of the mother and neglect of another person—the child—led to short-term thinking that minimized adoption possibilities. A study by the Child Welfare League of America reported that only one-fifth of adolescent mothers even considered adoption.[12] One study observed social workers and other counselors in ninety-four different settings who proceeded on the assumption that pregnant adolescents had little or no interest in adoption. That, of course, was a self-fulfilling prophecy, since given that belief counselors had little interest in giving full counsel.[13] Other studies found that "pregnant adolescents find little or no support if they wish to explore adoption as an alternative."[14] In the course of a generation, the marriage or adoption choices that had been normative became abnormal, and the hardship of single motherhood became standard. That alone represented an enormous decline in living standards.

By the end of the 1980s, the disaster was even clearer than before. Columnist William Raspberry wrote, "If I could offer a single prescription for the survival of America, and particularly of black America, it would be: Restore the family."[15] Charles Murray's research showed that "even after economic circumstances are matched, the children of single mothers do worse, often much worse, than the children of married couples."[16] Murray put it bluntly, "You can send in social workers and school teachers and clergy to tell a young male that when he grows up he should be a good father to his children, but he doesn't know what that means unless he's seen it."[17] And Richard John Neuhaus noted, "Millions of children do not know, and will never know what it means to have a father. More poignantly, they do not know anyone who has a father."[18]

Nevertheless, at the end of the 1980s programs continued to subsidize and encourage attempts at autonomy. If teen mothers could complete their education, the *Washington Post* suggested, all would be well.[19] In 1987, the newspaper reported that a seventeen-year-old mother wanted to go to school but couldn't afford day-care for her baby. The culprit in this case was "a recent change in public assistance rules" that took into account the seventeen-year-old's mother's income in addition to her own when figuring out her welfare eligibility.[20] By 1988, after twenty years of concern for single-parenting, the *Post* could report the opening of an infant care center in one of the District's junior high schools. Only two choices were possible, according to the infant care program coordinator: "There is a crisis in this city. We can ignore the fact that this is going on, or we can do something about it."[21]

The option seemed to be either ostrich behavior or "do something"— even if the "something" might cause further problems. It was necessary to have faith in things unseen. Another *Post* article in 1988 reported that the D.C. school system was considering opening a child-care center in an *elementary* school. The school board president, acknowledging concern that such a location might send the wrong message to grade school kids, said soberly, "All students in the school would see that this is not fun, it's responsibility."[22] Magazines in the 1960s were shocked by single-parenting among high school students. In the 1970s and early 1980s, stories about pregnant or parenting junior high school girls still retained some shock value. In the 1990s even tales from elementary schools were no surprise.[23]

"Do something," anything, would continue to predominate as long as "middle-class morality" remained unpopular. Historian Gertrude Himmelfarb noted, concerning nineteenth-century anti-poverty efforts in England, "So far from keeping the working class in a condition of inferiority and subservience, the single standard [of morality] was an invitation to economic improvement and social mobility."[24] Today, a single, family-based standard of morality, taught and communicated through every way possible and supported by state and private programs, remains the major antipoverty weapon. Urban analyst William Tucker is correct to state that, despite its other merits, "workfare will do nothing to put the black family back together. The main problem with single mothers, after all, is not that they don't work, but that they don't get married."[25] A poor woman is most likely to escape from poverty if she does not get pregnant. If she does have children, marriage is the best way to escape poverty.[26] And the single best way for children to escape from poverty is to have their mothers marry, or to be adopted; only 2 percent of adopted children are poor. The common factor in all of this is reaffiliation.

Groups that show the vitality of affiliation, instead of stressing autonomy, have registered considerable success. Jim and Anne Pierson of Lancaster, Pennsylvania, for example, bought a large, old house, named it House of His Creation, and over seven years provided shelter to two hundred pregnant women.[27] The Piersons learned that the family structure of their home was crucial, because most of the women who stayed with them had lacked a good family life. They had never seen a healthy mother-father or husband-wife relationship, and so had become cynics about marriage. Some of the residents at House of His Creation, freed from peer pressure to single-parent and able to see the importance of dual-parenting, chose to place for adoption. Most also began thinking about marriage in a new healthy way.

The Piersons' next step was to act as catalysts for the development of family-based maternity homes. They formed the Christian Maternity Home/Single Parent Association (CMHA), which has thirty-two member homes, each with two house parents and six to eight pregnant women in residence.[28] At one CMHA home, Sparrow House in Baltimore, houseparents draw each new resident into family life—for some, this is the only time in their lives that they have lived with a "mother" and a "father." The houseparents help each resident adjust to rules and responsibilities that may be new and hard to take at first. Since many of the young women have come from undisciplined lives, they are learning—maybe for the first time—to live with structure. They also learn to take their spiritual needs seriously. Sparrow House, like other CMHA homes, accepts needy women from any religious background, but the program's unapologetic base in Christian teaching is reminiscent of many in the late nineteenth century. Furthermore, dozens of volunteers from the church that supports Sparrow House become part of an extended family.[29]

Across the country, the Phoenix Christian Family Care Agency has a foster care program that provides supervision in a family setting to single-parenting teenage mothers. The foster home's primary goal is not to ease the burden of parenting for teenage mothers, but to combine lessons about reality with protection for infants. The housemother spends many hours with the teenage mother but she does not assume babysitting responsibilities; if a teenage mother is desperate, the house-mother takes over for a short time but only in exchange for doing laundry for the household or mowing the lawn. House-parents need to have

> inner strength and a conviction that the child will be better off in the long run by maintaining a hands-off situation. They have to let the child cry longer than they would let him cry. They have to let his diaper be wetter than they would allow. The teenager has to learn that it is her responsibility....[30]

CFCA's tough love leads about half of the teenage mothers to realize that for both their good and their children's, they should choose adoption; the other half raise their children with a new appreciation of marriage and an awareness of their own limitations. Crucially, that knowledge has come in the safe environment of a family home, not in the dangerous terrain of a solitary apartment filled with the sounds of a crying child and a tired and angry parent.

Many more compassionate programs for single mothers, usually with a theistic base, are developing in city after city.[31] To look quickly atone more: Beth Shalom, in Lancaster, Pennsylvania, is designed to "provide safe, affordable housing with emphasis on meeting the physical, emotional, and spiritual needs" of single mothers between the ages of sixteen and twenty-one. What makes this program different is that only women whose children are at least six months old are accepted into the program. Beth Shalom will not accept women straight from the hospital. The goal is to help women who do not need lectures on reality, because they have already experienced the difficulty of single-parenting and wish to change their lives and ways of thinking. In addition to helping these women avoid a repeat out-of-wedlock pregnancy, the program stresses homemaking and parenting skills, movement towards financial independence, and spiritual growth. Individual residents gain responsibilities and privileges as they move through the program, accomplishing particular goals.

These program listings could go on, but the point is that the people who start the successful ones are people who, for one reason or another, have not embraced the twentieth-century equation of compassion with "giving to." Repeatedly, volunteer leaders arrive at the same need for affiliation, employment, spiritual challenge, and so on, as did their counterparts a century ago. They also are well aware that their good charity is constantly threatened by bad charity. Every time AFDC pays for a young woman's apartment, affiliation is undercut. Every time dependence on government is equated with "independence," a child is hurt. The programs only have a chance because of the self-categorization of the pregnant women who come to Sparrow House and such places, desperate and vulnerable and in need of more than material kindness.

Working with young fathers is more difficult because they rarely see themselves as helpless. In fact, even when homeless, they have access to enormous amounts of material help offered both informally and formally. Shortly before Christmas 1989, a *Washington Post* reporter, Stephen Buckley, interviewed eight men who were living in Northwest Washington in a tent made by tying a bright blue tarpaulin over a grate that spewed hot air.[32] Buckley noted that the men had sleeping bags, gloves, scarves, and boots, and lots of food: "Party trays with chicken and turkey. Fruit. Boxes of crackers. Bags of popcorn. Canned goods. All donated by passersby." Some of the recipients probably were fathers, but they were not spending Christmas with their children.

Buckley also visited four men and two women who were camping on a heating grate on the eastern edge of the Ellipse, just south of the White House. The heat, along with "the generosity of private citizens who bring them food and clothes every night," meant that the campers "don't worry much about surviving the cold," Buckley reported. Indeed, visitors throughout the evening dropped off supplies: one woman brought fruit, nuts, and two dollars; three men brought a platter of cold cuts; and two other men hot chocolate, blankets, gloves, sweaters, and socks. One of the campers, a forty-one-year-old man who has been "largely homeless" for eleven years, noted that "the majority of clothes we have here now were dropped off by persons who were walking by and saw us here. They just thought they could bring something that would be helpful to us."[33]

Was such "compassion" helpful, or harmful? It was Christmas, of course, and—despite the cold—their life was easier than it might have been at less guilt-provoking times of the year. But three months later, another *Washington Post* reporter, Elizabeth Wiener, showed how "Vans Keep the Hungry Fed."[34] She quoted a theology student as saying, "Going out and serving homeless people is the most radical, hands-on thing you can do." She described one scene of service:

> It is about 5:30 p.m., and the white van laden with sand-
> wiches and hot soup is pulling up at Fifth Street and New
> York Avenue NW. Already a crowd, mostly men, has gath-
> ered. They jostle and thrust their hands through the win-
> dows for food...one feels almost overwhelmed by hungry,
> impatient people, a line that never seems satiated. "Yo, yo,
> pull up here," someone yells, and there are already arms
> reaching inside the van.[35]

The reporter saw this van and others as

> perhaps the steadiest of Washington's own points of light....
> Volunteers come from all over, from churches and
> schools... 8,600 volunteers over the past year. Motives vary,
> as do time and commitment, but this is such a fundamental
> transaction—giving food to the hungry—that people have
> trouble finding words to explain why they want to help.

Was this "compassion," evidently popular, helpful or harmful?

In 1989 and 1990 homeless shelters were busy, most believing they should provide a spot to all who came, whenever space allowed. In

New York, a shelter administrator was reprimanded after he wrote a memo proposing that residents of a men's shelter not be allowed to wear dresses, high heel shoes, and wigs. Reid Cramer, assistant director of the Coalition for the Homeless in New York City, pointed out the administrator's error:

> The memo is evidence of a real misconception of what the
> shelters are all about. Trying to curtail freedom of expres-
> sion, trying to shape the behavior of clients is completely
> inappropriate.[36]

Similarly, a director of Chicago's Center for Street People said the center's role was "to be supportive, not of a particular life-style in the sense of endorsing it, but supporting people...."[37] Was the center, by not supporting any particular life-style, truly supporting people?

In 1989 and 1990 Dan McMurry, a Tennessee sociology professor, continued his "participant observer" research in which he posed as a homeless man in cities throughout the United States. McMurry wrote that in city after city homeless individuals merely had to "line up and eat. No questions asked."[38] Homeless individuals in Nashville, a typical city in this regard, also received housing, towels, blankets, soap, medicine, dental care, stamps, newspapers, and a long list of other products. McMurry noted, "I was never asked to do anything I did not want on the streets. Of all the places I ate, I was never asked to bow my head; only once was I asked to take off my cap."[39] McMurry wrote of how he once

> intentionally smashed styrofoam cups and threw the pieces
> on the street as a kindly looking old gentleman stooped
> over with a Tuffy bag picking up the trash left by the men.

He saw me, saw what I was doing, bent over, picked up the
pieces, put them in his plastic bag, half rose, looked up at
me and smiled. Then he went on down the line.[40]

Was McMurry, when he was treated as an infant in a high chair (and
not even given a firm "no") treated with compassion?

I took a first-hand look at contemporary compassion toward the
poor early in March 1990. I put on three used T-shirts and two dirty
sweaters, equipped myself with a stocking cap and a plastic bag, removed my wedding ring, got lots of dirt on my hands, and walked with
the slow shuffle that characterizes the forty-year-old white homeless
male of the streets. In two days I was given lots of food, lots of pills of
various kinds, and lots of offers of clothing and shelter. I was never
asked to do anything, not even remove my tray after eating. But there
was one thing I did not get, even though I asked for it many times: a
Bible. For example, at Zaccheus' Kitchen, which provides very good
free breakfasts in the basement of the First Congregational Church
downtown, a sweet young volunteer kept putting food down in front
of me and asking if I wanted more. Finally I asked, mumbling a bit,
"Could I have a...Bible?" Puzzled, she tried to figure out what I had
said: "Do you want a bagel? a bag?" When I responded, "A Bible," she
said, politely but firmly, "I'm sorry, we don't have any Bibles."

That was my experience over two days on the streets—not enough
to draw any firm conclusions, but enough to raise questions. Most of
the helpers were nice. But were they compassionate? Were "homeless
advocates" compassionate when they worked hard to develop the myth
that the homeless are "people like us" who have been victimized by
situations beyond their control? Most are not ordinary folk down on
their luck, unless the "us" are alcoholics, addicts, shiftless, or insane.[41]

Robert M. Hayes, director of the National Coalition for the Homeless, recently acknowledged his role in developing that myth, but said he was just responding to the market demands of television news programs and congressional committees. Those reporting on homelessness, Hayes stated, always wanted "white, middle-class people to interview... someone who will be sympathetic to middle America"—and he had no choice but to oblige.[42]

The myths hurt generally and led to wasted effort among those who wished to help. Yes, there is a shortage of low-cost housing in some urban areas. Through urban renewal from the mid-1960s through the mid-1980s the U.S. lost half of its Single Room Occupancy (SRO) hotels.[43] Rent control kept new housing from being built and older housing from being properly maintained; the entire system became sticky, since people held on desperately to what they had.[44] Outmoded "safety" regulations (for example, requirements that copper rather than less-expensive but good PCV pipes be used) drove up costs and kept down construction of inexpensive housing.[45] But it still must be recognized, as Lawrence Schiff noted, that "many of the homeless are not homeless at all in the usual sense of the term"—homeless victim.[46] Many left their homes voluntarily because they did not want to be with their families or accept any obligations; others were thrown out temporarily because of drug abuse or violent behavior.

What is needed here is categorization and discernment, distinguishing those who are homeless because of lack of housing from those who are homeless because they lack the capacity to live in a home. In line with the myths, concerned individuals led by Donald Hendrix of Central City Concerns in Portland, Oregon, believed that homelessness generally was caused by lack of housing, so they worked hard to provide eight hundred SRO units and fill them with all who claimed a need for shelter—only to find that the "people coming into our buildings are people we can't house because of behavior problems." Crack use in particular, Hendrix noted, made these homeless individuals "aggressive and violent" whether they had homes or not. Hendrix's shock of recognition would have come as no surprise to Jacob Riis a century ago. At that time Riis described the plight of one owner of tenement buildings who

> undertook to fit his houses with stationary tubs, sanitary plumbing, wood closets, and all the latest improvements.... He felt that his tenants ought to be grateful for the interest he took in them. They were. They found the boards in the wood-closets fine kindling wood, while the pipes and faucets were as good as cash at the junk shop. In three months the owner had to remove what was left of his improvements. The pipes were cut and the houses running full of water.[47]

Riis was not arguing that nothing could be done, but he was pleading for discernment based on accurate knowledge of different groups among the homeless, rather than a blanket welcome that leads to frustration, recrimination, and Social Darwinism.

Similarly, we need to move from sentimentality to clear thinking about the problem of the mentally ill, who may constitute up to a third of the homeless.[48] All estimates of mental illness among the homeless need to be taken skeptically. Psychiatrist Schiff notes that the current Diagnostic and Statistical Manual of Mental Disorders (DSM-IIIR) lists alcohol and substance abuse as a mental disorder, as indeed they are,

but not necessarily in the psychiatric sense. Schiff points out that mental
health budgets depend on diagnosing patients as mentally ill, so that

> someone who is basically nasty or aggressive is no longer
> just nasty or aggressive, he's an Intermittent Explosive
> Disorder (DSM 312.34). Similarly, drug addicts have a way
> of becoming Dysthymic Disorders (DSM 300.40)... to
> let them be detoxified at general-hospital psychiatric
> units.... About the only diagnosis I've rarely seen em-
> ployed is No Pathology (DSM V71.09).[49]

Still, the "mentally ill" who are unable to help themselves are on the
streets because of the astoundingly sentimental deinstitutionalization
movement that swept through state mental hospitals during the
mixed-up days of the 1960s, when some had faith that the insane were
really sane and vice versa.[50] As college students read *One Flew Over
the Cuckoo's Nest* patient totals at state mental hospitals plummeted
from 550,000 to 110,000, and tens of thousands of the discharged
ended up on the streets, mumbling to themselves.[51]

The solution to this problem only seems difficult because of an
pervasive unwillingness to categorize. But it is clear to anyone who
walks the street that the insane homeless who are unable to help themselves desperately need asylum, both in the current meaning of that
word and in its original meaning of safety. Providing asylum fits well
within the American charitable tradition of caring unconditionally
for those unable (rather than merely unwilling) to help themselves. If
we find a little girl wandering the streets at midnight, few of us will
give her a chocolate chip cookie and feel that we have acted with

compassion. Why should we act differently to others who are also lost in the dark?

Basic categorization shows that the several hundred thousand homeless include, on one end, those who are mentally ill and cannot function by themselves, and on the other end, those abandoned women and children who are not yet within the welfare system, along with a few hard-luck men who would function perfectly well if they had better housing and a job offer.[52] The Mumbling Majority of the homeless, however, are men who are alone, who have been told that it is fine to be alone, and who have become used to receiving subsidy in their chosen life-style. Most of the homeless—three-fourths of all men in a Baltimore study conducted by clinicians from Johns Hopkins University—are substance abusers.[53] Many of the homeless alcoholics have families, but do not want to be with them. Those who have been married have often abandoned their wives and children. Many of the homeless have had jobs, but they just do not want to stick to them; some prefer the freedom of having odd jobs and being able to move around. In Schiff's psychiatric summary, "Almost all lack the sense of personal 'structuring' necessary to maintain steady employment."[54]

Sociologists have noted several significant changes in the composition of the homeless over the years, including a tendency toward youth (most of today's homeless are in their twenties or thirties) and minority status (most are black).[55] Sleeping in shelters or on the streets is dangerous, but for a person who has grown up amidst the bullets of drug wars and the knife thrusts of domestic and gang violence, the attraction of free food, medicine, clothes, and lots of leisure time may outweigh the disadvantages. As Dan McMurry notes, in any city some individuals are "barely hanging on"; the establishment of street services ends up "pulling the weakest loose from the fabric of the community onto the pavement. The stage is set for growth of the street persons to the limits imposed by the community. The greater the services, the larger the number."[56] Schiff's similar conclusion was, "The greater the monetary value of the benefits...the larger the number of people willing to consider homelessness as a viable option." Most of the homeless, of course, would prefer to have permanent residences that would include rooms with views, but they are "subsidized to not obtain the skills and make the sacrifices necessary to obtain such housing, when substandard accommodation is available free."[57]

Many Americans have not attained this insight because they rely on the mediated compassion offered by journalists who are philosophically committed to Social Universalism and professionally involved with the production of sentimentality. Accounts of those offering "help" to the homeless provide pleasant glows, but they end up harming the poor.[58] They lead good-hearted citizens to offer medicine more likely to harm than help. Those who want to help the homeless often work hard, sometimes as volunteers, to open new shelters, but

> shelters only make the drug problem among the homeless worse. Although shelters are supposed to be drug free, drug use is often open and widespread.... Many shelter residents actually have jobs, but they spend all their money on drugs....[59]

Addicts tend to use all available cash to feed their craving. Many addicts who could afford apartments prefer shelters with free room and board; such largesse allows them to avoid wasting money on low-priority items such as food. Of course, the choice after a while is no longer available: addiction not only puts people on the street but keeps them there. Most addicts do not want to go to work, and are physically unable to; they want to spend every dollar on drugs.

Are those who struggled to provide shelters, or paid taxes to support them, happy to be subsidizing addiction? Are they delighted to aid in the breakup of families, since shelter life makes it easier to avoid responsibility? Many New Yorkers contended that it was "compassionate" to allow individuals to stay in their largest railroad terminal, Penn Station, although one young man who slept there and was earning money explained that "if I had an address, my old lady would find me and make me pay alimony. I'm just 22, I don't have time for that s——."[60] Throughout the 1980s the typical stories of homelessness were rarely told; mediated compassion emphasized the sad but atypical instances of women and children with no place to go. But given that abandoned women and abandoning men are two sides of the same coin, one problem could worsen the other, and in time the fictions of homelessness could become the reality.

It does not have to be that way. One small church near Houston, Believers Fellowship, became concerned about homelessness in Texas early in the 1980s. The first decision church members made was the crucial one: they, like so many poverty-fighters before them, read the New Testament passage that included the apostle Paul's command to withhold support from anyone "who is idle and does not live according to...this rule: 'If a man will not work, he shall not eat.'" They took the injunction seriously and planned a campaign to allow the homeless to trade labor for food and lodging. Church members canvased neighborhood businesses for work projects. Members organized homeless men into work teams that cleared empty lots, swept sidewalks and parking lots, and performed other tasks that filled genuine needs of businesses. Members also set up an informal apprenticeship program so that people without skills could prepare for productive work.

The program worked well for two extrinsic and two intrinsic reasons. During the early 1980s Houston was the end of the road for some who had become newly unemployed through the closing of factories in old industrial cities of the North and Midwest. Few were alcoholics or addicts; many had good work habits and a desire to work. Furthermore, Houston social services were among the poorest in the country, which meant that many of the newcomers, instead of getting sucked into a welfare swamp, had little choice but to persevere in seeking work. The reasons for success intrinsic to the program included a willingness to refuse help to those unwilling to work, and a desire to go all out for those committed to hard work, which was easy. But church members did more; they applied a personal touch to those who needed to get their minds and hearts in shape.

The Believers Fellowship "work test" worked, largely with non-alcoholics. But a similar challenge worked with addicts and alcoholics in San Jose, California. There, CityTeam (formerly the San Jose City Mission) developed and managed throughout the 1980s a substance abuse program that had a success rate of over 75 percent.[61] The keys to success included one-on-one bonding of addicts with volunteers who were usually former addicts themselves, reaffiliation of addicts with family and community, a discerning refusal to accept excuses, and an emphasis on work and responsibility. The cornerstone of the new life, however, was spiritual; participants in the substance abuse program were expected to attend services regularly, read the Bible, and learn what God expected them to be. When county officials, impressed by City Team's success, proposed government funding to expand the program on the condition that the religious requirements be dropped, the offer had to be refused.

Again, a listing of particular programs could go on and on, but mention of one more might illuminate the current strengths and weaknesses of traditionally compassionate approaches. The Gospel Mission in inner city Washington, D.C., born over eighty years ago as part of the McAuley wave of missions, works on the homeless in the way Superintendent Lincoln Brooks, Jr., describes:

> We challenge them. We don't pat them on the back and say it's society's fault. They have to own up to their own faults. There's no free ride. If a guy's drunk and he comes to the back door, he can come in and go to sleep, but his bottle has to stay out. If he comes in and he's obnoxious, we have him walk around the block till he sobers up.[62]

Brooks offers, as the Gospel Mission's slogan,

> "use us but don't abuse us." We're long-suffering, but we'll keep confronting the alcoholic. Sometime we take a picture of a drunken guy passed out so he can see it when he wakes up. "Who's that on the sidewalk?" "That's you." We don't let people stay as they are. It's sickening to see a grown man go around bumming and begging. We have to put that pressure on.

The difficulty in applying the pressure, however, is that pressureless shelters are available only a few blocks away; again, bad compassion can drive out good. Brooks describes the choice of a person coming to the Gospel Mission:

Either he'll stop or (we hope not) he'll leave. Other places let him look at other things—Vietnam, Reaganomics, everything except the individual. They talk about the right to be homeless, people owing you a living. They want a Department of Homelessness.

But Brooks has concluded from his years of experience that "a program to be effective must be redemptive."

A Department of Homelessness *would be* the logical outcome of a century of Social Universalism, but new programs offering more material would be compassionate only as the "six-fingered" man in the movie, *The Princess Bride*, is compassionate. In that film a character named Inigo Montoya has chased for over twenty years a six-fingered man who killed his father. Finally he has the six-fingered man at swordpoint, and says in words he has long rehearsed: "My name is Inigo Montoya. You killed my father. Prepare to die." The vile murderer begins to plead for mercy. Inigo Montoya, says, "Offer me money." The six-fingered man says, "Yes." Montoya says, "Power, too, promise me that." "All I have and more." "Offer me everything I ask for." "Anything you want," the six-fingered man says. Inigo Montoya then runs him through with the sword, saying, "I want my father back, you son of a bitch."

Instead of offering money, we need to find ways to bring back the fathers.

CHAPTER THIRTEEN

Applying History

When the pilgrims came to the new world in 1620, they saw before them "a hideous and desolate wilderness," in the words of William Bradford, governor of the Plymouth colony.[1] Some Americans still read every Thanksgiving Bradford's description of the task he and his colleagues faced:

> For summer being done, all things stand upon them with a weatherbeaten face, and the whole country, full of woods and thickets, represented a wild and savage hue. If they looked behind them, there was the mighty ocean which they had passed and was now as a main bar and gulf to separate them from all the civil parts of the world.... What could now sustain them but the spirit of God and His grace?[2]

The Pilgrims, and other settlers in turn, could not spend much time looking back, or yearning for security; they had to set about turning the wilderness into neighborhood. They built churches and schools, town squares and bowling greens, barns and offices...and they spent most of their days at work and their nights at home amidst family life.

The pattern of neighborhood that pilgrims and pioneers created was interwoven with the understanding of compassion that they gained from reading their Bibles. Hebrew and Greek words commonly translated as "compassion" are used over eighty times in the Bible. Their most frequent use is not as an isolated noun, but as the culmination of a process. Repeatedly, in Judges and other books, the Bible shows that when the Israelites had sinned they were to repent and turn away from their sin. Only then, as a rule, would God show compassion. Second Chronicles 30:9 states the process precisely: "the Lord your God is gracious and compassionate. He will not turn his face from you if you return to him." Nehemiah 9:27 notes that "when they were oppressed they cried out to you. From heaven you heard them, and in your great compassion you gave them deliverers...."

American settlers often saw themselves as new Israelites entering a promised land; their analogy sometimes created problems, but at least they did not assume a promise that everything would always go well with them. They read angry biblical descriptions of Israel as "a people without understanding; so their Maker has no compassion on them...." They read in Jeremiah of God telling Israel, "You have rejected me...I can no longer show compassion." They saw compassion as mutual obligation, and they saw that rejection of God's love or man's neighborhood led back to wilderness.[3] Their understanding about marriage—it was not good for man to be alone—extended, in a looser sense, to their understanding of neighborhood: It was not good for man to be alone in a social wilderness. Through compassion they cut through vines and chopped down some of the trees. They used that wood to build good fences with swinging gates, and left some trees standing for shade and beauty.

Up until the past several decades, poor Americans as well as the better-off were privileged to live in neighborhoods, not wilderness. Even in poor sections of cities—except for those blocks taken over by "red light" and other vices—citizens did not need machetes to make their way along the streets. Only in modern times have the vines and wild forest growths reclaimed the ground of neighborhood. Although some leftist organizations still claim that governments must take the lead in rebuilding neighborhoods, the record of several decades shows that city wildernesses often were created by the very officials who claimed they were helping. Now, there is much wringing of hands, but a wide ocean separates many urban areas from the civilization left behind. Interestingly, those charged with assaulting the "Central Park jogger" acknowledged that on that occasion they were "wilding"— wilding, the natural sport of wilderness returned.

The eighteenth century in America was a time of journeying into the wilderness. Cotton Mather in 1710 said there was much to be done, and those who were idle must learn to help: "Don't nourish 'em and harden 'em in that, but find employment for them. Find 'em work; set 'em to work; keep 'em to work." Benjamin Colman in 1725 stressed the obligations of the better-off: "Christ seeks not yours but you.... Acts of Compassion and Mercy to our poor and needy Brethren [are] esteemed by the Lord of the Sabbath to be Holiness to himself." Individuals and churches cared for widows, orphans, and others who had suffered destitution by disaster or were unable to help themselves. Those who wanted to help knew how to do so effectively: they formed organizations to expand neighborhood and make sure that wilderness did not creep back.

The nineteenth century witnessed a vast war on wilderness. The increase of neighborhood came not everywhere, not at all times, and, woefully, not to a full extent for all races, but overall, the forward movement was remarkable. French observer Alexis de Tocqueville was amazed by how strong was the American "compassion for the sufferings of one another," and how—beginning with the establishment of the Female Humane Association for the aid of indigent Baltimore widows in 1798—women particularly were in the forefront of benevolent activity. Women founded and managed the Female Charitable Societies and Ladies Benevolent Societies that started up in the early 1800s in large Northern cities like New York and Philadelphia and in Southern cities such as Petersburg, Virginia, and Charleston, South Carolina.

These groups emphasized personal contact with the poor, even when some of their members were stunned by the firsthand experience. They refused to settle for the feed-and-forget principle or its equally depersonalizing but harsher opposite, the forget-and-don't-feed standard. They saw individuals made in the image of God, and when they saw someone acting disgracefully they responded, "You don't have to be that way. You're better than this. We expect more from you than an arm thrust out for food." Personal involvement became the hallmark of nineteenth-century compassion. A consistent line of understanding and action runs from Robert Hartley in the 1840s and Charles Brace of the orphan trains through the late nineteenth-century efforts of Humphreys Gurteen, Josephine Lowell, and other leaders of the Charity Organization Society movement. They wanted the rich to see without sentimentality. They wanted those with a pauper mentality to see the need to change and to know that they had neighbors willing to help. Their efforts were effective, as Jacob Riis and others pointed out.

But throughout the nineteenth century, the rock on which compassion stood was undergoing erosion. The chief erosion was theological:

the belief that sinful man, left to himself, would return to wilderness, seemed harshly pessimistic. Other erosion toward the end of the century was political and economic, as Social Darwinists and Social Universalists both assailed the idea that personal involvement could make a substantial difference. The erosion for a time did not seem crucial, but the long-term effect was severe enough to make the twentieth century not the Christian century, as celebrants in 1900 predicted, but the century of wilderness returning.

The return of wilderness is particularly striking because writings at the beginning of the century were so confident that it would be gone by its end. And yet, the essence of tragedy is overreaching. Books and articles at the beginning of this century were filled with an unwillingness to go on laboring patiently, one-by-one. The process of turning wilderness into neighborhoods seemed too slow. A changed view of the nature of God and the nature of man led to impatience. The older view saw God as both holy and loving; the new view tended to mention love only. The older anthropology saw man as sinful and likely to want something for nothing, if given the opportunity. The new view saw folks as naturally good and productive, unless they were in a competitive environment that warped finer sensibilities. In the new thinking, change came not through challenge, but through placement in a pleasant environment that would bring out a person's true, benevolent nature.

Such thinking packed a political pistol, for it soon became customary to argue that only the federal government had the potential power to create a socioeconomic environment that would save all, and that those who were truly compassionate should rally behind the creation of new programs. When a major economic crisis emerged in the early 1930s, it seemed not only natural but inevitable to rely on governmental programs run by professionals and to emphasize material transfer rather than individual challenge and spiritual concern. During the Depression, when millions of individuals were not responsible for their own plight, and jobs were not readily available, many governmental programs made moral sense (although some may have prolonged overall economic misery) as temporary expedients. But later, when programs were institutionalized at a time when jobs were available, the potential problem grew. Throughout the 1940s and 1950s governmental systems were like a guillotine poised to sever compassion from thought. Yet, as long as most families were intact and most people saw benefits not as rights but as backups only for use during dire emergencies, the blade did not fall.

The blade did fall, however, in the 1960s, when—under conditions of prosperity rather than duress—a cultural revolution led to attacks on any kind of categorization and investigation of welfare applicants.[4] The War on Poverty of the 1960s was a disaster not so much because of its new programs but because of their emphasis on entitlement rather than need. Opportunities to give aid with discretion disappeared as welfare hearings became legal circuses and depersonalization triumphed. Talk of affiliation and bonding was seen merely as an attempt to fight wars on poverty cheaply. And small efforts at categorization and discernment were seen as plots to blame the poor rather than the socioeconomic system that trapped them. "Freedom" came to mean governmental support rather than the opportunity to work and move up the employment ladder. A *Time* magazine cover asked whether God was dead: He certainly seemed to be, considering much of what went by the name of philanthropy.

In the new dispensation, Professor Richard Ely's compulsory philanthropy became standard, and those who complained about income transfer through taxation were thought to lack compassion. Telethons and jogathons became the most dramatic private charitable activities: stars would appear on television for twenty-four hours at a stretch, or long-distance runners would run at so much per mile, to raise money to pay professionals to help the needy. These were good-hearted activities, even if the horseshoes pitched were at best leaners rather than ringers. Government groups and many charities, in turn, tended to offer "velcro compassion"—the poor, like children unable to tie their own shoes, were treated to a continual supply of sneakers with velcro closers.[f]

And yet, with all this interest in helping the poor, were the poor really helped? A question Ronald Reagan asked during his 1980 election campaign that helped make him president was: "Are you better off now than you were four years ago?" If we were to borrow the time-travelling device from *Back to the Future* and transport a woman needing help from 1970, at the height of the new welfare consciousness, to 1890, in which year would she be better off? Twenty years ago, *Time* magazine reported that government "home-making" help was given to all who needed it, but certain rules had to be followed:

> A Brooklyn woman—in the late stages of pregnancy, injured and confined to bed—was left that way, without a "homemaker" to help her, until her toilet was repaired. Under the rules, no homemaker may stay where there is no functioning toilet.

Eighty years earlier, the poor could not legally demand the kindness of strangers. And yet, "slum angels" visiting apartments without toilets were "making gruel for the sick, washing dirty babies," and—according to magazine articles—doing this "gladly" because of "Jesus' love."[6]

Coming back to the present, the perspective from 1990 shows that the social revolution of the 1960s has not helped the poor. More women and children are abandoned and impoverished. The poor generally, and homeless individuals specifically, are treated like zoo animals at feeding time—some as carnivores who need cuts of meat thrown into their cages, and some as cute-looking pandas who feed on bamboo shoots. Using the same device, let's transport an able-to-work, homeless person from the present to 1890 and ask the question, "Are you better off now or then?" Then he would have been asked to take some responsibility for his own life, and to help others as well, by chopping wood or cleaning up trash. Then, he would have had to contact other people, whether relatives or former colleagues. Now, he is free to be a "naked nomad," shuffling from meal to meal.

And what of the children? Let's transport an abandoned child from the present to 1890 and compare treatment now—shuttling from foster home to foster home, or growing up in a home without a daddy—to treatment then, when adoption into two-parent families was a priority preached about in churches and facilitated by a lack of bureaucracy. Then, the New York Children's Aid Society alone found permanent homes for seventy thousand children, and Jacob Riis wrote, "The records show that the great mass, with this start given them, become useful citizens."[7] Then, Charles Brace worried about the moral tendencies among many children who grew up apart from parental direction and love:

> The faculties of the individual are mainly bent on securing support by other means than industry. Cunning, deception,

flattery, and waiting for chances become the means of livelihood. Self-respect is lost, and with it go the best qualities
of the soul.[8]

Now, although there are many exceptions, these vices are becoming
typical.

And let's time-travel with charitable individuals who want to be
effective in their work: Are they better off now or then? Demoralization
among the poor in 1990 is matched by "compassion fatigue" among
the better off, whether on the political Left or the Right. We've already
looked at the angst of culturally liberal columnists such as Ellen
Goodman, but evangelical Christians are also frustrated by the restrictions often placed on their actions. When one organization, Family
Ministries, brought twenty orphans out of Cambodia in 1975, it considered only members of evangelical churches as potential adoptive
parents. Family Ministries was challenged in court, on the grounds
that the agency could not discriminate on a religious basis because it
was licensed by the state; since the state must be neutral in religion,
any private agency it chartered should be neutral also. When Family
Ministries fought the case to the appeals court level the Los Angeles
County Department of Adoption finally allowed the organization to
proceed, but the cost of litigation forced the liquidation of the
ministry.

The legal direction in regard to such questions is now unclear. But
the rationale for putting up barriers to plans of private or church compassion can be traced to Social Universalism: anything that is not universal is antisocial. But since that all-or-nothing approach has often
produced nothing positive, surely it is time for a different idea. If the
Bible-based program of CityTeam in San Jose is far more successful in

getting people off drugs than the secularized county program, CityTeam should receive encouragement and perhaps even government grants, without antireligious strings attached. When Islamic or Jewish groups are effective, they too should be encouraged rather than restricted. Isn't it time, with rats running wild, that we adopt a policy of moral realism that prizes cats of any sort as long as they can catch rats? As matters stand, many government agencies and private charities are dispensing aid indiscriminately; in doing so they ignore the moral and spiritual needs of the poor and are unable to change lives. Isn't it time that we start managing by results, even if that means returning social services to those private and religious institutions that emphasize challenging compassion?[9]

There are two indications that moral realism in support of neighborhood-building may make a comeback. First, our eyes have seen the gory results of departure from that vision. Just as communism was a shining idol early in the century but is now proven wrong in history as well as in theory, so we have seen from the failure of the Great Society that there are no shortcuts in fighting poverty. There are no effective alternatives to investigating the claims of applicants, to requiring work, to demanding that fathers provide for their children. There is no good substitute for personal contact. Textbooks may still teach students about "the incompatibility of policies that simultaneously preach compassion and stress deterrence," but it has been proven again and again that programs are truly compassionate only when deterrence is stressed.[10]

The second bit of good news is that if we absorb the lessons of the past, we know the right questions to ask. Professor Robert Thompson put it concisely in 1891: "You can judge the scale on which any scheme of help for the needy stands by this single quality, Does it make great demands on men to give themselves to their brethren?" In 1990, let us ask: Does government program X increase affiliation and bonding or decrease them? Does charity practice Y make it more or less likely that recipients will get jobs? Is church program Z based on categorization and discernment, or does it pat itself on the back for promiscuous material distribution? An emphasis on neighborhood runs against the atomistic individualism of our age, but the able-bodied poor should not expect to gain a form of "independence" by becoming dependent on government or learning to howl for food-wagon suppers in the wilderness.

Let's be specific. Today, when confronted with a needy individual, do we find out "who is bound to help in this case," or do we immediately proffer aid? Studies show that many homeless alcoholics have families, but they just do not want to be with them. Those who have been married have often abandoned their wives and children. Many of the homeless have had jobs, but they just do not want to stick to them. When we hand out food and clothing indiscriminately, aren't we subsidizing disaffiliation? Other questions: Do government and private programs increase the likelihood that a pregnant, unmarried teenager will be reunited with those on whom she actually is dependent, whether she wishes to admit it or not—parents, the child's father—or do they offer a mirage of independence? Do programs encourage single-parenting? Do fathers now effectively have the choice of providing or not providing?

On the question of bonding, let's look particularly at what many religious institutions do. Are boards of deacons often mere distributors of a "deacon's fund" of cash donations and cans of food, or do they act as a switchboard to connect better-off congregation members with the needy? Let's remember the century-old wisdom of Nathaniel

Rosenau of the United Hebrew Charities: "If every person possessing the capability should assume the care of a single family, there would not be enough poor to go around."[11] Individuals and families all have different callings—some may adopt hard-to-place children, others may give refuge to abandoned pregnant women, and so on—but everyone can do something. Do churches and synagogues convey through both words and programs the biblical messages of personal involvement and mutual obligation?

Are there ways that governmental programs can encourage bonding? Cash contributions are tax deductible, but what about offering a room to a homeless person or to a pregnant and abandoned woman? Going back to the seventeenth century, town councils sometimes covered the out-of-pocket expenses of those who took in the destitute, and a tax deduction of this kind—carefully fenced, designed not to create a new victim class, with precautions against fraud—could be useful. Or perhaps it would not—troublesome consequences could arise—but this is the type of question that should be asked. Similarly, when farmers took in older orphans they provided care but also received work, and there was nothing wrong in that economic tradeoff. The economy today does not allow the same agricultural incentives, but tax deductions for all adoptions similar to those for the medical expenses of birth, and significant tax credits for the costs of adopting hard-to-place children, could be another way to lower economic barriers to bonding. Government action can be only a secondary affecter of attitudes, of course, but if political leaders want to do something useful, they may consider such ideas.

We could also use some of the categorizing sensibility of a century ago. One *Charities Review* article described the "floating population of all large modern cities" as including some "strangers seeking work" and needing temporary help, but a larger number of "victims of intemperance and vice."[12] That's not all that different from today, with studies showing a majority of the homeless in major cities suffering from alcohol or drug abuse. What we have often forgotten in our rush to help "the homeless" generally is the Baltimore Charity Organization Society's warning that the worst kind of "wastefulness" was that which "squanders brotherly love in the doing of useless or mischievous work."[13] Don't we need to stop talking about "the homeless" in abstraction and start distinguishing between those who need a hand (such as the mentally ill and abandoned women with small children) and those who desperately need a push? Shouldn't we say, with Jacob Riis a century ago, that the bad alternatives of the latter must be closed off?

"We must reform those mild, well-meaning, tender-hearted, sweet-voiced criminals who insist upon indulging in indiscriminate charity," a *Charities Review* author wrote in 1893.[14] If the indiscriminate were to have their way, *Charities Review* feared, the desirous would simply see a pool of available money "of which they may as well get their share"; that problem "does not yet threaten our municipal existence, but the time will come when it will...."[15] One hundred years later, that time has come. Alcoholics and addicts feel they are entitled to food and shelter, and their sweet-voiced "helpers" do not see that refusal would be the first step toward true compassion. In Washington, when Jack M. White

> started a residence two years ago to help homeless men find jobs and apartments, he began by simply asking the men not to use drugs or abuse alcohol. Only five percent made it through the four-month programs. He then decided to institute random urine tests for the residents and staff and to evict anyone using drugs. His success rate is now 75 percent.[16]

But even that step was controversial among those who contend that anything short of unlimited tolerance is injustice to the oppressed.

In the absence of categorization, not only do many of the poor continue to wallow, but frustration among the better-off grows. Actions by fed-up citizens from coast to coast are beginning to speak louder than the rhetoric of feed-lot compassion. "Sympathy Wanes for Homeless," the *Washington Post* noted.[17] "Homeless face growing hostility," the *San Francisco Chronicle* reported at the top of its front page: "Compassion is rapidly turning to disgust and anger, even their advocates agree."[18] Panhandlers are being rousted not only in Atlanta but in Berkeley, California.[19] Anita Beatty, director of the Georgia task force on the homeless, complained that Atlanta police were pushing "the homeless" away from the city's big convention hotels because "this city is built on an advertising image.... It depends on visuals. Visuals don't work with the guys you stumble over in the park."[20] The story of media fascination with homelessness may be a tale of live by the image, die by the image.[21] One frustrated "advocate for the homeless" in Georgia blamed the public: "I don't think the American people like problems that stare them in the face."[22] She did not understand that the real dislike was aimed at people who spit in other people's faces.

Under these circumstances, work test requirements for the able-bodied at shelters, if alternative handouts were not available, would have the same effect as those of a century ago. First, only the truly needy would come. Second, they would sort themselves out. Third, most would learn to help themselves and others, not by chopping wood these days, but by cleaning up streets and parks or working at other tasks. For example, thousands of crack babies, born addicted to cocaine and often deserted by their mothers who care only for the next high, languish in hospitals under bright lights and with almost no human contact. Some volunteers hold the trembling, sometimes

twitching babies, and that is wonderful, but why shouldn't the homeless women and men who are healthy and gentle be assigned to hold
a baby for an hour in exchange for a meal?

As providers of false comfort were confronted and defunded, programs that stressed employment, sometimes in creative ways, could
receive new emphasis. For example, more of the able-bodied might
receive not housing but the opportunity to work for a home. One head-
line from 1990, "Out of the Ashes: A South Bronx Street Rises Through
the Toil of Poor Homesteaders," told of a self-imposed work test:

> Poor people in need of decent housing, they banded to-
> gether in 1977 and stopped the city from demolishing three
> empty tenements in the 900 block of Kelly Street. After
> working all day driving taxis or operating machines, they
> worked an additional eight hours in shoulder high debris,
> restoring the abandoned shells that landlords had left to rot
> and burn. The apartments finally sold for $250 to those who
> had invested at least 600 hours of labor. Out of those first
> three buildings grew housing for 21 families....
>
> For Mr. Madrigal and others like him, "sweat equity"
> arrangements, in which labor constitutes most of the down
> payment, have provided an otherwise unobtainable ticket
> to home ownership and, in many respects, to the middle
> class. Mr. Madrigal now proudly houses his family in a
> spacious five-bedroom, two-bath apartment he spent
> 2,800 hours renovating. "We are poor," he says, "but we
> have something that is ours. When you use your own blood,
> sweat and tears, it's part of your soul. You stand and say, "I
> did it."[23]

Many who start, of course, drop out with complaints that too much sweat is required. They find champions who would prefer to see a Department of Housing and Animal Development passing out free cages.

At stake here are not only successful efforts but the freedom to work. In 1984 Washington resident Ego Brown decided to be "a pioneer shoeshine vendor" on the downtown streets. Brown, wanting to show "class and charisma," wore a tuxedo, black felt hat, argyle socks, and spit-shined oxblood loafers. He recruited fifty to sixty teenagers and homeless people who desired to work. He provided each with training, a shower, a shoeshine kit, and a stand. Brown explained, "Not only was I pulling myself up by the bootstraps, I was helping others pull themselves up by the bootstraps."[24] The others paid him part of their earnings for the day, and Brown, with that income and his own shoeshine work, typically made $100 to $150 a day. But in the summer of 1985 the city closed down his operation because of a law prohibiting bootblacks from using public space, even though virtually every other type of vendor had access.[25]

That law was a remnant from the Jim Crow era, when Southern cities tried to thwart black enterprise. After four years of skirmishing by the Center for Civil Rights of the Landmark Legal Foundation, Brown won the right to work—but why should it have taken four years? Why shouldn't husbands and wives be able to work at home, teach their children at home, or adopt needy children from any race, without having to leap over numerous walls and even some tall buildings? Officials of the Georgia Department of Human Resources removed nine girls from the Ruth Home of Compassion (organized by the Faith Baptist Church of Thomaston, Georgia) because it did not have a state license for group-care homes. The officials were unable to cite any health or safety hazard on the premises, or find any indication that the children were neglected or abused; the children were defined as "deprived" merely because the home did not have a license. There is nothing wrong with *reasonable* health, building code, and fire protection requirements, but many state regulations, in an attempt to mandate universalistic uniformity, have gone far beyond reason.[26]

An emphasis on freedom also should include a willingness to step away for a time and let those who have dug their own hole "suffer the consequences of their misconduct."[27] The early Calvinists knew that time spent in the pit could be what was needed to save a life from permanent debauch (and a soul from hell). C. S. Lewis wrote of the illogic that seizes many modern minds as we remove the organ and demand the function.[28] We laugh at honor, and are then amazed to find traitors among us. We castrate, then bid the geldings to be fruitful. Similarly, when the poor are left with neither incentive nor penalty, we are surprised to find them immobile. When many children grow up without knowing a father either on earth or in heaven, we are surprised to find them wilding in the social wilderness.

Who pushes for change once wilderness is spreading? If the goal is to supply material, neither government nor recipient is likely to demand change. Universalizing depersonalizers are popular among those of the poor who do not want anyone to challenge them. The welfare system prospers in the same way that grade inflation and declining academic standards come about. Many college students find it easier to sit in large halls listening to joke-filled and content-less lectures, than to learn through the pressure of personal interchange. Few students complain, particularly if they get on the honor roll without studying up a sweat. Many professors find impersonality less cumbersome.

Who will fight such an arrangement? Only those who live by a different ethic and are unwilling to see it die.

And so we come back to the practical applications of theology. It seems that our ideas about poverty always reflect our ideas about the nature of man, which in turn are tied to ideas about the nature of God. New ways of fostering affiliation, bonding, categorizing, discernment, employment, and freedom are important—but in the end, not much will be accomplished without a spiritual revival that transforms the everyday advice people give and receive, and the way we lead our lives. Two stories, one from a Christian source, one from a Jewish source, may illustrate this point.

The Christian story was told by John Timmer, a minister in Michigan who was a child in Holland half a century ago. His parents at that time hid Jews from the Nazis. In 1990 he asked, "Why did my parents do it? Why did they risk their own lives and possibly those of their six children? What madness possessed them to take such risks?"[29] Timmer wrote, "The only reason I remember my father giving was this: 'As God shows compassion to us, so we must show compassion to others.'" Timmer added, "These are words in which rescuers make themselves the equal of the rescued because both are equally dependent on the compassion of God."[30] That realization suffused American charity a century ago. Without it, the will to put up with all the problems of dealing with poverty, and the will to maintain moral realism, disappear.

The Jewish story was told by a concentration camp survivor, Joseph Horn. He discussed his reactions when a black teenager stole several hundred dollars from him and was later arrested. Horn thought back to 1945 and how, shortly after deliverance from camp, he stole a German bicycle and was arrested by English military police.

When a Jewish chaplain came to visit, Horn told him the theft was justified: the Germans had killed the other members of his family and taken his possessions. "And then I asked, why am I not entitled to this miserable bike?"[31]

The answer, evidently, was that we are made in God's image and should not smear that reflection by stealing or acting in disgraceful ways. Horn noted that the teenager who stole his money in 1990 "may have been convinced, just as I was, that he was simply taking back what his peers tell him was justifiably his, if it had been properly distributed in the first place." Every time we tell someone he is a victim, every time we say he deserves a special break today, every time we hand out charity to someone capable of working, we are hurting rather than helping. Horn's column concluded, "My question is this: Will this young man meet a real chaplain who will help him, the way I was helped?"[32]

When I walked around Washington as a homeless person, I met people who felt they were doing good, but no real chaplains. No one ever pointed me in the right direction, even when I hinted where I wanted to go, toward some spiritual help. And yet, only full-orbed counseling will revive compassion. The task will not be easy, particularly after a century of demoralization. Anyone who talks about *suffering with* is likely to be attacked not only by liberals committed to the present culture of delegated compassion, but by those conservatives who want to ignore problems. Few on the Left will admit, as Clifford Orwin pointed out a decade ago, that "compassion resembles love: to demand it is a good way to kill it."[33] And even some on the Right will not agree with Robert Thompson's comment on state-run charity a century ago:

> The sooner it goes out of business the better. Its almshouse and workhouses and poor-houses are nothing but a rough

contrivance to lift from the social conscience a burden that
should not be either lifted or lightened in that way.[34]

Certainly, our political leaders can break down some programmatic
barriers to compassion, but isn't it time we realized that there is only
so much that public policy can do? Certainly it's good to "empower"
the poor so they are not in thrall to the welfare establishment, but isn't
it time to realize that only a richness of spirit can battle a poverty of
soul?

Most of us have grown up with personal peace and affluence, to use
theologian Francis Schaeffer's phrase, as the great goal. We like the way a
welfare system, corrupt and inefficient though it is, removes the burden
of basic material care from our consciences, and protects us from the
mean streets that we traverse only by day. We react to any prospect of
removing the wall of pseudo-compassion in the same anxious way some
reacted to changes in Central Europe: agreed, the unbreached Berlin Wall
was an atrocity, but it symbolized for four decades a certain sad stability.
We had become accustomed to its face, as we have become accustomed
to the welfare system.[35] Nevertheless, we need to realize that we do not
increase compassion by expanding it to cover everything. Instead, we kill
a good word by making it mean too much, and nothing.

Change in poverty-fighting is needed, but Americans need to be
clear about the reasons for change. Governmental welfare programs
need to be fought not because they are too expensive—although,
clearly, much money is wasted—but because they are inevitably too
stingy in what is really important, treating people as people and not
animals. At the same time, the crisis of the modern welfare state is not
just a crisis of government. Too many private charities dispense aid
indiscriminately and thus provide, instead of points of light, alternative

shades of darkness. The century-old question—Does any given "scheme of help…make great demands on men to give themselves to their brethren?"—is still the right one to ask.

Each of us needs to ask that question not in the abstract, but personally. We need to ask ourselves: Are we offering not coerced silver, but our lives? If we talk of crisis pregnancies, are we actually willing to provide a home to a pregnant young woman? If we talk of abandoned children, are we actually willing to adopt a child? Most of our twentieth-century schemes, based on having someone else take action, are proven failures. It's time to learn from the warm hearts and hard heads of earlier times, and to bring that understanding into our own lives.

NOTES

Introduction

1. Steven Burger quoted in *Moody*, May 1990, p. 19.
2. Ellen Goodman, "Compassion Fatigue," *Washington Post*, February 3, 1990, p. A25.
3. *Washington Post*, December 16, 1989, p. A31.
4. James S. Fishkin, *The Limits of Obligation* (New Haven: Yale University Press, 1982), p. 171.

Chapter One

1. *Detroit News*, May 6, 1982, clip in Hogg Foundation Library, Austin, TX.
2. William Shakespeare, *Love's Labours Lost*, Act V, Scene 2.
3. William Bradford, *Of Plimoth Plantation*, many editions (here, Boston: Wright & Potter, 1898), p. 111.
4. Included in Ralph and Muriel Pumphrey, eds., *The Heritage of American Social Work* (New York: Columbia University Press, 1961), p. 22.
5. Quoted in Eleanor Parkhurst, "Poor Relief in a Massachusetts Village in the Eighteenth Century," *The Social Service Review* XI (September 1937), p. 452.
6. Ibid., pp. 454–456. In emergency situations involving large demands individual families would help out, but they would receive town reimbursement and the town, in turn, might even be aided by the province or state. When French authorities expelled Acadians from Nova Scotia during the French and Indian Wars, many came to Massachusetts and lived in private homes, but the families that were willing to feed and house the needy had their expenses covered.
7. Pumphrey, p. 29.
8. Harry S. Stout, *The New England Soul: Preaching and Religious Culture in Colonial New England* (New York: Oxford University Press, 1986), p. 3.
9. Benjamin Colman, *The Merchandise of a People: Holiness to the Lord* (Boston: J. Draper, 1736), from sermons preached in 1725 and 1726.
10. Stout noted, "Twice on Sunday and often once during the week, every minister in New England delivered sermons lasting between one and two

hours in length. Collectively over the entire span of the colonial period, sermons totalled over five million separate messages in a society whose population never exceeded one-half million.... The average weekly churchgoer in New England (and there were far more churchgoers than church members) listened to something like seven thousand sermons in a lifetime, totaling somewhere around fifteen thousand hours of concentrated listening." (pp. 3–4)

11. The Earl of Shaftesbury quoted by Gertrude Himmelfarb in *The Idea of Poverty: England in the Early Industrial Age* (New York: Knopf, 1984), p. 37.

12. Quoted in Himmelfarb, p. 32.

13. Benjamin Colman, *The Merchandise of a People: Holiness to the Lord* (Boston: J. Draper, 1736), from sermons preached in 1725 and 1726.

14. Citations of Hosea 12:8, Amos 8:5, Mic: 2:1–3, Jer 22:13–17, Ezek. 22:29, and other verses indicate concern over injustice; frequent citing of Proverbs (such as Prov. 6:6–11, 10:15, 11:24–26, 13:4, 18:11, 19:15, 20:13, 21:25, 24:30–34, 28:19, and 30:24–28) shows animus toward sloth.

15. It was believed that the worst situation for a person was not poverty but exclusion from God's presence (which might also lead to material impoverishment, as it did for Adam and Eve).

16. Ibid., p. 33.

17. Robert H. Bremner, *American Philanthropy* (Chicago: University of Chicago Press, 1960), p. 14.

18. Ibid.

19. Cotton Mather, *Bonifacius: Essays to Do Good* (Boston: J. Draper, 1710).

20. Charles Chauncey, *The Idle-Poor secluded from the Bread of Charity by the Christian Law. A Sermon Preached in Boston, before the Society for encouraging Industry and employing the Poor*, August 12, 1752 (Boston: Thomas Fleet, 1752), pp. 16–17.

21. Ibid.

22. Ibid. Quoted in Eleanor Parkhurst, "Poor Relief in a Massachusetts Village in the Eighteenth Century," *The Social Service Review*, vol. XI (September 1957), pp. 462–463.

23. Thomas Bacon, *A Sermon Preached at the Parish Church of St. Peter's, in Talbot County, Maryland: On Sunday the 14th of October, 1750. For the Benefit of a Charity Working School...for the Maintenance and Education of Orphans and Other Poor Children, and Negroes....* London, 1751), quoted in Dann, p. 129.

24. See John Christie Dann, *Humanitarian Reform and Organized Benevolence in the Southern United States, 1780–1830*, Ph.D. dissertation, The College of William and Mary, 1975, pp. 77–78.

25. Salmon P. Chase, ed., *The Statutes of Ohio and the Northwestern Territory* (Cincinnati: Corey & Fairbanks, 1833), vol. I, p. 176.

26. Ibid., I, p. 182.
27. David M. Schneider, *The History of Public Welfare in New York State, 1609–1866* (Montclair, N.J.: Patterson Smith, 1969), p. 188.
28. Ibid., p. 189.
29. Quoted in Keith Melder, "Ladies Bountiful: Organized Women's Benevolence in Early 19th-Century America," *New York History* XVIII (July, 1967), p. 238.
30. Quoted in Suzanne Lebsock, *The Free Women of Petersburg* (New York: Norton, 1984), p. 202. The typical pattern for involvement began when one woman helped another, and the latter then was inspired to go on and help others. For example, one Sarah Freeland compassionately cared for a Mary Cumming and her husband William in the fall of 1812 when both were helpless with fever; Mary soon wrote, "I do not know what I should have done during my illness if it had not been for Mrs. Freeland. I never experienced so much kindness and attention from any stranger." Soon Mary Cumming was a mainstay, along with Sarah Freeland, of the Petersburg orphanage. (Lebsock, pp. 209–210)
31. In upstate New York, for example, the society set up homes in Poughkeepsie in 1847, Rochester in 1849, and Albany in 1852.
32. The emphasis on spirit and material was evident in organizational formation from colonial days; in 1773 a group of New Yorkers formed an American Society for Promoting Religious Knowledge Among the Poor.
33. Dann, p. 145.
34. *Southern Evangelical Intelligencer*, vol. 2 (1820–1821), pp. 244–247.
35. Ibid., vol. 1 (1819–1820), p. 215.
36. Lebsock, pp. 217–218. Petersburg men also supported a few widows and orphans through the Petersburg Benevolent Mechanic Association, an organization of artisans and manufacturers founded in 1825 to take care of those left in economic distress through tragedy. In the 1840s and 1850s the organization is recorded as making regular cash payments to six widows.
37. Schneider, p. 191.
38. Homer Folks, *The Care of Destitute, Neglected, and Delinquent Children* (New York: The Charities Review, 1900), pp. 34–36.
39. Dann, p. 145.
40. *The Charities of New York, Brooklyn and Staten Island* (New York: Hurd and Houghton, 1873), p. 46.
41. Ibid., p. 48.
42. See John Griscom (committee chairman), *The First Annual Report of the Managers of the Society for the Prevention of Pauperism in the City of New York* (New York: J. Seymour, 1818), pp. 12–22.
43. Ibid.

44. Association of Delegates from the Benevolent Societies of Boston, *First Annual Report* (Boston: I.R. Butts, 1835), pp. 7–44.
45. Ibid.
46. See, for example, Freeman Hunt, *Lives of American Merchants* (New York: Hunt's Merchants' Magazine, 1856), vol. 1, p. 276.
47. Ibid.
48. Benevolent Societies of Boston, *Annual Report*, vol. 1 (1835), p. 17.
49. Association of Delegates from the Benevolent Societies of Boston, *First Annual Report* (Boston: I.R. Butts, 1835), pp. 7–44.
50. Dorothy G. Becker, "Exit Lady Bountiful: The Volunteer and the Professional Social Worker," *Social Service Review* 38 (March 1964), p. 58. Becker herself notes the superficiality of the condemnatory views.
51. Kathleen D. McCarthy, *Noblesse Oblige: Charity and Cultural Philanthropy in Chicago, 1849–1929* (Chicago: University of Chicago Press, 1982), p. 11.
52. Benjamin Klebaner, "Poverty and its Relief in American Thought, 1815–1861," *Social Science Review* 38:4 (December 1964), p. 385.
53. Ibid.
54. Francis G. Peabody, "The Modern Charity Worker," included in the 22nd Annual Report of the United Hebrew Charities of the City of New York, p. 49.
55. D. Griffiths, Jr., *Two Years' Residence in the New Settlements of Ohio, North America: with Direction to Emigrants* (London: Westley and Davis, 1835), p. 37.
56. Ibid., pp. 76–77.
57. Alexis de Tocqueville, *Democracy in America*, book 3, chapter 1, available in many editions; in the 1945 Vintage edition (New York), II, 176. Caring did have its limits, Tocqueville noted sardonically: Americans, he wrote, "are happy to relieve the griefs of others when they can do so without much hurting themselves...."
58. Ibid., II, p. 185 (book 3, chapter 4).
59. Society for the Prevention of Pauperism, *Annual Report*, 1858, p. 6. The essayist, in describing the first half of the century from the vantage point of 1858, noted that "The poor were personally subjects of knowledge and cognizance to the more favored classes. Every man was known by his neighbor." In New York by the eve of the Civil War, that situation was changing.
60. Klebaner, p. 387.
61. Mona Charen, "Charities, ideology, and. . .," *Washington Times*, January 5, 1990, p. F4.

62. Thomas S. Grimke, *An Address on the Character and Objects of Science…
Delivered in the First Presbyterian Church* (Charleston: Literary and
Philosophical Society, 1827), p. 54.

Chapter Two

1. Chalmers also argued that "relief of the poor from public funds resulted in
taking money from the thrifty and giving it to the thriftless." He predicted
that the small grants that the poor fund could provide would disappoint
many and lead to jealousy and envy.
2. Thomas Chalmers, *The Sufficiency of the Parochial System Without a Poor
Rate* (Glasgow: W. Collins, 1841).
3. Ibid. In those days of differential education, his church members also
pledged to teach every boy to read and every girl to sew.
4. D.O. Kellogg, "The Pauper Question," *Reports and Papers* 17 (July 1883) of
the New York Charity Organization Society, p. 16.
5. Rev. Robert E. Thompson, *Manual for Visitors Among the Poor* (Philadelphia:
Lippincott, 1879), p. 245.
6. Quoted in Frank Dekker Watson, *The Charity Organization Movement in
the United States* (New York: Macmillan, 1922), p. 36. The Chalmers plan
continued in effect through 1837, but resentment developed as those in the
parish were asked to contribute for their own area and were also taxed for
the maintenance of public outdoor relief elsewhere.
7. Society for the Prevention of Pauperism in the City of New York, *First
Annual Report* (New York: Society…, 1818).
8. Watson, p. 79.
9. See New York Association of Improving the Condition of the Poor
(NYAICP), *Third Annual Report* (New York: NYAICP, 1847).
10. Included in Ralph and Muriel Pumphrey, eds., *The Heritage of American
Social Work* (New York: Columbia University Press, 1961), pp. 110–111.
11. Ibid.
12. Walter I. Trattner, *From Poor Law to Welfare State: A History of Social
Welfare in America* (New York: Free Press, 1974).
13. Quoted in Watson, p. 80.
14. *The Economist* (New York: NYAICP, 1847), p. 12.
15. Watson, p. 84.
16. Ibid., p. 85.
17. NYAICP, *Third Annual Report*, pp. 12–13.
18. II Thessalonians 3:11–12 (New International Version).
19. *Directory to the Charities of New York* (New York: The Bureau of Charities,
1874), p. 8.

20. Nathan I. Huggins, *Protestants Against Poverty: Boston's Charities, 1870–1900* (Westport, Conn.: Greenwood, 1971), p. 27.

21. Ibid., p. 16.

22. Ibid., p. 48.

23. NYAICP, *Twelfth Annual Report*, p. 14.

24. NYAICP, *Eleventh Annual Report* (New York: John F. Trow, 1854), p. 39.

25. Michael B. Katz, *In the Shadow of the Poorhouse: A Social History of Welfare in America* (New York: Basic Books, 1986), p. 59.

26. NYAICP, *Eleventh Annual Report* (New York: John F. Trow, 1854), p. 39.

27. Suzanne Lebsock, *The Free Women of Petersburg* (New York: Norton, 1984), p. 215.

28. The secret, perhaps, was not a hidden monetary fund, but a spiritual bank that included a verse which Americans liked to apply to themselves and others: "Do not make light of the Lord's discipline, and do not lose heart when he rebukes you, because the Lord disciplines those he loves, and he punishes everyone he accepts as a son." (Hebrews 12:5, 6, after Proverbs 3:11, 12)

29. William Ruffner, *Charity and The Clergy* (Philadelphia: Lippincott, 1853), pp. 142–143.

30. Ibid., pp. 144–146.

31. NYAICP, *First Annual Report* (New York: AICP, 1845), p. 26.

32. Ibid.

33. Charles Loring Brace, *The Dangerous Classes of New York and Twenty Years' Work Among Them* (New York: Wynkoop & Hallenbeck, 1880), pp. 93–94 (third edition; first edition published in 1872).

34. Ibid., pp. 56–57.

35. Ibid., p. 58.

36. Ibid., p. 60.

37. Ibid., p. 60.

38. Ibid., pp. 22–23.

39. Ibid., p. 80.

40. Ibid., p. 82.

41. Ibid., p. 393.

42. Ibid., pp. 224, 236.

43. Ibid., p. 82.

44. Ibid., p. 396. Concerning children who were working as newspaper boys or messengers, Brace wrote, "Our Lodging-housekeepers soon learn that the best humanity towards the boys is 'to take, not give.' Each lad pays for his lodging, and then feels independent; if he is too poor to do this, he is taken in 'on trust,' and pays his bill when business is successful. He is not clothed at once, unless under some peculiar and unfortunate circumstances, but is

induced to save some pennies every day until he have enough to buy his own clothing" (p. 394).

45. Miriam Z. Langsam, *Children West: A History of the Placing-Out System of the New York Children's Aid Society, 1853–1900* (Madison: State Historical Society of Wisconsin, 1964), pp. 17, 70.

46. Quoted in Langsam, p. 18.

47. Brace, pp. 226–227.

48. "First Circular of the Children's Aid Society," in Edith Abbott, ed., *Some American Pioneers in Social Welfare* (Chicago: University of Chicago Press, 1937), pp. 132–134.

49. Brace, p. 227.

50. Ibid., pp. 228–229.

51. Ibid., pp. 231–232. Brace added, "In every American community, especially in a Western one, there are many spare places at the table of life.... They have enough for themselves and the stranger too."

52. Ibid., p. 233.

53. See Henry W. Thurston, *The Dependent Child* (New York: Columbia University Press, 1930), pp. 123–125.

54. Letter from C. R. Fry, reprinted in Brace, p. 256.

55. Quoted in Brace, p. 261.

56. Ibid.

57. Ibid., pp. 230–231.

58. Ibid., p. 282.

59. See Kathleen D. McCarthy, *Noblesse Oblige. Charity & Cultural Philanthropy in Chicago, 1849–1929* (Chicago: U. of Chicago Press, 1982), p. 9. Farmers who received children in this fashion were expected to pay part of the COA's expenses by donating fresh produce or other products.

60. Brace, p. 240.

61. Ibid., p. 240; Langsam, pp. 56–62; Schneider and Deutsch, p. 76. One report of neglect reads, "We visited the lad, and discovered that he had not been schooled as he should, and had sometimes been left alone at night in the lonely log-house. Yet this had roused the feelings of the whole countryside; we removed the boy, amid the tears and protestations of the 'father' and 'mother,' and put him in another place."

62. See Hastings H. Hart, "Placing Out Children in the West," *Proceedings of the National Conference of Charities and Correction* (Boston: George H. Ellis, 1885), pp. 144–145.

63. When the match did not work out and a change was requested by either party or ordered by an agent, the Society paid children's expenses back to New York or to another home.

64. Langsam, p. 24.
65. Today such practice raises eyebrows. McCarthy archly notes at the end of one paragraph of description, "Only the child netted dubious gains." But that is the late twentieth-century view; then, work was seen as an important part of education, and the life in a family was seen as immensely superior to life in an institution.
66. John O'Grady, *Catholic Charities in the United States* (Washington: National Conference of Catholic Charities, 1930), p. 99.
67. Brace, p. 239.
68. Ibid., p. 238. Brace himself acknowledged that those over fourteen might already have become so hardened that additional precautions were needed, but he was reluctant to impose formal restrictions.
69. Quoted in Brace, p. 269.
70. See Langsam, pp. 56–62.
71. Ibid.
72. Brace, p. 243.
73. Ibid.
74. Langsam, p. 25. Even critics acknowledged that it cost only a tenth as much to send a child West as it did to place and keep him in a jail or asylum, where he was likely to receive an education in how to commit more serious crimes.
75. Brace, p. 282.

Chapter Three

1. Robert L. Rose, "For Welfare Parents, Scrimping Is Legal, But Saving Is Out," *The Wall Street Journal*, February 7, 1990, pp. A1, A11.
2. Ibid., p. A1.
3. Ibid., p. A11.
4. Franklin quoted in Philip Klein, *From Philanthropy to Social Welfare* (San Francisco: Jossey-Bass, 1968), p. 282.
5. Walter Trattner, *From Poor Law to Welfare State: A History of Social Welfare in America*, third edition (New York: Free Press, 1984), p. 53.
6. Thomas Cooper, *A Manual of Political Economy* (Washington, D.C., 1834), p. 95.
7. Delaware House of Representatives, *Journal*, 1824, p. 15.
8. *American Quarterly Review* 14 (1835), p. 78.
9. Ibid., p. 68.
10. Nathan I. Huggins, *Protestants Against Poverty: Boston's Charities, 1870–1900* (Westport, Conn.: Greenwood, 1971), p. 25.
11. Ibid.
12. Josiah Quincy, chairman, Committee on Pauper Laws of the General Court, *Report of the Committee to Whom was Referred the Consideration of the*

Pauper Laws of this Commonwealth (1821), reprinted in *The Almshouse Experience* (New York: Arno, 1971), p. 4.

13. Ibid.
14. Ibid.
15. Ibid., p. 9; Quincy concluded "that of all modes of providing for the poor, the most wasteful, the most expensive, and most injurious to their morals and destructive to their industrious habits is that of supply in their own families."
16. *Report of the Committee Appointed by the Board of Guardians of the Poor of the City and Districts of Philadelphia*... (Philadelphia: Samuel Parker, 1827), p. 24.
17. Michael B. Katz, *In the Shadow of the Poorhouse: A Social History of Welfare in America* (New York: Basic Books, 1986), pp. 17–18.
18. *Report of the Secretary of State on the Relief and Settlement of the Poor*, reprinted in State Board of Charities of the State of New York, 34th Annual Report (1900), vol. I, pp. 939–963. Yates argued that "overseers not infrequently granted relief without sufficient examination into the circumstances or the ability of the party claiming it."
19. *Report of the Committee*, p. 5.
20. Ibid., p. 26.
21. Samuel Chipman, *Report of an Examination of Poor-Houses, Jails, &c in the State of New York* (Albany: New York State Temperance Society, 1834), p. 76.
22. *American Quarterly Review* XIV (1833), p. 90.
23. *U.S. Commercial and Statistical Register* VI (1842), p. 363.
24. Ibid., p. 25.
25. *Report of the Committee*, p. 29.
26. Ibid.
27. Thomas Chalmers, *The Christian and Civic Economy of Large Towns* (Glasgow: Chalmers and Collins, 1823), vol. II, pp. 59–60.
28. Ibid.
29. *Benevolent Societies of Boston, Report* (Boston, 1834), pp. 4–5.
30. Nathaniel Ware, *An Exposition of the Weakness and Inefficiency of the Government of the United States of North America* (New York: Leavitt, Trow, 1845), p. 191.
31. For example of quotation, see Robert Thompson, *The Divine Order of Human Society* (Philadelphia: Wattles, 1891), p. 244.
32. Ibid., pp. 25–26. British programs had some work requirement, but the commissioners were concerned that a recipient's "subsistence does not depend upon his exertions," so the association of labor with reward is lost, and the recipient "gets through his work, such as it is, with the reluctance of a slave" (pp. 27–28). The commission report concluded that, "The bane

of all pauper legislation has been the legislating for extreme cases. Every exception, every violation of the general rule, to meet a real case of unusual hardship, lets in a whole class of fraudulent cases by which that rule must in time be destroyed. Where cases of real hardship occur, the remedy must be applied by individual charity, a virtue for which no system of compulsory relief can be or ought to be a substitute" (p. 59).

33. Concern about the effect of dependence on character also was evident: "No man's principles can be corrupted without injury to society in general; but the person most injured is the person whose principles have been corrupted," the commissioners concluded.

34. S. Humphreys Gurteen, *A Handbook of Charity Organization* (Buffalo, published by the author, 1882), p. 24.

35. NYAICP, *Twelfth Annual Report* (1855), p. 13.

36. William Ruffner, *Charity and the Clergy* (Philadelphia: Lippincott, 1853), p. 138.

37. Ibid., p. 141.

38. *Congressional Globe* XXVIII, 2 (1854), p. 1062. Pierce added, "I cannot find any authority in the Constitution for making the Federal Government the great almoner of public charity throughout the United States."

39. Ibid.

40. Quoted in Philip Klein, *From Philanthropy to Social Welfare* (San Francisco: Jossey-Bass, 1968), p. 283.

41. Horace Greeley, *Hints Toward Reforms* (New York: Harper & Bros., 1850), p. 86.

42. Greeley agreed with statements by Unitarian leader William Ellery Channing citing "avarice" as "the chief obstacle to human progress.... The only way to eliminate it was to establish a community of property." Channing later moderated his communistic ideas concerning property, but he typified the liberal New Englander's approach to the problem of evil. Evil was created by the way society was organized, not by anything innately evil in man.

43. Brook Farm, which attracted for a time some leading literary lights, became the best known of the communes; Nathaniel Hawthorne's *The Blithedale Romance* shows his sarcastic reaction to Brook Farm.

44. Toast by Albert Brisbane, quoted in William Harlan Hale, *Horace Greeley: Voice of the People* (New York: Harper & Brothers, 1950), p. 105.

45. Quoted in Charles Sotheran, *Horace Greeley and Other Pioneers of American Socialism* (New York: Humboldt, 1892), p. 193.

46. Ibid., p. 195.

47. *New York Tribune*, November 20, 1846.

48. *New York Courier and Enquirer*, November 23, 1846 (hereafter noted as *Courier*).

49. *Courier*, December 24, 1846.
50. Ibid.
51. *Courier*, January 6, 1847.
52. Ibid.
53. *Tribune*, January 13, 1847.
54. Ibid.
55. *Courier*, January 20, 1847.
56. Ibid.
57. *Tribune*, January 29, 1847. Greeley observed that charity might merely encourage dependency: "Do not all agree that Alms-giving, though laudable and vitally necessary, does not tend to remove the evils which it palliates, but the contrary? Does any one believe that there will be fewer paupers here next Winter for all that Public and Private Charity is so nobly doing this Winter? Is it not rather probable that there will be more?"
58. *Tribune*, February 17, and *Courier*, March 5, 1847.
59. *Courier*, January 20, 1847.
60. Ibid., March 5, 1847.
61. Ibid.
62. *Tribune*, March 12, 1847.
63. Ibid., March 26, 1847.
64. *Courier*, April 16, 1847.
65. Ibid.
66. Ibid.
67. Ibid.
68. Ibid.
69. *Lowell Daily Journal and Courier*, December 24, 1857.
70. Andrew W. Young, *Introduction to the Science of Government, with a Brief Treatise on Political Economy* (New York: Young, 1860), p. 324.
71. Henry C. Carey, *Principles of Social Science* (Philadelphia: J. B. Lippincott, 1859), III, p. 438.
72. Benjamin Joseph Klebaner, *Public Poor Relief in America 1790–1860*, Ph. D. dissertation, Columbia University, 1951, chapter six (no page number; typescript published in 1976 by Arno Press, New York).
73. Katz, p. 37.
74. Benjamin Klebaner, "Poverty and its Relief in American Thought, 1815–1861," *Social Science Review* 38:4 (December, 1964), p. 382.
75. Samuel Austin Allibone, *A Review by a Layman of a Work Entitled 'New Themes for the Protestant Clergy...'* (Philadelphia: Allibone, 1852), pp. 81, 88.
76. 1852 survey reported in Klebaner, op. cit., p. 387.
77. New York State Senate, Documents 1857, I, No. 8.

78. *New Haven Morning Journal and Courier*, October 28, 1857.

79. *New York Times*, November 11, 1857.

80. NYAICP, *20th Annual Report*, p. 8.

81. Ibid., p. 14.

82. *Providence Journal*, December 16, 1857; an editor responded that this idea was "full of danger, and full of discouragement to industry...."

83. Klebaner, loc. cit.

84. Boston, *City Documents*, 1859, no. 27, pp. 21–22.

85. *Waltham Sentinel*, March 12, 1858.

86. Klebaner, p. 287.

87. Ibid.

88. Alfred T. White, "The Story of Twenty-five Years," *Charities* XXX (1904), p. 7.

89. Brooklyn was then an independent city.

90. Schneider and Deutsch, p. 48.

91. Ibid. Eventually, three of the "county commissioners of charities" were tried and convicted of malfeasance in office.

92. Many of those lining up were immigrants not used to the yeoman independence that reportedly had characterized much of the American citizenry in antebellum times. It's also possible to speculate that some Northern citizens during the Civil War had become used to relying on others for sustenance.

93. Charles D. Kellogg, "Charity Organization in the United States," *Proceedings of the National Conference of Charities and Correction, 1893* (Boston, 1893), pp. 68–69; cited in Robert H. Bremner, " 'Scientific Philanthropy,' 1873–93," *Social Science Review* 30 (June, 1956), p. 169.

94. Hartley, the long-time head of the New York Association for Improving the Condition of the Poor, scorned indiscriminate charity, particularly the "soup-kitchens, free lunches, free dormitories, and others of a kindred class."

95. Ibid.

Chapter Four

1. Otto L. Bettmann, *The Good Old Days—They were Terrible* (New York: Random House, 1974), pp. 88–89.

2. Ibid., p. 152.

3. Ibid., pp. 6, 10, 19.

4. Arthur Bonner, *Jerry McAuley and His Mission* (Neptune, N.J.: Loizeaux Brothers, 1967), p. 27.

5. Horace Greeley, *Recollections of a Busy Life* (New York: J. B. Ford, 1869), p. 193.

6. Ibid., p. 199.

7. Ibid. To an historian, Greeley is a delightful rascal. He was almost always foolish and wrong but vividly self-confident. He almost always reversed himself, sometimes days but often years later, without ever apologizing.

8. Josephine Shaw Lowell, *Public Relief and Private Charity* (New York: Putnam's, 1884; reprinted by Arno, 1971), p. 55.

9. Ibid., p. 56.

10. Ibid.

11. The United Hebrew Charities' *Twenty-Fifth Annual Report* (New York: Philip Cowen, 1899), p. 15, looked back at the situation when it was founded.

12. "The Causes of Pauperism," quoted in Lowell, op. cit.

13. Paul T. Ringenbach, *Tramps and Reformers, 1873–1916: The Discovery of Unemployment in New York* (Westport, Conn., 1973), p. 15. The state legislature did not respond to the board's major concerns at this point, but did pass (in May 1880) "An Act Concerning Tramps." The act, essentially an antivagrancy measure, prohibited individuals from going from "place to place begging."

14. State of New York, *Annual Report of the State Board of Charities* (Albany, 1876, 1879, and 1884), 9:133, 12:30, and 17:160.

15. "The Causes of Pauperism," op. cit.

16. Edward L. Pierce, "Experience of the Overseers of the Poor, Collated and Reviewed," in "Report of the Secretary," *Eighth Annual Report of the Massachusetts Board of State Charities*, January 1872, pp. 41–53. Pierce defined a compassionate system as one "which shall deter, as far as may be, from unnecessary resort to public charity without doing violence to humane and honorable instincts."

17. Ibid.

18. Ibid., p. 170.

19. Associated Charities of Boston, *Fourth Annual Report* (1883), pp. 43–44.

20. Raymond A. Mohl, "Abolition of Public Outdoor Relief," in Walter I. Trattner, ed., *Social Welfare or Social Control?* (Knoxville: University of Tennessee Press, 1983), pp. 45–46.

21. Ibid.

22. Ibid., p. 57.

23. Ibid., pp. 45–46.

24. Frances Smith quoted in Nathan I. Huggins, *Protestants Against Poverty: Boston's Charities, 1870–1900* (Westport, Conn.: Greenwood, 1971), p. 66.

25. Ibid., p. 68.

26. Frances Smith also pointed out that governmental charity was less efficient than the private variety, since governmental agents "did not ask for personal reform, or were not able to press their point effectively."

27. Huggins, p. 67. Smith asked, "Cannot this thrift be encouraged by benevolent societies and individuals taking the relief and aid of the aged into their own hands, granting it in such ways as shall most encourage the rising generation to grow up self-sustaining, even in their old age?" The "old age" for many of these individuals came during the Depression, when the popularity of Townsend Plans among the elderly led to passage of the first Social Security bill.

28. *Lend a Hand,* I (November 1886), 647, 690.

29. Edward T. Devine, "Relief and Care of the Poor in Their Homes," *The Charities Review* X (1900), p. 268.

30. S. Humphreys Gurteen, *A Handbook of Charity Organization* (Buffalo: published by the author, 1882), p. 25.

31. Devine, loc. cit.

32. Brace, *The Dangerous Classes of New York,* p. 384.

33. Ibid.; Brace noted, "Perhaps not one citizen in a thousand could so well recite the long list of charitable societies and agencies in New York, as one of these busy dependents on charity."

34. Sometimes the change was rapid: in Chicago, the great fire of 1871 destroyed much of the old city, and rebuilding tended to occur along economic lines. In most cities, such as New York, the change was more gradual, and thus less obvious.

35. Ray Stannard Baker counted 72 wealthy New York churches moving up or out between 1867 and 1909 (Baker, p. 71).

36. Louise de Koven Bowen, *Growing Up with a City* (New York: Macmillan, 1926), p. 50, and quoted in McCarthy, pp. 28–29.

37. Kathleen D. McCarthy, *Noblesse Oblige: Charity & Cultural Philanthropy in Chicago, 1849–1929* (Chicago: U. of Chicago Press, 1982), p. 30. Many ministers criticized this trend; the Reverend Harry C. Vrooman, for example, complained that "Jesus never instituted a charity ball where amid the voluptuous swell of the dance, the rustle of silks, the sparkle of diamonds, the stimulus of wine and women dressed decollete, He could dissipate His love for the lowly." [Harry C. Vrooman, "Charity, Old and News," *Arena* 11 (January, 1895), p. 274]

38. Ibid.

39. From "The Gospel of Wealth," in O'Connell, ed., p. 98.

40. Jane Addams, "A Modern Lear," in Christopher Lasch, ed., *The Social Thought of Jane Addams* (Indianapolis: Bobbs-Merrill, 1965), p. 112.

41. Charles Loring Brace, *The Dangerous Classes of New York and Twenty Years' Work Among Them* (New York: Wynkoop & Hallenbeck, 1880), p. 383.

42. Ibid.
43. Ibid.
44. Ibid., pp. 384–385.
45. Walter Trattner, *From Poor Law to Welfare State: A History of Social Welfare in America*, third edition (New York: Free Press, 1984), p. 81.
46. Ibid., p. 81.
47. Richard Hofstadter, *Social Darwinism in American Thought, 1860–1915* (Philadelphia: University of Pennsylvania, 1944), p. 21.
48. David Schneider and Albert Deutsch, *The History of Public Welfare in New York State 1867–1940* (Montclair, N.J.: Patterson Smith, 1969), p. 27.
49. William Graham Sumner, *What Social Classes Owe To Each Other* (Caldwell, Idaho: Caxton, 1974), p. 20; originally published in 1883.
50. Ibid.
51. Ibid., p. 108.
52. Ibid., p. 114.
53. Ibid.
54. Simon Newcomb, *Principles of Political Economy* (New York: Harper & Brothers, 1886), p. 527.
55. Ibid., p. 527.
56. Ibid., p. 527.
57. Ibid., pp. 529–530.
58. Ibid., p. 529.
59. Ibid., p. 532.
60. Ibid., p. 536.
61. Ibid.
62. J. G. Schurman, "The Growth and Character of Organized Charity," *The Charities Review* I (March 1892), p. 200. Schurman argued that just because "the profoundest thinker of antiquity recognized it as a matter of course that infanticide should be resorted to as a prudential means of solving an ugly problem," Americans of the 1890s and thereafter were not obligated to do the same; a better way needed to be found, or "our republic is doomed and our civilization is doomed" (p. 192).
63. Associated Charities of Boston, *Ninth Annual Report* (Boston: George Ellis, 1888), p. 10.
64. Ibid.
65. Mohl, p. 41.
66. Seth Low, "Out-Door Relief in the United States," *Annual Conference of Charities, 1881* (Boston: George Ellis, 1881), pp. 144–154.

67. See Michael B. Katz, *In the Shadow of the Poorhouse: A Social History of Welfare in America* (New York: Basic Books, 1986), pp. 50–52.

68. Low, op. cit. He added, "No reason… occurs to this writer why a similar experience would not follow the abolition of out-door relief in any city or town sufficiently large to enable private benevolence to organize and act in concert."

69. Josephine Shaw Lowell, *Public Relief and Private Charity* (New York: Putnam's, 1884), p. 100.

70. S. Humphreys Gurteen, *A Handbook of Charity Organization* (Buffalo, publisher by the author, 1882), p. 20.

71. Ibid., p. 32.

72. Ibid., p. 188.

73. Ibid., pp. 20, 32.

74. Ibid., p. 20.

75. Ibid., p. 32.

76. Ibid., pp. 20, 32.

77. Ibid., p. 39.

78. Ibid., pp. 35, 54.

79. *Laws of 1875*, chapter 140, quoted in Schneider and Deutsch, p. 27.

80. Gurteen, p. 31.

81. Ibid., p. 141.

82. Ibid., p. 33.

83. Ibid.

84. Ibid., p. 31.

85. Ibid., p. 34.

86. Ibid., p. 192.

87. Lowell, p. 66.

88. Ibid., p. 89.

89. Ibid., pp. 84, 92.

90. Interestingly, late nineteenth-century studies of "tramping" showed that Jews and blacks were rarely tramps: Jews were cared for by fellow Jews, and blacks, because of discrimination, found it very difficult to beg successfully; tramping, for a black, was not "socially acceptable." (Paul T. Ringenbach, *Tramps and Reformers, 1873–1916: The Discovery of Unemployment in New York* (Westport, Conn., 1973), p. 71).

91. Charity Organization Society of New York, *Fifth Annual Report*, January 1, 1887, p. 29.

92. *Directory of the Charitable and Beneficent Organizations of Baltimore and of Maryland* (Baltimore: Friedenwald Press, 1892, Second edition,), p. 2.

93. Ibid., p. 2.

94. Ibid.

95. Lowell, p. 66. Lowell's worldview also led her to emphasize effect on character: the problem with "outdoor relief," she wrote, is that "it fails to save the recipient of relief and community from moral harm, because human nature is so constituted that no man can receive as a gift what he should earn by his own labor without a moral deterioration…."

96. Ibid.

Chapter Five

1. *Directory of the Charitable and Beneficent Organizations of Baltimore and of Maryland* (Baltimore: Friedenwald Press, 1892, Second edition), p. 29.

2. Ibid. Women who did not know how to sew could learn at the "Electric Sewing-Machine Rooms," run by a nonprofit organization that provided a woman with one or two months of free sewing machine use (during which she received the proceeds from sales of whatever she produced) and then placed her in a job.

3. Baltimore Directory, p. 28.

4. Other Baltimore groups were devoted specifically to the Jewish needy. The Hebrew Hospital and Asylum provided care to the "needy sick" and was "free to residents of Maryland who are unable to pay board." The Hebrew Orphan Asylum and the Hebrew Orphan's Aid Society, and the Society for Educating Hebrew Poor and Orphaned Children, provided shelter. The Young Men's Hebrew Association had four hundred members and featured a chess club and orchestra. (Baltimore Directory, p. 86)

5. Illinois Conference of Charities and Corrections' *Handbook of Chicago's Charity* (Chicago: Colvin, 1892), pp. 26, 36, 78.

6. Statement by the Chicago Relief and Aid Society in Ibid., p. 46.

7. Volunteers at Helping Hand were to offer counsel and challenge, but not to do for those living there what they should do for themselves: "All the work in the institution, such as scrubbing the floors, laundrying, etc., is done by the occupants." Many shelters today do not require any work from their occupants.

8. *Handbook of Chicago's Charity*, pp. 105, 116.

9. Some additional examples: The New York Bible and Fruit Mission to Public Hospitals provided Bible readers to visit among the poor in public hospitals, and the Christmas Message Association distributed 35,000 letters of encouragement to people who were alone in December. The New York Dorcas Society was one of many sewing circles that produced clothing for the poor. The better-off could also help in a more indirect way, ads noted: "By having your washing done at the Park Avenue Laundry of the Charity Organization Society… you will enable the society to train and employ many poor women. No chemicals are used." Another ad: "Buy your kindling wood from The

Woodyard of the Charity Organization Society, 514 E. 23rd St. This woodyard is maintained to supply relief agencies and private persons with the means of helping able-bodied men who ask for help, without demoralizing them by direct gifts of alms, and of testing their willingness to work." [*New York Charities Directory* (New York: New York Charity Organization Society, 1892), p. ix].

10. Many other organizations carried on interesting and important work in New York. The Earle Guild, the Ladies' Fuel and Aid Society, and other groups provided food, clothing, and fuel for the "worthy poor," and ice in summer for sick children. Lodging houses of the Children's Aid Society sheltered 1,252 boys and girls in 1891. The Ecole Francaise Gratuite was a free school for children of French descent. The Wilson Industrial School for Girls taught two hundred girls sewing and other skills and supplied free material, allowing the girls to use credit marks for diligence to "buy" the garments they made. The Association for Protection of Children and Young Girls protected children from "dissolute parents." The Society for Giving Free Entertainments to the Poor and Unfortunate provided entertainment at shelters and penal institutions, and the West Side Protective League worked to restrict liquor traffic. The House of Mercy, House of the Good Shepherd, Goodnight Mission (156 residents), Margaret Strachan Home, and the Magdalen Society (228 residents) were for the aid of "fallen women." The Women's Prison Association and Home and the Isaac T. Hopper Home (219 women) helped ex-prisoners gain employment.

11. Some groups were ethnically rather than religiously based. The Belgium Society of Benevolence, the Chinese Hospital Association, the French Benevolent Society, the German Ladies' Society, the Hungarian Association, the Irish Immigrant Society, and so on, were among those with New York offices.

12. The *New York Charities Directory*, 1892, listed many other organizations, including the Young Men's Hebrew Association, which had many programs and provided a reading room and library. The Sanitarium for Hebrew Children offered medical aid and excursions to 18,124 boys and girls in 1891. The Hebrew Free Association of the City of New York provided free schools for 3,197 pupils.

13. *The American Hebrew* LI (May 27, 1892), p. 123.

14. United Hebrew Charities, *22nd Annual Report* (1896), p. 51.

15. United Hebrew Charities, *23rd Annual Report* (New York: Seixas, 1898), p. 20.

16. United Hebrew Charities, *25th Annual Report* (New York: Philip Cowen, 1899), p. 19: only seventy of one thousand applicants from 1894 still were receiving aid.

17. *The American Hebrew* LII (February 11, 1898), p. 445.

18. Aaron Ignatius Abell, *The Urban Impact on American Protestantism, 1865–1900* (Cambridge: Harvard University Press, 1943), p. 46.

19. *Illustrated Christian Weekly*, October 16, 1875, p. 502.

20. *War Cry*, September 24, 1898, p. 8, and August 23, 1902, p. 9.

21. Ibid., July 20, 1901, pp. 9, 12, and August 31, 1901, pp. 9, 12.

22. See Josiah Strong, *Religious Movements for Social Betterment* (New York: Baker & Taylor, 1900).

23. *New York Charities Directory*, pp. 302–313 and 319–389, lists activities of Protestant churches.

24. Abell, pp. 150–151.

25. The leaders realized that there would be social pressures to join with others, but they were not averse to this as long as the individuals were warned that statements of faith were not to be made lightly. Some, of course, still might insincerely confess, but the churches were willing to take that risk, and suggested that personal contact was a guard against excess.

26. *Lend a Hand* and other magazines carried accounts of these activities. Strong provides a good summary, and Abell (pp. 150–151) mentions some others. Strong's list of schools specifically established to aid minorities (pp. 90–97) also is interesting.

27. The goal was to offer both material and spiritual help and to explain the connection between the two. Some ministers saw potential danger in this effort of bringing into the fold what in Chinese missions came to be called "rice Christians"—individuals who would indicate a spiritual change so as to gain material benefits. But Conwell and others typically guarded against this, with some success, by making their programs or deliveries of food or medicine available to all who would come and listen, whether or not they made statements of faith.

28. Ibid., p. 50.

29. New York Mission and Tract Society, *Christian Work in New York* (New York: Society, 1878), p. 35: The effect of false benevolence "is to encourage the least needy and least deserving among the poor to rely for their support upon the alms of others, rather than upon their own exertions. Thus the amount of relief that might otherwise be rendered to the really worthy and needy poor is materially decreased."

30. "Vigorous Church Work," *Outlook* (November 30, 1901), p. 804. For a general discussion of Presbyterian response to social pressures, see chapter nine of Gary Scott Smith, *The Seeds of Secularization: Calvinism, Culture, and Pluralism in America, 1870–1915* (Grand Rapids: Christian University Press, 1985).

31. Some of the missions concentrated on men, while others worked primarily among women and offered cooking schools, classes in dressmaking, and kindergartens.

32. *Outlook*, November 2, 1895, p. 358.

33. *New York Charities Directory*, pp. 390–398.

34. United Hebrew Charities, *26th Annual Report* (New York: Cowen, 1900), pp. 25–27; see also *New York Charities Directory*, 1896, pp. 314–318.

35. Baltimore Directory, p. 41.

36. Placement required agreement of boys and, in the case of abandoned children, living parents who could be found.

37. Robert M. Offord, ed., *Jerry McAuley: An Apostle to the Lost* (New York: American Tract Society, 1907), p. 138.

38. Ray Stannard Baker, *The Spiritual Unrest* (New York: Stokes, 1910), p. 143.

39. She was called Gallus Mag because she kept up her skirt with suspenders, or galluses.

40. Arthur Bonner, *Jerry McAuley and His Mission* (Neptune, NJ: Loizeaux Brothers, 1967), p. 32.

41. *New York Herald*, September 5, 1868.

42. Ibid.

43. For other biographical details see Jerry McAuley, as told to Helen E. Brown, *Transformed; or, the History of a River Thief* (New York: self-published, 1876).

44. Ibid., p. 48.

45. Ibid., p. 62.

46. Offord, p. 125.

47. Brown, pp. 63–64.

48. Samuel H. Hadley, *Down in Water Street* (New York: Revell, 1902), p. 102.

49. Offord, p. 184.

50. Ibid., p. 185.

51. Ibid., pp. 186, 188, 189.

52. Ibid., p. 187.

53. Bonner, p. 47.

54. Quoted in Bonner, p. 60.

55. Ibid.

56. Offord, p. 115.

57. Helen Brown's introduction to *Transformed*, p. 5.

58. Remarks at Sept. 21, 1884, memorial service for McAuley, Offord, p. 136.

59. Brown, p. 7.

60. Bonner, p. 74.

61. The mission received its name because Jaegar said, "the question is not, 'Shall a man drink?' but 'What shall he drink?' "—and Jaegar's goal was to apply Jesus' teaching, "If any man thirst, let him come unto Me."

62. "Ministry to the Poor," *New Englander*, March 1877, pp. 169–183.
63. *Christian Herald*, June 17, 1891, pp. 369, 372; April 5, 1893, pp. 225, 227; January 15, 1896, p. 47.
64. The *Christian Herald* not only provided publicity, but took over management of several activities, including New York's Bowery Mission.
65. *The Outlook*, November 30, 1901, pp. 804–805.
66. Norris Magnuson, *Salvation in the Slums* (Metuchen, NJ: Scarecrow Press, 1977), p. 91.
67. *Christian Herald*, June 19, 1914, p. 564.
68. In the twentieth century, the mission movement also spread through the work of the Convention of Christian Workers, the Winona Lake Bible Conference (in Indiana, with key meetings between 1900 and 1906), the National Gospel Mission Union, and the National Federation of Gospel Missions, which in 1913 turned into the International Union of Gospel Missions.
69. Offord, p. 148.

Chapter Six

1. See Department of the Interior, Census Office, *Eleventh Census* (Washington: Government Printing Office, 1895).
2. Edward E. Hale, *If Jesus Came to Boston* (Boston: Lamson, Wolffe, 1895), p. 23.
3. Mrs. Campbell, quoted in Bonner, p. 64.
4. Ray Stannard Baker, *The Spiritual Unrest* (New York: Stokes, 1910), p. 157.
5. Despite his positive reaction, the mission's existence (evidence of societal failure) and its one-on-one emphasis (evidence of desire to transform individuals rather than masses) bothered Baker.
6. Jacob Riis, *How the Other Half Lives*, orig. pub. 1890 (New York: Dover, 1971), p. 148.
7. Ibid., p. 199.
8. Ibid., p. 151.
9. Ibid., p. 69.
10. Edward T. Devine, "The Value and the Dangers of Investigation," *Proceedings of the Section on Organization of Charity*, 1897, pp. 92–93, 95.
11. Ibid., p. 28.
12. Bosanquet et al., *Philanthropy and Social Progress* (Boston: Crowell, 1893), p. 261.
13. Ibid.
14. Associated Charities of Boston, *Fourth Annual Report* (1883), pp. 43–44.
15. Ibid.

16. Ibid., p. 15.

17. See Barry J. Kaplan, "Reformers and Charity: The Abolition of Public Outdoor Relief in New York City, 1870–1898," *Social Science Review* 52 (June 1978), pp. 202–214.

18. Rev. Robert E. Thompson, *Manual for Visitors Among the Poor* (Philadelphia: Lippincott, 1879), p. 21.

19. *The American Hebrew* LII (February 11, 1898), p. 448.

20. John H. Holliday, "Proceedings of the Eighth Annual State Conference, Indiana State Conference on Social Work, October 3–5, 1899," published in the *Indiana Bulletin*, June 1900, p. 8. Holliday referred to a famous Social Darwinist study: "Many of you remember the important study of Mr. McCulloch, 'The Tribe of Ishmael,' showing that 420 criminal pauper families were related to each other by birth and marriage. Twenty years of work has wrought a change in that tribe and quite a number of members are now decent and self-supporting." Holliday said that the woman in question, through careful, personal work and challenge, "was brought back to a life of work and economy, and her former associates would not now know her, in a clean home surrounded by well-kept children."

21. United Hebrew Charities, *23rd Annual Report* (New York: Seixas, 1898), p. 20.

22. Walter Johnson in *Lend a Hand*, quoted in *The American Hebrew* LI (May 27, 1892), p. 123.

23. Associated Charities of Boston, *Ninth Annual Report* (Boston: George Ellis, 1888), p. 12.

24. Robert W. De Forest, "What is Charity Organization?" *The Charities Review* I (November, 1891), p. 2.

25. Nathan I. Huggins, *Protestants Against Poverty: Boston's Charities, 1870–1900* (Westport, Conn.: Greenwood, 1971), pp. 76–77.

26. The Associated Charities *Nineteenth Annual Report*, (November 1898, pp. 61–62) provides an example, cited by Lubove, of how this type of categorization worked out in practice, as seen in a district agent's typical day's work: She advised an "undoubted tramp" to earn his keep at Stephen's Lodging-house; she authorized a contribution for a sick woman "known to be good and industrious"; she turned down a request from a young woman for rent money, saying that the applicant was one of a family of six, but only one was willing to work; she obtained sewing work for a needy client.

27. In addition, 33 families and 37 single persons were sent out of the city to places where they could be self-supporting (20 and 14, respectively, stayed in their new homes, and the rest returned). Homes in the city were found for 83 families or individuals; 16 families were broken up to save children from abuse; fraud was exposed 42 times.

28. Charity Organization Society of New Orleans, *Third Annual Report* (New Orleans: James Buckley, 1899), p. 10.

29. Ibid.

30. The New Orleans COS in one year also reported that visiting nurses made 1833 visits to 435 individuals and supplied medicine 501 times. Six thousand individuals received lodging in COS shelters, and 104 women who were given work in the sewing department made 11,600 garments for the poor. Some 475 families received groceries and 112 fuel.

31. St. Louis Provident Association; 33rd annual report, 1893, pp. 20, 22–23. Quoted in Robert and Jeanette Lauer, "Will a Private War on Poverty Succeed? The Case of the St. Louis Provident Association," *Journal of Sociology and Social Welfare* X (March 1983), p. 16.

32. Ibid. The report noted, "Hypocrisy is shrewd as well as inquisition; and deceit has many obstructions to the glare of the search-light."

33. Reported in *The American Hebrew* LII (February 11, 1898), p. 447. The UHC reported aid given to another woman "in the belief that she was a widow with none to depend upon and unable to earn her livelihood. One day we discovered that she had another residence in the northern part of the city, extremely well furnished, with a piano of good make, where she lived with three adult sons."

34. Riis, *How the Other Half Lives*, p. 196.

35. Ibid., p. 28.

36. Mary Richmond, *Friendly Visiting Among the Poor* (Montclair, N.J.: Patterson Smith, 1969; originally published in 1899), p. 4.

37. Ibid., p. 13.

38. Francis G. Peabody, "The Modern Charity Worker," included in United Hebrew Charities of the City of New York, *22nd Annual Report*, p. 49.

39. Lauer, p. 17.

40. United Hebrew Charities, *25th Annual Report* (New York: Philip Cowen, 1899), p. 15, and *22nd Annual Report* (New York: Irving Friedman, 1896), p. 54.

41. Peabody, p. 55.

42. Charity Organization Society of New Orleans, *Third Annual Report* (New Orleans: James Buckley, 1899).

43. S. Humphreys Gurteen, *A Handbook of Charity Organization* (Buffalo: published by the author, 1882), p. 190.

44. H. L. Wayland, "A Scientific Basis of Charity," *Charities Review* III (1893–94), p. 268.

45. *Charities Review* I (November 1891), p. 2.

46. Frederic W. Farrar, *Social and Present Day Questions* (Boston: Bradley & Woodruff, 1891), p. 85.

47. John Glenn, "Cooperation Against Beggary," *The Charities Review* I (December 1891), p. 67.
48. Quoted in Mohl, p. 46.
49. Philip W. Ayres, "Relief in Work," *The Charities Review* II (November 1892), p. 36.
50. Alfred Bishop Mason, in "Things to Do," *The Charities Review* I (March 1892), quoted a prominent New York advertisement: "The Charity Organization Society is ready, with its woodyard and its laundry, to give temporary work to every man who will use a saw on a log of wood, and to every woman who will try to wash a shirt." (p. 213)
51. Procedures varied, but the principle was common: Year after year speakers at annual meetings of the National Conference of Charities and Correction affirmed the importance of work requirements. See, for example, *Proceedings of the Section on Organization of Charity*, 1897 (St. Paul: Pioneer Press, 1897), pp. 81–83.
52. S. O. Preston, "Night Work in the Woodyard," *The Charities Review* II (November 1892), p. 42.
53. Exceptions to the "no work-no food" principle for the able-bodied occasionally were made in order "that no one shall starve," as New York charity leader Josephine Lowell wrote, but her goal always was "to make this provision in such a way as shall do as little moral harm as possible, both to the recipient of relief and to the community at large."
54. Glenn, p. 46.
55. Lowell, pp. 93–94.
56. *How the Other Half Lives*, p. 191.
57. Mishnah Abot 2:2, quoted in Frisch, p. 125.
58. Rabbi Jochanan, Pesachim 113a, in Ephraim Frisch, *An Historical Survey of Jewish Philanthropy* (New York: Cooper Square Publishers, 1969), p. 59.
59. Amos G. Warner, *American Charities: A Study in Philanthropy and Economics* (New Brunswick: Transaction, 1989; orig. published in 1894), pp. 367–368.
60. Ibid., pp. 368–369.
61. Joseph Henry Crooker, *Problems in American Society* (Boston, 1889), p. 112.
62. Frederic Almy, "The Problem of Charity from Another Point of View," *Charities Review* IV (1894–95).
63. Mary Richmond, *Friendly Visiting Among the Poor* (Montclair, N.J.: Patterson Smith, 1969; originally published in 1899), p. 151.
64. Bosanquet, *Philanthropy and Social Progress*, p. 261.
65. *Legal Aid Review*, vol. 2, January 1904, p. 1.

66. Quoted in Raymond A. Mohl, "Abolition of Public Outdoor Relief," in Walter I. Trattner, ed., *Social Welfare or Social Control?* (Knoxville: University of Tennessee Press, 1983), p. 46.
67. *Legal Aid Review*, op. cit.
68. Succah 49b, in Frisch, p. 92.
69. Emma Whittemore, *Records of Modern Miracles* (Toronto: Mission of Biblical Education, 1931), p. 131.
70. Ibid., p. 130.
71. Riis, p. 148.
72. Ibid., p. 221.
73. Ibid., pp. 151, 221.

Chapter Seven

1. Housing problems and other causes contributed to the deaths of three thousand people during an August 1896 New York heat wave.
2. Otto L. Bettman, *The Good Old Days—They were Terrible* (New York: Random House, 1974), pp. 12, 96, 115, 129.
3. Ibid.
4. Jacob Riis, *The Children of the Poor* (New York: Scribner's, 1892), pp. 277–78.
5. Jacob Riis, *How the Other Half Lives* (New York: Dover edition, 1971), p. 199.
6. Frederick Law Olmstead, "Public Parks and Enlargement of Towns," *Journal of Social Science* (1871), p. 5.
7. United Hebrew Charities *26th annual report* (1900), pp. 7–8.
8. Ray Stannard Baker, *The Spiritual Unrest* (New York: Stokes, 1910), p. 157.
9. Ibid., p. 159.
10. Ibid.
11. Ibid., p. 161.
12. *American Magazine*, July, 1909, p. 3.
13. Again, many mission workers modeled their practice of compassion after the biblical pattern in which God frequently let the Israelites see the consequences of their beliefs and would not show compassion until they repented.
14. Edward T. Devine, "Relief and Care of the Poor in Their Homes," *The Charities Review* X (1900), pp. 91–92.
15. Ibid.
16. Quoted in Bonner, p. 64.
17. *New York World*, January 18, 1893.

322   *Notes*

18. John H. Holliday, "Proceedings of the Eighth Annual State Conference, Indiana State Conference on Social Work, October 3–5, 1899," published in the *Indiana Bulletin*, June 1900, p. 8.

19. Edward Bellamy, *Looking Backward* (New York: Signet Classic, 1960; original publication in 1888), p. 75. Bellamy's economic views were based on a pantheistic faith; he wrote in one essay, "The Religion of Solidarity," that "there is a conscious solidarity of the universe toward the intuition of which we must struggle, that it may become to us, not a logical abstraction, but a felt and living fact.... Believe that your sympathy with infinite being, infinite extension, infinite variety, is a pledge of identity." [This essay, written in 1874, is contained in Arthur E. Morgan, *The Philosophy of Edward Bellamy* (Westport, CT: Hyperion Press, 1979)].

20. See Arthur Mann, *Yankee Reformers in the Urban Age* (Cambridge, Harvard University Press, 1954), pp. 81–91.

21. Richard Ely, *Social Aspects of Christianity* (New York: T. Y. Crowell, 1889), p. 92.

22. From a speech given December 4, 1891, before the Evangelical Alliance convention in Boston. Given Ely's stress on government, a stress on deep personal commitment that was conventional among some took on the ominous sound of potential totalitarianism: "What is the extent of our obligations? It is measured by nothing less than our capacity—everything must be devoted to the service of humanity. The old Mosaic ten-per-cent rule was given for the hardness of men's hearts. We now live under a hundred-per-cent rule." (p. 77)

23. George Herron, *Between Caesar and Jesus* (Boston: T.Y. Crowell, 1899).

24. Introduction to William G. Fremantle, *The World as the Subject of Redemption* (New York: Longmans, Green, 1895, second edition), p. x. The book was published initially in 1885 and based on a series of eight lectures that Fremantle (Canon of Canterbury and Fellow of Balliol College, Oxford) delivered at Oxford in 1883. The lectures excited little attention either then or immediately upon their initial publication in 1885, but during the 1890s Ely's promotion of the book was extremely successful. By the middle of the decade, as Fremantle proudly noted, his work was "placed in the line of succession, reaching down from Aristotle's Politics...." (p. x).

25. Ibid., pp. 278–280.

26. Ibid., pp. 278–279.

27. Ibid., p. 281.

28. Ibid., p. 309.

29. Robert Bremner, *From the Depths: The Discovery of Poverty in the United States* (New York, 1956), p. 61.

30. *Handbook of Chicago's Charity*, p. 82.

31. Jane Addams, *Twenty Years at Hull-House* (New York: Macmillan, 1910), p. 310.

32. National Council of Charities and Correction, *Proceedings*, 1897; quoted in Frank J. Bruno, *Trends in Social Work, 1874–1956* (New York: Columbia University Press, 1948), p. 114.

33. In Cathryne Cooke Gilman, "Neighbors United," typescript in Minnesota Historical Society; quoted in Clarke A. Chambers, *Seedtime of Reform: American Social Service and Social Action, 1918–1933* (Minneapolis: University of Minnesota Press, 1963), p. 122.

34. Ibid.

35. Ibid.

36. Bremner, op. cit.

37. Ibid., p. 110.

38. Correspondence of Mary Richmond, June 3, 1899, included in Ralph and Muriel Pumphrey, eds., *The Heritage of American Social Work* (New York: Columbia University Press, 1961), p. 266.

39. Ibid., p. 267.

40. Ibid.

41. Jane Addams, "The Subjective Necessity for Social Settlements," paper delivered at the Ethical Culture Societies summer school at Plymouth, Massachusetts, 1892, in *Philanthropy and Social Progress* (Boston: T. Y. Crowell, 1893), pp. 119–120.

42. Charles Loring Brace, *The Dangerous Classes of New York and Twenty Years' Work Among Them* (New York: Wynkoop & Hallenbeck, 1880), p. 385.

43. David Schneider and Albert Deutsch, *The History of Public Welfare in New York State 1867–1940* (Montclair, N. J.: Patterson Smith, 1969), p. 37. The bureau was also "to ascertain and report to the public the most simple methods of testing and verifying applications for aid, and of directing deserving claimants to the agency adapted to their respective cases."

44. During its first year the Bureau put together a directory of 194 private welfare agencies in New York, and a registry of 14,000 recipients of relief. The bureau folded in 1875, however, and a similar bureau begun in Brooklyn in 1876 also failed.

45. Roy Lubove, *The Professional Altruist* (Cambridge: Harvard University Press, 1965), p. 2; Nathan I. Huggins, *Protestants Against Poverty: Boston's Charities, 1870–1900* (Westport, Conn.: Greenwood, 1971), p. 122.

46. Occasionally the result was ludicrous. William Randolph Hearst, owner of the *New York Journal*, sent pale children on jaunts to the beach and sent along reporters as chaperones and horn-blowers. One reporter later wrote that she was given only one container of ice cream to be dealt out on a Coney Island trip: "When at last I placed a dab on each saucer, a little fellow in ragged knickerbockers got up and declared that the Journal was a fake and I thought

there was going to be a riot. I took away the ice-cream from a deaf and dumb kid who couldn't holler and gave it to the malcontent. Then I had to write my story beginning: 'Thousands of children, pale-faced but happy, danced merrily down Coney Island's beaches yesterday and were soon sporting in the sun-lit waves shouting, God bless Mr. Hearst.' " (*Park Row*, p. 81.)

47. *The Forum*, vol. 17, May 1894; quoted in Brown, p. 44.

48. Ibid. Coit phrased his statements, somewhat awkwardly, as a series of rhetorical questions.

49. John G. O'Grady, *Catholic Charities in the United States* (Washington: National Conference of Catholic Charities, 1931), p. 1, notes that at first home placement was successful: "All that was necessary was to have the pastors make an appeal from their pulpits to the generosity of the people. As a result of the appeal large numbers of applications for children began to pour into the church rectories. Each application was endorsed by the pastor and forwarded to the institution which immediately furnished the family with a child...." Over time, however, demand for Catholic homes far exceeded supply, and the emphasis turned to orphanages.

50. As stated by the National Conference of Catholic Charities' history, ibid., p. 101.

51. Ibid., p. 381.

52. Ibid., p. 389.

53. For example, see Leroy A. Halbert's paper in National Conference of Charities and Correction, *Proceedings*, 1913.

54. Rev. Robert E. Thompson, *Manual for Visitors Among the Poor* (Philadelphia: Lippincott, 1879), pp. 240–241. The book was based on a series of lectures Thompson gave at Princeton Theological Seminary earlier in that year.

55. Ibid.

56. Ibid.

57. Quoted in Mayer Zald, *Organizational Change: The Political Economy of the YMCA* (Chicago: University of Chicago Press, 1970), p. 54: As the YMCA "spread across the United States it began to resemble an organization for general evangelism."

58. *Directory of the Charitable and Beneficent Organizations of Baltimore and of Maryland* (Baltimore: Friedenwald Press, 1892, second edition), p. 85.

59. Norris Magnuson, *Salvation in the Slums* (Metuchen, N. J.: Scarecrow Press, 1977), p. 100.

60. *The Conqueror* VI (April 1897), p. 89. The Salvation Army also urged the industrious to move out of central cities and, with help, set up a small farm of their own; the goal was to turn a "hobo" (who was willing to change) into a "hopebo" and then a "homebo."

61. Magnuson, p. 93.

62. *War Cry*, August 14, 1897, p. 12.

63. Ibid., March 26, 1898, p. 4, and December 9, 1899, p. 3.
64. Ibid., June 4, 1898, p. 7.
65. Frederick Booth-Tucker, *The Social Relief Work of the Salvation Army in the United States* (Albany, New York, 1900), pp. 10–11, notes that the Salvation Army also provided better housing than homeless men were used to, for some homeless shelters were "of the meanest character," without heat or blankets on bitterly cold nights; bed-bugs along with a cacophony of "hacking coughs" made sleep difficult. Salvation Army shelters, however, had blankets, stoves, and hot baths. They were generally devoid of bedbugs but furnished with both a reading room and an "officer in command [who] takes a kindly interest in the men." The charge was ten cents a night, or a private room for five cents more. By 1903 the Salvation Army recorded a monthly average of 137,000 lodgings and 365,000 meals at its sixty shelters.
66. Paul T. Ringenbach, *Tramps and Reformers, 1873–1916. The Discovery of Unemployment in New York* (Westport, Conn., 1973), p. 91.
67. Ringenbach, p. 138. Temperance crusader Francis Murphy had long proposed that the way to change was to "inoculate the community with the Gospel of Jesus Christ." (*Christian Union*, March 27, 1878, p. 266.) The Women's Christian Temperance Union, founded in 1874, mixed Gospel temperance meetings with the establishment of houses for inebriate women, coffee rooms, and other types of social mission work.
68. *War Cry*, December 31, 1898, p. 5.
69. Ibid., February 23, 1899, p. 5.
70. Magnuson, p. 8. Ballington Booth wanted a more "democratic" organization, and over the years volunteers placed more emphasis on prison work, but the two groups had more similarities than differences in both theology and practice.
71. *Ten Talks on the Salvation Army* (New York, 1902), pp. 62–63.
72. Aaron Ignatius Abell, *The Urban Impact on American Protestantism, 1865–1900* (Cambridge: Harvard University Press, 1943), p. 126.
73. *War Cry*, May 16, 1891, p. 8. Booth-Tucker wrote that "Sacrifice is the language of love"—but Salvation Army wariness about mere "sentiments of emotional affection" kept such a declaration above the level of sentiment. The focus at that time was not only on a profession of faith but on repentance and follow-up, including practical movement away from bearing grudges and slandering others. Those who came to the woodyards were told that it could be a new start, if they took personal responsibility for their past failures and renewed prospects. (*War Cry*, March 4, 1899, p. 9; March 3, 1894, p. 7. See also October 21, 1899, p. 5; August 17, 1901, p. 11; and October 3, 1908, p. 6.)
74. *War Cry*, February 22, 1908, p. 7; see also June 4, 1887, p. 8; July 23, 1887, p. 8; July 30, 1887, p. 9.

Chapter Eight

1. *Christian Century*, January 4, 1900, p. 1.
2. *New York Journal*, December 24, 1899, p. 39.
3. Ibid.
4. Ibid., December 31, 1899, p. 30.
5. Ibid., January 1, 1901, editorial page.
6. Ibid., December 31, 1899, p. 30.
7. Ibid., December 30, 1900, editorial page.
8. *Christian Century*, November 23, 1899, p. 4.
9. Ibid., November 30, 1899, p. 8.
10. Ibid., May 10, 1900, p. 5.
11. *New York Journal*, December 24, 1899, p. 39.
12. John Haynes Holmes quoted in Paul T. Ringenbach, *Tramps and Reformers, 1873–1916: The Discovery of Unemployment in New York* (Westport, Conn., 1973), p. 168.
13. *Christian Century*, December 27, 1900, p. 10.
14. Ibid.
15. "Where Shall We Find God?" *Christian Century*, September 2, 1909, p. 873.
16. "Fundamentalism, Modernism and the Bible," *Christian Century*, April 3, 1924, pp. 424–426; see also editorials of March 27 (pp. 388–390) and April 17 (pp. 495–497).
17. William D. P. Bliss, ed., *The Encyclopedia of Social Reform* (New York: Funk & Wagnalls, 1897), p. 270.
18. Frank Dekker Watson, *The Charity Organization Movement in the United States* (New York: Macmillan, 1922), p. 332.
19. Ibid., p. 527.
20. Simon N. Patten, *The New Basis of Civilization* (Cambridge: Harvard University Press, 1968; originally published in 1907), p. 205. Patten noted his allegiance to the "heretical doctrine that the depraved man is not the natural man."
21. Watson, pp. 398–399.
22. Ibid.
23. Hall Caine, "Mission of the Twentieth Century," *Chicago Tribune*, December 30, 1900, p. 37.
24. Walter Rauschenbusch, *Christianity and the Social Crisis* (New York: Macmillan, 1907). See also Dwight D. Murphey, *Liberal Thought in Modern America* (Lanham, Maryland: University Press, 1987), p. 60, and Ralph Henry Gabriel, *The Course of American Democratic Thought* (New York: Ronald Press, 1956) second edition, p. 274.
25. The period before World War I, of course, was when socialist parties were attaining their American peak and had particular strength among

intellectuals, so it is not surprising that some ecclesiastical academics went with the flow.

26. Frank Luther Mott, *American Journalism* (New York, 1941), p. 539.
27. Roy Everett Littlefield III, *William Randolph Hearst: His Role in American Progressivism* (Lanham, Md.: University Press of America, 1980), p. 103.
28. William Salisbury, *The Career of a Journalist* (New York: B. W. Dodge, 1908), pp. 146–147.
29. Ibid., p. 153.
30. *New York Times*, February 14 and November 1, 1905. When Hearst was unable to win elections, however, the Left turned on him. Hearst in turn lost his patience with radicals and by the 1930s was stoutly opposing governmental control of the economy.
31. Many socialists also considered the settlement house movement insignificant, except as a political organizing tool. Husock, p. 88, notes that New York's East Side House described itself in 1914 as "a radiant center of spiritual, moral and intellectual light in a thickly settled neighborhood of 150,000"—but its clubs enrolled 1,346.
32. U.S. Congress, Senate, *Conference on Care of Dependent Children: Proceedings*, 60th Cong., 2d sess., 1909, S. Doc. 721.
33. Ibid.
34. Ringenbach, p. 182.
35. Edward T. Devine, "Pensions for Mothers," in Edna D. Bullock, ed., *Selected Articles on Mothers' Pensions* (White Plains, N.Y.: H. W. Wilson, 1915), pp. 176–183. See also Mark H. Leff, "Consensus for Reform: The Mothers'-Pension Movement in the Progressive Era," *Social Service Review* 47 (September, 1973), p. 251.
36. Ibid.
37. Bruno, p. 181.
38. Ibid., pp. 87–89.
39. By 1935, all states except South Carolina and Georgia were giving aid to widows with children.
40. Law quoted in Leff, p. 248.
41. See Muriel and Ralph Pumphrey, "The Widows' Pension Movement, 1900–1930," in Walter I. Trattner, ed., *Social Welfare or Social Control?* (Knoxville: University of Tennessee Press, 1983), p. 58.
42. Quoted in Walter I. Trattner, *Homer Folks: Pioneer in Social Welfare* (New York: Columbia University Press, 1968), p. 108.
43. Trattner, *Homer Folks*, p. 113. The original appropriation was $1,252,000 for a five year period, later extended to seven.
44. Ann Geddes, *Trends in Relief Expenditures, 1910–1935* (Washington, D.C.: Government Printing Office, 1937), pp. 8–9. The cities were New York, Chicago, Philadelphia, Detroit, Cleveland, St. Louis, Baltimore, Boston,

Pittsburgh, San Francisco, Milwaukee, Buffalo, Washington, New Orleans, Cincinnati, and Newark.

45. Geddes, p. 99.
46. See Willford I. King, *Trends in Philanthropy* (New York: National Bureau of Economic Research, 1928), p. 68.
47. Watson, p. 400.
48. Minutes of National Federation of Settlements business meeting, 1922, quoted in Clarke A. Chambers, *Seedtime of Reform: American Social Service and Social Action, 1918–1933* (Minneapolis: University of Minnesota Press, 1963), p. 136.
49. Quoted in the *New York Times*, May 8, 1921.
50. Ibid.
51. Quoted in Merritt Ierley, *With Charity for All* (New York: Praegar, 1984), p. 137.
52. In 1893, Anna Dawes delivered a paper on "The Need for Training Schools for a New Profession"; in 1897 Mary Richmond followed with a much-discussed paper, "The Need of a Training School in Applied Philanthropy."
53. Names during the transitional period were the New York School of Philanthropy and the New York School of Social Work.
54. Quoted in Roy Lubove, *The Progressives and the Slums: Tenement House Reform in New York City, 1890–1917* (Pittsburgh: University of Pittsburgh Press, 1962), p. 199.
55. Ibid., pp. 199–200.
56. Ibid., p. 41.
57. Owen R. Lovejoy, "The Faith of a Social Worker," *Survey* 44:6 (May 8, 1920), p. 208.
58. Ibid., p. 210.
59. Ibid., p. 208.
60. Ibid.
61. Ibid., pp. 208, 210.
62. Ibid., p. 209.
63. Ibid.
64. Ibid.
65. Ibid.
66. Ibid., pp. 211, 212.
67. While Lovejoy disparaged the idea of sacrificial atonement, he played around with Christological imagery as he implied that the better-off caused slum problems: "The tenement sections of our great cities are the scapegoat of the prosperous sections. The woman of the red light district is the scapegoat of the protected daughter of the avenue" (p. 211). This was the domestic equivalent of the most recent view that the West is responsible for "third world" poverty.

68. Ibid., p. 209.
69. Ibid., pp. 210, 212.
70. Ibid., p. 211.
71. J. Gresham Machen, *Christianity and Liberalism* (Grand Rapids: Eerdman's, 1923), p. 64.
72. Ibid.
73. William H. Matthews, "Breaking the Poverty Circle," *Survey* 52:2 (April 15, 1924), pp. 96–98.
74. Rogert Baldwin, "The Challenge to Social Work of the Changing Control of Industry," quoted in Jacob Fisher, *The Response of Social Work to the Depression* (Boston: G.K. Hall 1980), pp. 32–33.
75. Ibid.
76. Reinhold Niebuhr, *The Contribution of Religion to Social Work* (New York: Columbia University Press, 1932), p. 61.
77. Ibid.
78. Kathleen D. McCarthy, *Noblesse Oblige: Charity & Cultural Philanthropy in Chicago, 1849–1929* (Chicago: U. of Chicago Press, 1982), p. xii.
79. Ibid., p. 136.
80. Ibid., p. 146.
81. Ibid., p. 147.
82. Ibid., p. 167.
83. The professional social workers' contribution to the destruction of voluntarism is an acknowledged but embarrassing fact in some books that recount social work history. Frank Bruno's standard history merely notes, "It is futile to imagine what development the use of volunteers would have reached, in the primary functions of the charity organization societies, had it not been blocked in the early twentieth century by the rise of a professional personnel" (*Trends in Social Work*, p. 104).
84. Clarence Elmer Glick thesis quoted in McCarthy, pp. 167–168.
85. "Billions for Practical Piety," *Literary Digest* 100 (January 26, 1929), p. 28.
86. Results of interviews by Harvey W. Zorbaugh quoted in McCarthy, p. 170.
87. See Charles Crittenton, *The Brother of Girls* (Chicago, 1910); see also Charlton Edholm, *Traffic in Girls and Florence Crittenton Mission* (Chicago: Woman's Temperance Publishing Union, 1893).
88. During that period other Florence Crittenton homes and missions opened in San Jose, Sacramento, Los Angeles, San Francisco, Denver, and Chicago, and also in Portland, Oregon; Fargo, North Dakota; and Norfolk, Virginia. There were twenty Crittenton homes in 1895.
89. Crittenton officials sometimes seemed unsure about how their program worked; they proclaimed that "the only lasting power is transformation through the power of the Cross," and at the same time stated that "honest industry lies at the bottom of true character." (Magnuson, p. 24)

90. Magnuson, p. 22.
91. Albert J. Kennedy, "Social Settlements," in Fred S. Hall, ed., *Social Work Year Book* (New York: Russell Sage Foundation, 1933), p. 481.
92. Ibid.
93. Fred S. Hall, ed., *Social Work Year Book* (New York: Russell Sage Foundation, 1933), pp. 57, 257, 373.
94. Ibid., p. 235.
95. Walter Gifford, chairman of the Organization on Unemployment Relief in 1932, predicted with considerable accuracy that if reliance on government became standard, in the long run "individuals would tend to withdraw much of the invisible aid they are now giving." [S. 164 and S. 262 hearings (unemployment relief), U.S. Senate Committee on Manufactures, 72d Congress, 1st Session (Washington: Government Printing Office, 1932), p. 313.] But few observers seemed to care.
96. Allan Herrick, *You Don't Have to be Rich* (New York: Appleton-Century, 1940), pp. 201, 202. Herrick noted that relief had been "personal, direct, frank, and above board," but in the new pattern "the giver never sees the object of his bounty.... Whether the recipient is made happy or is embittered by the gift, is unknown to him. Giving is impersonal, indirect, mechanized."
97. Ibid.

Chapter Nine

1. Michael B. Katz, *In the Shadow of the Poorhouse: A Social History of Welfare in America* (New York: Basic Books, 1986), p. 212.
2. "Unemployment in 1937," *Fortune* 16 (October, 1937), p. 106.
3. Ibid.
4. Gladys L. Palmer and Katherine D. Wood, *Urban Workers on Relief*, Part I (Washington: Works Progress Administration, 1936), p. 32.
5. Ibid.
6. Letter from Martha Gellhorn to Harry Hopkins, December 10, 1934, quoted in James T. Patterson, *America's Struggle Against Poverty, 1900–1985* (Cambridge: Harvard University Press, 1986), p. 37.
7. James T. Patterson, *America's Struggle Against Poverty, 1900–1985* (Cambridge: Harvard University Press, 1986), p. 53.
8. Quoted in *Time*, February 8, 1971, p. 18.
9. E. Wright Bakke, *Citizens Without Work: A Study of the Effects of Unemployment Upon the Workers' Social Relations and Practices* (New Haven: Yale University Press, 1940), pp. 362–366.
10. Ibid., pp. 26–29.
11. Ibid., pp. 363–364.

12. Josephine Chapin Brown, *Public Relief 1929–1939* (New York: Octagon Books, 1971), pp. 10–11. Laws in many localities and at least nine states also indicated, through retention of a "pauper's oath" or the equivalent, that relief was to be given only in dire circumstances; an applicant for relief to swear to his absolute destitution.

13. The federal program was modeled after New York's landmark unemployment relief program, begun in 1931 and labeled the Temporary Emergency Relief Administration.

14. *Louisville Courier-Journal*, October 27, 1985; quoted in Butler and Kondratas, p. 36.

15. Hearing Pursuant to S.Res. 36 (unemployment and relief), U.S. Senate Special Committee to Investigate Unemployment and Relief, 75th Congress, 3d session (Washington: Government Printing Office, 1938), vol. 2, p. 1228.

16. Bonnie Fox Schwartz, *The Civil Works Administration: The Business of Emergency Employment in the New Deal* (Princeton: Princeton University Press, 1984), p. 227.

17. Grace Adams, *Workers on Relief* (New Haven: Yale University Press, 1939), p. 11.

18. *New York Times*, January 5, 1935.

19. Ibid., November 30, 1935.

20. See Joanna C. Colcord's paper on the role of professional social workers in directing and framing the first federal relief programs, in National Conference of Social Work, *Proceedings*, 1943.

21. Frank Bruno, *Trends in Social Work, 1874–1856* (New York: Columbia University Press, 1948), p. 300.

22. Josephine Chapin Brown, *Public Relief 1929–1939* (New York: Octagon, 1971), p. 85.

23. Milford conference 1932–1933 report quoted in Jacob Fisher, *The Response of Social Work to the Depression* (Boston: G. K. Hall, 1980), p. 71.

24. Ibid. AASW members increasingly tended to identify themselves with their clients; for example, when relief was cut in 1935 as the economy improved for a time, AASW chapters in dozens of cities held protest meetings and sent telegrams to Washington. The American Public Welfare Association, meanwhile, lobbied for increased federal activity and against giving aid only to those who fell within the mother/orphan categories. In 1936 the APWA resolved that the federal government was obliged to meet the relief requirements of all needy persons.

25. Fisher, p. 71.

26. *Social Forces* XIV (1935), p. 92.

27. National Conference on Social Work, *Proceedings of the National Conference of Social Work*, 1934 (Chicago, 1934), pp. 473–485. See also Fisher, pp. 74–75.

28. Mary van Kleeck, "Our Illusions Concerning Government," *Proceedings of the National Conference of Social Work*, 1934 (Chicago, 1934), pp. 284–303.

29. Ibid.

30. Ibid.

31. Gertrude Springer, "Rising to a New Challenge," *Survey* 70 (June 1934), p. 179.

32. *Proceedings*, pp. 504–516.

33. Springer, p. 180.

34. White wrote that "the yeast of Edward Bellamy" changed him, as it changed others, from a "thoroughgoing conservative" to a person with "an open-minded attitude about the political, social, and economic problems." How highly was Bellamy regarded during the Depression? In 1935, when Columbia University asked John Dewey, historian Charles Beard, and *Atlantic Monthly* editor Edward Weeks each to make a list of twenty-five books of the preceding half century that had most influenced the thought and action of the world, first on each list was Karl Marx's *Das Kapital*, and second was Edward Bellamy's *Looking Backward*.

35. "When Will America Begin to Plan?" *Christian Century* March 11, 1931, pp. 334–336.

36. Ibid.

37. See Arthur M. Schlesinger, Jr., *The Age of Roosevelt: The Crisis of the Old Order, 1919–1933* (Boston: Houghton Mifflin, 1957), p. 25, and John Ehrenreich, *The Altruistic Imagination* (Ithaca: Cornell University Press, 1905), p. 104.

38. Eduard C. Lindeman, "Basic Unities in Social Work," *Proceedings of the National Conference of Social Work*, 1934, pp. 504–516.

39. S. 164 and S. 262 hearings (unemployment relief), U.S. Senate Committee on Manufactures, 72d Congress, 1st Session (Washington: Government Printing Office, 1932), p. 226.

40. Representative Sirovich in the *Congressional Record*, April 16, 1935, p. 5786.

41. In the 1930s the liberal hope, as described by Eleanor Roosevelt, was still for a time when no married woman would have to work. By 1977, however, the program provided support for not only 650,000 children whose fathers had died or were disabled, but ten times as many—6.5 million—with fathers reported as "absent." [See discussion of AFDC changes in Alvin L. Schorr, *Explorations in Social Policy* (New York: Basic Books, 1968). About one-fourth of the absences were due to divorce and one-third to abandonment; 40 percent of the children were born out of wedlock.]

42. Hearing, First Deficiency Appropriation Bill for 1936, U.S. House Committee on Appropriations, 74th Congress, 2d Session, 1936, p. 29.

43. Quoted in Donald S. Howard, *The WPA and Federal Relief Policy* (New York: Russell Sage, 1943), p. 806.
44. Schlesinger, *The Age of Roosevelt*, 275.
45. See Bakke, op. cit.
46. Memo of November 28, 1934, quoted in Arthur W. Macmahon et al., *The Administration of Federal Work Relief* (Chicago: Public Administration Service, 1941), p. 37.
47. Merritt Ierley, *With Charity for All* (New York: Praeger, 1984), p. 159.
48. Patterson, p. 46.
49. Harry L. Hopkins, *Spending to Save: The Complete Story of Relief* (New York: Norton, 1936), p. 109.
50. WPA Release 4-1177, May 26, 1936, quoted in Howard, p. 778.
51. "WPA and the Negro," quoted in Howard, p. 812.
52. Margaret C. Bristol, "Personal Reactions of Assignees to W.P.A. in Chicago," *Social Service Review* 12 (March 1938), p. 93.
53. *Our Job with the WPA* (Washington: Government Printing Office, 1936), p. 27.
54. Macmahon, pp. 3–6.
55. Grace Adams, p. 9.
56. J. Donald Adams, "The Collapse of Conscience," *The Atlantic Monthly* 161 (January 1938), p. 56.
57. Allan Herrick, *You Don't Have to be Rich* (New York: Appleton-Century, 1940), p. 202.
58. Ibid.
59. Grace Marcus, "The Status of Social Casework Today," *Compass* 16 (June 1935), pp. 5–12.
60. Ellery F. Reed, *Social Forces* XIV (1935), pp. 87–93. Reed was director of the Research Department at the Cincinnati Community Chest. Cited in Pumphrey & Pumphrey, p. 414.
61. Ibid.
62. Presidential address, *Proceedings of the National Conference of Social Work*, 1937.
63. Dorothy C. Kahn, "Some Professional Questions About Relief," in *Four Papers on Professional Function* (New York: American Association of Social Workers, 1937), pp. 38–39. Even worse, Kahn said, ideas about relief were "accompanied by a tendency to believe that any provision for able-bodied workers, which does not result directly from their own efforts, is bound to have a demoralizing effect on the individual and tends to increase the numbers of such persons in any community."
64. Ibid.
65. Quoted in Bruno, p. 314.

66. Bruno, p. 320.
67. Howard, p. 652.
68. Ibid., p. 653. New York Mayor Fiorello La Guardia had made similar arguments in 1939; he wanted Washington to take a larger role because "the Federal Government has unlimited credit. It has no constitutional tax limitation. It has no constitutional borrowing limitation." (Hearings on J.J. Res. 83 [work relief], U.S. House Committee on Appropriations, 76th Congress, 1st Session, 1939, p. 184.)
69. The growth of social science approaches led to other attempts to disparage local government. George Benson, in *The New Centralization: A Study of Intergovernmental Relationships in the United States*, complained that "state and local units do not seem generally to have functioned as satisfactory experimental laboratories. It is true that new devices and programs are often tried out in restricted areas, but the utility of such 'experiments' is questionable if no scientific recording or evaluation of results occurs.... [The problem is that] men who have had no previous opportunity or occasion to study governmental problems are elected for relatively short terms" (pp. 38–39).
70. Howard., pp. 753, 755.
71. Ibid., pp. 829–830.
72. Ibid., p. 807.
73. Ibid., p. 831.
74. Ibid., p. 65.
75. Ibid., p. 755. Howard also provided a different slant on the meaning of "democracy." He wrote sarcastically, "The claim that local and even state administration as practiced in the various sections of the country represents the prize flower of democratic free government is not one that wins easy acceptance." Federal providing of employment, however, was "a greater contribution to the preservation of democratic government than would have been likely to result from turning over to state and local authorities greater responsibilities for meeting needs arising from unemployment" (pp. 757–758).
76. Ibid., p. 832.
77. Howard did not understand in this context that the more they change, the more they stay the same.
78. Ibid., p. 835.
79. *Saturday Evening Post*, December 10, 1949, p. 122.
80. Ibid., p. 125.
81. Fletcher Knebel, "Welfare: Has it Become a Scandal?" *Look*, November 7, 1961, p. 31.
82. Ibid.

83. Quoted in Bruno (second edition, 1957), p. 388.

Chapter Ten

1.   *Operation Big City: A Review of How the Needs of People Coming to Public Welfare Agencies Are Met in Six Metropolitan Areas* (Washington: U.S. Department of Health, Education, and Welfare, Bureau of Family Services: 1965).
2.   Quoted in James T. Patterson, *America's Struggle Against Poverty, 1900–1985* (Cambridge: Harvard University Press, 1986), p. 88.
3.   Buster Soaries, "The Moral Foundation of the Civil Rights Movement," *The Heritage Lectures* 246 (February 1990), p. 5. Soaries, pastor at Shiloh Baptist Church in Trenton, New Jersey, noted that "the African American understanding of God's will" included "the responsibility to rise above the shackles of slavery, that was Egypt. But on the other hand, we needed to expunge the degenerate ways of Egypt from our hearts. That was sin."
4.   Frances Fox Piven and Richard A. Cloward, *Regulating the Poor: The Functions of Public Welfare* (New York: Pantheon, 1971), pp. 218–219.
5.   Walter Williams, "Recollections at a birthday party," *Washington Times*, June 11, 1990, p. D4.
6.   Michael Harrington, *The Other America: Poverty in the United States* (New York: Penguin, 1981, revised edition; originally published in 1962), p. 37.
7.   See *Organization Trends*, March 1990, p. 2.
8.   Elizabeth Wickenden and Winifred Bell, *Public Welfare: Time for a Change* (New York: The Project on Public Services for Families and Children, New York School of Social Work of Columbia University, 1961), p. 25. See also Wickenden material in the White House central file, box nine, LBJ Library.
9.   Ibid.
10. Ibid., pp. 26–27.
11. Ibid., p. 29.
12. Ibid., p. 48.
13. Ibid.
14. Ibid., pp. 52, 54.
15. Martin Quigley, "Philanthropic Stew, a Recipe Derived from an Annual Report of the Ford Foundation, Circa 1952," quoted in Martin Morse Wooster, "The Ford Foundation: New Directions in Social Welfare?" *Alternatives in Philanthropy*, September 1989.
16. See Daniel P. Moynihan, *Maximum Feasible Misunderstanding* (New York: Free Press, 1969), pp. 35, 40–41. Ylvisaker headed the Ford Foundation's Public Affairs Program.
17. James N. Morgan, Martin H. David, Wilbur J. Cohen, and Harvey J. Brazer, *Income and Welfare in the United States* (New York, 1962), p. 3.

18. Ibid., p. 7.
19. Harrington, p. 163.
20. "The Problem of Poverty in America," *Economic Report of the President* (Washington: Government Printing Office, 1964), p. 60.
21. Quoted in Patterson, p. 79.
22. Statement of February 24, 1966; quoted in K. L. Billingsley, *From Mainline to Sideline: The Social Witness of the National Council of Churches* (Washington, D.C.: Ethics and Public Policy Center, 1990), p. 160.
23. Ibid.
24. Statement of December 3, 1966, quoted in Billingsley, p. 160.
25. Ibid.
26. Robert James St. Clair, "Now it's the Social Welfare Gospel," *United Evangelical Action* 20 (January 1962), p. 10.
27. Carl F. H. Henry, "Evangelicals in the Social Struggle," *Christianity Today* 10 (October 8, 1965), pp. 3–11.
28. Howard E. Kershner, "The Church and Social Problems," *Christianity Today* 10 (March 4, 1966), p. 35.
29. R. M. MacIver, ed., *The Assault on Poverty: And Individual Responsibility* (New York: Institute for Religious and Social Studies, with distribution by Harper & Row, 1965), p. 2. The placement of a colon followed by "and" in the title seems unusual, but was apparently designed to emphasize the responsibility of those reading the book to take action. The War on Poverty turned out to be a war on individual responsibility also, without the colon.
30. Ibid., p. 3.
31. Ibid.
32. Ibid., p. 1.
33. *Public Papers of the Presidents of the United States*, Lyndon B. Johnson, 1963–64, no. 431, p. 819.
34. Patterson, p. 135.
35. *Newsweek*, February 17, 1964, p. 38.
36. Ibid.
37. See Doris Goodwin, *Lyndon Johnson and the American Dream* (New York: Harper & Row, 1976), p. 209.
38. Quoted by Herbert J. Kramer in an oral history interview housed at The University of Texas LBJ Library, Kramer Interview, p. 21.
39. Merritt Ierley, *With Charity for All* (New York: Praegar, 1984), p. 179.
40. Quoted by Stewart Alsop, "After Vietnam—Abolish Poverty?" *Saturday Evening Post*, December 17, 1966, p. 12.
41. Alsop, p. 12. Alsop, however, predicted that social universalistic proposals would be a hard sell if they resulted in transferring income, no questions asked, to "the drunks and the drug addicts, as well as bad people, immoral

people and just plain lazy people." He explained that "the deepest and most instinctive opposition to the idea derives from 'the Puritan ethic,' " and only if that ethic were attacked could universalistic proposals receive widespread acceptance.

42. See Scott Briar, "Welfare From Below: Recipients' Views of the Welfare System," in Jacobus ten Broek, ed., *The Law of the Poor* (San Francisco: Chandler Publishing, 1966), p. 46.

43. J. Skelly Wright, "The Courts Have Failed the Poor," *New York Times Magazine*, March 9, 1969, p. 26.

44. Piven and Cloward, p. 289.

45. Ibid., pp. 291–292.

46. Ibid., pp. 295–296.

47. John Ehrenreich, *The Altruistic Imagination* (Ithaca: Cornell University Press, 1985), p. 171.

48. Piven and Cloward, pp. 270–271.

49. Moynihan, pp. 141–142.

50. Ehrenreich, p. 179.

51. Quoted in Joseph Kershaw, *Government Against Poverty* (Washington, 1970), p. 166.

52. Quoted in Patterson, p. 152.

53. *Time*, February 8, 1971, p. 14.

54. Richard Cloward, "Strategy of Crisis," *American Child* 48 (Summer, 1966), p. 24.

55. Ibid., p. 21.

56. Ibid.

57. See T. George Harris, "Do We Owe People a Living?" in *Look*, April 30, 1968, p. 27. As *Look* reported and Piven and Cloward readily acknowledged, the radicals' "strategy of deliberate disruption" also had a larger goal: to "overload the welfare bureaucracy, break it and bring on, they hoped, a guaranteed income" (*Look*, April 30, 1968, p. 27).

58. Ibid. Wiley in 1966 had run for president of CORE and had lost to Floyd McKissick in a bitter contest. Personal ups and downs clearly play a part in history; as one of Wiley's close colleagues remarked, "If George had not lost, NWRO would not have been founded." [Carl Rachlin quoted in Guida West, *The National Welfare Rights Movement* (New York: Praeger, 1981), p. 25.] And yet, if NWRO had not been founded, something else very much like it probably would have been, because it met the needs of the political and theological Left.

59. West, pp. 98–99.

60. Nicholas and Mary Lynn Kotz, *A Passion for Equality: George A. Wiley and the Movement* (New York: Norton, 1977), p. 199.

61. *Time*, February 8, 1971, p. 18.
62. Kotz, p. 219.
63. West, pp. 98–99.
64. Ibid., p. 31.
65. Kotz, p. 183.
66. Ibid., p. 245.
67. West, pp. 162–163.
68. See Harvey Cox, "The 'New Breed' in American Churches: Sources of Social Activism in American Religion," in William McLoughlin and Robert N. Bellah, eds., *Religion in America* (Boston: Houghton Mifflin, 1968), pp. 366–382.
69. Ibid.
70. The National Welfare Rights Organization financial statement for October 1968 through September 1969 showed $164,000 of its $457,000 budget coming from liberal church groups, primarily the Inter-Religious Foundation for Community Organization. (*Prospectus*, March 1970, p. 7; cited in West, p. 29.)
71. Nelson Bell, "The Church and Poverty," *Christianity Today* 14 (March 27, 1970), p. 27.
72. Francis A. Schaeffer, "Race and Economics," *Christianity Today* 18 (January 4, 1974), p. 19.
73. *Time*, May 17, 1968, p. 32.
74. Ibid.
75. *Time*, July 8, 1971, p. 18: A Nixon administration official interviewed at HEW headquarters said of NWRO, "I tell you, they've educated a lot of people. They've brought the problem right into this building, and believe me, it's had an impact."
76. Patterson, p. 143.
77. West, p. 33.
78. Richard Rogin, "Now Its Welfare Lib," *New York Times Magazine*, September 27, 1970, p. 31; see also Sar A. Levitan, *The Great Society's Poor Law: A New Approach to Poverty* (Baltimore: Johns Hopkins Press, 1969), p. 179. The OEO gave its Legal Services arm sufficient funding—$24 million in 1964, an amount that would triple in a decade—to establish 850 neighborhood law offices.
79. The most significant Supreme Court case was *King v. Smith* (1968).
80. Piven and Cloward, p. 311.
81. See Charles A. Reich, "The New Property," *Yale Law Journal*, 1964, pp. 733–787, and U.S. Supreme Court, *Goldberg v. Kelly*, March 24, 1970.
82. West, p. 327.

83. *Legal Aid Review* I (July, 1903), p. 1: The society's language may now appear quaint, and it can legitimately be asked whether some of the wealthy were also put through the same educational process, but the concept of an attorney's responsibility is remarkable: When "an applicant comes to the offices of the society indignant at treatment he has received," it may be "the duty of the attorney to point out to this person that the treatment he has received is not unjust, but that the rules and regulations are necessary to the social and political well-being of the community." The Legal Aid attorneys were to gain satisfaction not just from winning cases: "in addition to the feeling that they are accomplishing a great and good work, they have the satisfaction of knowing that they have instilled in many an individual who previously thought only of his own individual advantage, the first appreciation of the duties of good citizenship."

84. Piven and Cloward, p. 327.

85. *Look*, April 30, 1968, p. 27.

86. Ibid.

87. According to *Time* (February 8, 1971, p. 18), AFDC numbers from 1960 to 1970 went from 3 million to 9.5 million.

88. Patterson, p. 174.

89. James Welsh, "Poor Have New Outlook," Newark *Star Ledger*, November 3, 1970; quoted in West, p. 296.

90. For a spirited discussion of the various theories, see Piven and Cloward, pp. 183–284.

91. Welsh, op. cit.

92. Battle in January 1971 reported in West, pp. 301–302.

93. *Time*, February 8, 1971, p. 18.

Chapter Eleven

1. Quotation from William Wordsworth in *The Oxford Dictionary of Quotations* (Oxford: Oxford University Press, 1979), p. 577.

2. Quoted in Mark R. Arnold, "We're Winning the War on Poverty," *The National Observer*, February 19, 1977, p. 1.

3. Robert H. Haveman, "Poverty and Social Policy in the 1960s and 1970s," in Haveman, ed., *A Decade of Federal Antipoverty Programs: Achievements, Failures, and Lessons* (New York: Academic Press, 1977), p. 18.

4. Husock notes that when some "VISTA workers and New Left activists followed the settlement example of taking up residence among the poor, few were driven by the idea of assisting the poor in self-improvement. Indeed, many of them rejected the very notion that the poor needed improvement; 'the system' was the problem." (p. 90)

5. William Whyte, *Street Corner Society*, quoted in Husock, p. 88.
6. Guida West, *The National Welfare Rights Movement: The Social Protest of Poor Women* (New York: Praeger, 1981), pp. 98–99. Some maintained a desire to conform to middle-class goals and were happy to have real needs met.
7. See Charles Murray, *Losing Ground: American Social Policy, 1950–1980* (New York: Basic Books, 1984).
8. See, for example, *Time*, February 8, 1971, p. 15.
9. Arthur Bonner, *Jerry McAuley and His Mission* (Neptune, N.J.: Loizeaux Brothers, 1967), p. 110.
10. Ibid., p. 112.
11. Ibid., p. 114.
12. Maris Vinovskis, *An "Epidemic" of Adolescent Pregnancy?* (New York: Oxford, 1988), p. 25.
13. Quoted in *The Family in America*, April 1987.
14. Judith S. Musick, Arden Handler, and Katherine Downs Waddill, "Teens and Adoption: A Pregnancy Resolution Alternative?" *Children Today* (November/December 1984), p. 26. See also Arden Handler and Katherine Downs, *A Statewide Study of Teenage Parents and Adoption*, final report for the Ounce of Prevention Fund, Chicago, 1984.
15. Christopher Jencks, "Deadly Neighborhoods," *The New Republic* (June 13, 1988), p. 29. Jencks' article also critiques economic determinist explanations of delinquency and crime.
16. The effect on the real fathers in some urban communities was equally severe: Since there was no moral pressure or economic need to work hard to support a family, job incentive decreased. The social and economic components of the entitlement revolution, in short, led to a vast increase in children growing up without a father and fathers never growing up.
17. West, p. 168.
18. *Time*, February 8, 1971, p. 17.
19. Nathaniel Dunford, "N.Y.C., True to Form," *New York Times*, April 10, 1990, p. A21.
20. Ralph M. Kramer, *Voluntary Agencies in the Welfare State* (Berkely: University of Chicago, 1981), pp. 57–76; cited in Katz, p. 263.
21. Ibid., p. 68.
22. Ibid., p. 67: From 1950 to 1975 the growth rate of government was at least four times that of the voluntary sector, with a ten-to-one spending ratio of governmental to nongovernmental organizations. In the field of health, the federal government spent only 15 percent more than private philanthropy in 1930; by 1973 it was spending nearly seven times as much.
23. *Time*, October 1, 1975, pp. 34–35; *Time* also noted the "right to own a TV set."

24. The press was generally sympathetic to welfare mothers but could not resist reporting the machinations of others who learned to play the welfare game, as in this report: "Item: a regulation-wise hippie commune in Berkeley reconstituted itself into eight paper 'households' and collected $1,000 a month in aid." (*Time*, February 8, 1971, p. 17.)

25. The Harris Survey, February 1976; cited in Martin Anderson, *Welfare* (Stanford: Hoover Institution Press, 1978), p. 62.

26. Nathan Glazer, "Reform Work, Not Welfare," *The Public Interest*, No. 40 (Summer, 1975), p. 4.

27. *Christian Science Monitor*, April 4, 1985.

28. *Los Angeles Times*, April 20–25, 1985; quoted in Butler and Kondratas, p. 37.

29. *Time*, February 8, 1971, p. 15.

30. Ibid., p. 16.

31. *The Mary Thomas Story*, NBC, December 3, 1989.

32. Anderson, p. 43.

33. U.S. Congress, Joint Economic Committee, Subcommittee on Fiscal Policy, *Income Security for Americans: Recommendations of the Public Welfare Study* (Washington, D.C., 1974), p. 77.

34. Put another way: Familial man and economic man are always fighting with each other; when the federal government put its thumb on the scale, economics became supreme. Economics are not finally determinative, but the poverty wall became solid when the moral wall was destroyed.

35. Speech given May 17, 1970, Thomas P. Collins and Louis M. Savary, eds., *A People of Compassion* (New York: The Regina Press, 1972), p. 41.

36. April 5, 1968; p. 122.

37. For more examples of the misuse of the word "compassion," see Marvin Olasky, "Reclaiming Compassion," *Heritage Lectures 228*, December (1989).

38. Christina Feldman, "Nurturing Compassion," p. 23, and Jack Kornfield, "The Path of Compassion," p. 25, in Fred Eppsteiner, ed., *The Path of Compassion: Writings on Socially Engaged Buddhism* (Berkeley: Parallax Press, 1988).

39. David E. Purpel, *The Moral & Spiritual Crisis in Education: A Curriculum for Justice and Compassion in Education* (Granby, Mass.: Bergin & Garvey, 1989), p. 35. Regarding education, Purpel asks, "Why do we single out a group for 'graduating with honor?' Does this mean that those who are not in the group are without honor? (p. 37).

40. Sar A. Levitan (George Washington University), *Programs in Aid of the Poor*, 5th ed. (Baltimore: Johns Hopkins University Press, 1985), p. 138.

41. Leslie Dunbar, *The Common Interest: How Our Social Welfare Policies Don't Work and What We Can Do About Them* (New York: Pantheon, 1988), p. 110. Dunbar was senior program associate of the Ford Foundation's Project on Social Welfare and the American Future.

42. Douglas John Hall, *The Steward: A Biblical Symbol Come of Age* (New York: Friendship Press, 1982), p. 79.
43. Ibid., pp. 80–81. Hall states—and puts in italics for emphasis—his belief that there is "no major problem in the world today that can be confronted without human solidarity" (p. 75). Try sin.
44. See Clifford Orwin, "Compassion," *The American Scholar* (Summer, 1980), pp. 309–333.
45. John Agresto, "Educating About Compassion," *American Educator*, Summer, 1982, p. 20. Agresto noted, "Who hasn't witnessed the indifference and even cruelty of students toward their classmates, then seen those same students tearful and distraught over the loss of the class gerbil?"
46. George Will, "Faced up to victims, and reality," *Spokane Chronicle*, May 14, 1989, p. A18.
47. Mickey Kaus, "Up from Altruism: The Case Against Compassion," *The New Republic*, December 15, 1986, p. 17.
48. *Washington Post*, December 22, 1987, p. A2.
49. Ibid., November 17, 1984. A1.
50. Ibid., February 18, 1988, p. A23.
51. Dwight Lee, *Public Compassion and Political Competition*, booklet published in the Contemporary Issue Series (no. 35) by the Center for the Study of American Business, Washington University, St. Louis, September 1989, pp. 14–15. Lee also observed, "To suggest that government transfers should be reduced, or even tightly constrained, is to risk being rebuked as heartless."
52. Larry Burkett, "Is Welfare Scriptural?" *Fundamentalist Journal* 4 (April 1985), p. 21.
53. George Grant, *In the Shadow of Plenty* (Fort Worth, TX: Dominion, 1986), p. 76.
54. William E. Diehl, "A Guided Market Response," in Robert G. Clouse, ed., *Wealth and Poverty: Four Christian Views of Economics* (Downers Grove: InterVarsity, 1984), pp. 68–69.
55. Ronald J. Sider, *Rich Christians in an Age of Hunger* (Downer's Grove, IL: InterVarsity Press, 1977); David Chilton, *Productive Christians in an Age of Guilt Manipulators* (Tyler, TX: Institute for Christian Economics, 1985) is a hard-hitting response to Sider.
56. Chris Hedges, "For Mainline Protestantism, the Inner City Grows Remote," *New York Times*, May 31, 1990, pp. A1, B4.
57. Ibid., p. B4.
58. *Los Angeles Times*, September 30, 1989, II, p. 1.
59. *The American Spectator*, November 1989, p. 20.
60. *Washington Post*, September 24, 1989, p. F2. Three days later, readers were told to carry on "compassionate service in the spirit of Claude Pepper" (September 27, 1989, p. D3).

61. *Chicago Tribune*, September 28, 1989, p. 2.
62. *Los Angeles Times*, September 28, 1989, p. II-1.
63. *Los Angeles Times Magazine*, September 24, 1989, p. 7.
64. *Washington Post*, September 29, 1989, p. D1; see also *Chicago Tribune*, September 29, 1989, p. 14.
65. *Chicago Tribune*, September 28, 1989, p. 13E.
66. Ibid., September 27, 1989, p. VI-9.
67. Ibid., September 24, 1989, p. 3. The actor was Danny Aiello. Actresses are taught to give come-hither looks, actors looks of compassion.
68. *New York Times*, September 21, 1989, p. B1.
69. Noah Webster, *American Dictionary of the English Language* (New York: N. and J. White, 1834), p. 167.
70. *The Compact Edition of the Oxford English Dictionary* (New York: Oxford University Press, 1971); see also *Webster's New Twentieth Century Dictionary of the English Language* (Cleveland: World Publishing Co., 1945), which in 1945 had been "newly revised" by "a staff of eminent scholars, educators, and office editors." The eminent scholars, educators, and office editors defined compassion as "A suffering with another: hence sympathy" (p. 348). These men made suffering too easy by turning it into mere sympathy
71. *Webster's Third New International Dictionary* (Springfield, Mass: Merriam-Webster, 1986), p. 462.
72. *New York Times*, September 28, 1989, p. C13; *Washington Post Book World*, September 24, 1989, p. 1. The latter redundancy is probably hard to avoid at a time with folks also say, "I personally spoke with...."
73. *Oxford English Dictionary*, loc. cit., p. 3054.
74. Perhaps we need a movie entitled *Invasion of the Compassion Snatchers*.

Chapter Twelve

1. Christopher Jencks, "Deadly Neighborhoods," *The New Republic* (June 13, 1988), p. 30.
2. Edmund Mech, *Orientation of Pregnancy Counselors Toward Adoption*, report prepared for the Office of Adolescent Pregnancy Programs, Dept. of Health and Human Services, 1984, p. 71.
3. *Time*, September 6, 1971, p. 48. *Time* even seemed pleased about vacancy rates at maternity homes that showed "more and more unwed pregnant women feel no need to hide out."
4. *The Green Book* (Austin: Teenage Parent Council, 1987), p. 3.
5. *Time*, September 6, 1971, p. 48.
6. The number of programs for teens was so great that even a Ford Foundation study in 1982 could not count them all, but noted merely that "Throughout the United States a large variety of public and private institutions offer... a

range of services including educational, counseling, social, and medical services." (McGee, p. 21)

7. Ibid.

8. In 1988, the poverty rate among intact families was 5.6 percent, and the poverty rate for female-headed families was 33.5 percent (Census Bureau statistics, as reported by Kate O'Beirne and Robert Rector).

9. Susan Newcomer and J. Richard Udry, "Parental Marital Status Effects on Adolescent Sexual Behavior," *Journal of Marriage and the Family*, May 1987, pp. 235–240. (Cited in "New Research" section of *Family in America*, August 1987.)

10. See, for example, Selwyn M. Smith, Ruth Hanson, and Sheila Noble, "Social Aspects of the Battered Baby Syndrome," in *Child Abuse: Commission and Omission*, eds. Joanne V. Cook and Roy T. Bowles (Toronto: Butterworths, 1980), pp. 217–220; these researchers found that premarital pregnancy, illegitimacy, and absence of fathers are among the most common precursors of "baby battering." For reports on additional research see *The Family in America*, February and April 1989.

11. *Family in America*, February 1989.

12. Shelby H. Miller, "Childbearing and Childrearing Among the Very Young," *Children Today*, May-June 1984, p. 27.

13. Edmund Mech, *Orientation of Pregnancy Counselors Toward Adoption*, report prepared for the Office of Adolescent Pregnancy Programs, Department of Health and Human Services, 1984.

14. Judith S. Musick, Arden Handler, and Katherine Downs Waddill, "Teens and Adoption: A Pregnancy Resolution Alternative?" *Children Today* (November/December 1984), p. 26.

15. *Detroit News*, July 19, 1989.

16. Charles Murray, "Underclass," London *Sunday Times Magazine*, November 26, 1989. As Murray wrote, "The lack of fathers is associated with a level of physical unruliness that makes life difficult.... In communities without fathers, the kids tend to run wild. The fewer the fathers, the greater the tendency."

17. Ibid., p. 30.

18. *Detroit News*, July 19, 1989. Neuhaus asks "whether, in all of human history, we have an instance of a large population in which the institution of the family simply disappeared.... the answer is almost certainly no."

19. *Washington Post*, October 1, 1987, p. 1B; *Post*, January 14, 1988, p. B1.

20. Ibid., October 1, 1987, p. B1.

21. Ibid., January 14, 1988, p. B1. The *Post* quoted one school board member who "had bristled" at the idea of infant care in a junior high, but now said,

"I've got to bite the bullet." The *Post*, acknowledging that some critics would see the infant center as encouraging teen childbearing, claimed that the program would help develop parenting skills, including skill at taking advantage of other governmental programs: "By intervening at the earliest possible stage, the center's planners hope to involve the children of teenagers in a series of government programs, from the infant center to a toddler center at Ballou and on to Headstart and other early childhood programs." The *Post* did not ask whether such programs pushed pregnant teens toward a decision to single-parent.

22. Ibid., January 15, 1988, p. C3.
23. Ibid., May 28, 1987, p. A17; the *Post* reported that teen pregnancy had cost taxpayers nearly $17.9 billion in 1986. The solution, according to the report's source (The Center for Population Options), was more birth control funding.
24. Gertrude Himmelfarb, "Victorian Values/Jewish Values," *Commentary*, February 1989, p. 25.
25. William Tucker, *The Excluded Americans: Homelessness and Housing Policies* (Chicago: Regnery Gateway, 1989).
26. The poverty rate for black families headed by a single mother is 50 percent, which is more than four times the rate for intact, two-parent black families. (Robert L. Woodson, "Race and Economic Opportunity," *NPI Policy Review Series*, National Center for Neighborhood Enterprise, 1989, p. 3.)
27. See Piersons, *Mending Hearts, Mending Lives*.
28. Residents decide to live in these maternity homes for many reasons. Some feel uncomfortable at home, or are pushed out by parents angry or embarrassed about a pregnancy. Others seek a supportive environment in which to explore adoption, or the friendship of women in similar situations.
29. Some volunteers decorate or do maintenance, and others help as labor coaches, prayer parents, backup house parents, and drivers. Yearly training helps prepare new volunteers and keeps the church sensitive to the needs of Sparrow House residents.
30. Interview with agency director Kay Ekstrom, May 1989.
31. For more information on these, see Susan and Marvin Olasky, *More Than Kindness: A Compassionate Approach to Crisis Childbearing* (Westchester, IL: Crossway, 1990).
32. Stephen Buckley, "On the Grate, Camaraderie Gives Warmth," *Washington Post*, December 23, 1989, p. B1. The men were at 21st and Virginia NW.
33. *Washington Post*, December 23, 1989, p. B7.
34. Ibid., March 30, 1990, p. E1.
35. Ibid., pp. E1-E2.

346 Notes

36. Donna Minkowitz, "Shelter for Macho Men Only," *The Village Voice*, 1989, clip from Scanlon file, The Heritage File. The memo was withdrawn.
37. Doug Doabmeyer, quoted in Dick Simpson, *The Politics of Compassion and Transformation* (Athens, Ohio: Swallow Press/Ohio University Press, 1989), p. 211. Simpson, "minister of urban mission" of the Wellington Avenue United Church of Christ, which acted as fiscal agent for the project, noted that "The center did not intend to 'reform' street people" (p. 210).
38. Dan McMurry, "Hard Living on Easy Street," *Chronicles*, August 1988, p. 15.
39. Ibid., p. 19
40. Ibid., p. 19.
41. A Philadelphia expert "estimated that 75 to 80 percent of homeless men and women are addicts." A New York study researcher gave a figure of 75 percent, and a Washington manager of a residence for the homeless (Joshua House, Tom Taylor) estimated that at least 90 percent of the men he saw were addicts. Other estimates of addiction range from 44 to 68 percent, and estimates of the percentage of homeless who are mentally ill range as high as 30 percent. (See Gina Kolata, "Twins of the Streets: Homelessness and Addiction," *New York Times*, May 22, 1989, pp. A1, A13.)
42. Ibid. See also "Drugs, Homelessness Increasingly Linked," *Washington Post*, December 21, 1989, p. A6.
43. Many studies have discussed this problem; see, for instance, *Living Between the Cracks: Hearing Before the Senate Special Committee on Aging*, 98th Congress, 2d Sess. 64 (1984).
44. In the words of Swedish socialist economist Assar Lindbeck, "...rent control appears to be the most efficient technique presently known to destroy a city—except for bombing." The best recent book on the role of rent control and other housing policies is William Tucker, *The Excluded Americans: Homelessness and Housing Policies* (Chicago: Regnery Gateway, 1989). Interesting monographs include Richard Bourdon, *Bigger and Better Homes Help Explain House Price Increases*, CRS Report for Congress (Washington: Congressional Research Service, 1989). Articles include William Tucker, "Home Economics: The Housing Crisis That Overregulation Built," *Policy Review*, Fall, 1989, pp. 21–24; Tucker, "Where Do The Homeless Come From?" *National Review*, September 25, 1987, pp. 32–43; Stephen Chapman, "Housing the poor by doing less," *Washington Times*, May 17, 1989, p. F1; Warren Brookes, "Housing crisis hokum?" *Washington Times*, February 23, 1989, p. F1.
45. Chicago became especially famous for its byzantine plumbing and wiring guidelines. Union-protection legislation also drove up costs.

46. Laurence Schiff, "Would They Be Better Off in a Home?" *National Review*, March 5, 1990, p. 33.
47. Jacob Riis, *How the Other Half Lives*, orig. pub. 1890 (New York: Dover, 1971).
48. E. Fuller Torrey, discussion at the Heritage Foundation, 1989, and Torrey, *Nowhere to Go: The Tragic Odyssey of the Homeless Mentally Ill* (New York: Harper & Row, 1989); Torrey, "Thirty Years of Shame: The Scandalous Neglect of the Mentally Ill Homeless," *Policy Review*, Spring, 1989, pp. 10–15. Torrey reports that up to 180,000 mentally ill individuals are on the streets, compared to 68,000 mentally ill in public mental hospitals. Torrey states that of the one million people incarcerated in the United States on any given day, about 100,000 of them are schizophrenic or suffer from some other psychosis. Over three thousand seriously mentally ill persons can be found in the Los Angeles County jail on any given day, making that the largest mental hospital in the United States.
49. Schiff also noted that most psychiatrists prefer to be in private practice where they can make large salaries from caring for neurotics. In municipal and state hospitals, he wrote, most psychiatrists are from foreign countries, have little familiarity with American culture (particularly ghetto culture), speak English poorly, and are attracted to the state system by secure salaries and the lack of intimate patient contact. A deal is struck: Take medicine, don't make waves, and I'll call you mentally disabled and help you obtain government benefits. Schiff calls this "a full-employment program for drug dealers," since that is where much of the income thus received ends up. Schiff's conclusion: "In my work with the homeless I have in general been struck not by how many are mentally ill, but by how many of those so diagnosed show virtually no real signs and symptoms of mental illness." (Schiff, *National Review*, March 5, 1990, p. 32–35)
50. State budget-cutting, helped by federal programs that allowed shifting of the burden of care to Washington, formed half of the chute, with ideology contributing the other half. The impetus was federal legislation in 1963 that gave communities the opportunity to empty their mental health facilities and promised alternatives. Those alternatives were not provided, however, as federal community mental health programs headed toward the wonderland of stress management rather than the wilderness of helping the wild.
51. In a more recent example, when 160 patients were discharged from a Columbus, Ohio, mental hospital in 1985, 35 percent were on the streets six months later, and 13 percent were in jail. For constructive proposals, see

Paul S. Appelbaum, "Crazy in the Streets," *Commentary*, May 1987, pp. 34–39.

52. Many recent studies have shown that the estimates of three to four million homeless Americans that have been offered by "homeless advocates" are wildly out-of-line. For a summary of the social science literature see Randall K. Filer and Marjorie Honig (City University of New York), *Policy Issues in Homelessness: Current Understanding and Directions for Research* (New York: Manhattan Institute, 1990).

53. Ibid.

54. Schiff, p. 35.

55. Peter H. Rossi, *Down and Out in America: The Origins of Homelessness* (Chicago: University of Chicago Press, 1989), p. 40.

56. McMurry, p. 19.

57. Schiff, p. 35.

58. John Agresto, "Educating About Compassion," *American Education*, Summer, 1982, p. 20. Agresto's distinction between compassion and sentimentality is good: "Unlike compassion, sentimentality makes us feel good. We feel warm all over and lumpy in the throat. We can get rid of it with a good cry. Through it we enjoy a glow of feeling without incurring a debt of obligation. Unlike compassion, sentimentality is often easy and pleasant."

59. Gina Kolata, *New York Times*, May 22, 1989, p. A1.

60. Quoted by David Frum in his article, "Why Would Anyone Live in Penn Station?" *Wall Street Journal*, May 30, 1990, p. A 12.

61. The rate of freedom from addiction one year after an individual completed the CityTeam program.

62. Interview at the Mission, February 1990.

Chapter Thirteen

1. William Bradford, *Of Plymouth Plantation*, excerpted in Perry Miller, ed., *The American Puritans: Their Prose and Poetry* (Garden City, N.Y.: Doubleday, 1956), p. 17.

2. Ibid., pp. 17–18.

3. In relation to God, they believed there was nothing they could do to be worthy of his mercy; their hope lay in forgiveness of sins rather than their own attempts to do good.

4. The moral difference between the programs of the 1960s and those of the 1930s can perhaps be brought out with an analogy from media law. When a reporter has to proceed against a deadline, it's regrettable but

understandable if he mixes up a couple of names, and courts tend to be lenient; if the reporter errs in the course of an unpressured magazine article, "reckless disregard" is apparent.

5. Or, to try another analogy. We need to ask ourselves whether the goal is to teach swimming or support floating. If the former, then flotation devices will be available for those who need them, but they will not be handed out with the expectation that all will use them. If it is a matter of pride to swim, most people will do so even if flotation devices are free.

6. *War Cry*, October 12, 1889, p. 9, and December 15, 1894, p. 1.

7. Riis, *The Children of the Poor*, p. 160.

8. Brace, p. 390.

9. In thinking about the role of government in poverty-fighting, it's crucial that the initial question not be, "How much should government be involved?" Instead, the emphasis should be on what needs to be accomplished. Does government have sufficient flexibility to emphasize the individual and the spiritual? If we start with goals and then examine means, the likely conclusion is that government cannot accomplish what must be accomplished.

10. Victor A. Thompson, *Without Sympathy or Enthusiasm: The Problem of Administrative Compassion* (University, Alabama: The University of Alabama Press, 1975), p. 50.

11. United Hebrew Charities, *23rd Annual Report* (New York: Seixas, 1898), p. 20.

12. *Charities Review*, vol. II, November 1892, p. 42.

13. Amos G. Warner, "Introduction," *Directory of the Charitable and Beneficent Organizations of Baltimore and of Maryland* (Baltimore: Charity Organization Society, 1892), p. xii.

14. H. L. Wayland, "A Scientific Basis of Charity," *Charities Review* III (1893–94), p. 268.

15. Ibid., p. 272.

16. *Washington Post*, May 21, 1990, p. A1.

17. Ibid.

18. *San Francisco Chronicle*, July 15, 1990, p. A1. The article noted a crackdown against panhandlers even in Berkeley.

19. In New York in May 1990, a federal appeals court upheld a transit authority ban on subway panhandling. In Washington, the city council abandoned a six-year-old guarantee of free shelter for all, regardless of conduct. In Atlanta, police made arrests for loitering and public drunkenness.

20. *Washington Post*, May 21, 1990, pp. A1, A6.

21. A Children's Defense Fund spokeswoman decried "a growing tendency to classify all homeless people—individuals and families—as dysfunctional drug or alcohol addicts." She argued that an unfair generalization of that kind "allows people to be less sympathetic." However, generalizations that pushed people to be more sympathetic have been satisfactory.

22. *Washington Post*, May 21, 1990, pp. A1, A6.

23. Ellen Graham and Joseph N. Boyce, "Out of the Ashes," *Wall Street Journal*, August 22, 1989, pp. A1, A6.

24. Information provided by Glint Bolick.

25. Ibid.

26. Lynn R. Buzzard and Samuel Ericsson, *The Battle for Religious Liberty* (Elgin, Illinois: David C. Cook Publishing Co., 1984), pp. 239, 244–248.

27. AICP, *Annual Report*, 1847, pp. 12–13.

28. C. S. Lewis, *The Abolition of Man* (New York: MacMillan Publishing Co., 1978).

29. John Timmer, "Half a Century Ago," *The Banner*, May 7, 1990, p. 10.

30. Ibid., p. 11.

31. Joseph Horn, "Robbed by a Young Black," *New York Times*, May 15, 1990, p. A25.

32. Ibid.

33. Orwin, p. 331.

34. Thompson, p. 246.

35. Furthermore, when we call for an end to programs that have established a wall of oppression in the name of compassion, we need to examine our own motives. If we are not careful, we can easily be like the lawyer who asked Jesus the question, "Who is my neighbor?" merely to justify his own lack of kindness. It would be wrong, and futile, to do a song-and-dance about compassion in order to develop complacent conclusions that justify country-club conservatism. The Bible points us to more effort, not less—but it is different from the cheap grace proferred by liberalism.

Index

AASW. *See* American Association of
  Social Workers
Abbott, Edith, 204–5
Abbott, Grace, 196, 206
Addams, Jane, 81, 154–57, 176
adolescents
  child-care centers for, 186
  single parenting and, 237–38, 257, 259
adoption, 102, 254, 256, 258, 260, 282,
  286
  single parenting and, 236
affiliation, mark of compassion, 126–28,
  136, 140, 142
AICP. *See* New York Association for
  Improving the Condition of the Poor
Aid to Families with Dependent
  Children, 49, 238
  Capetillo case, 49–50
alcoholism, xix 8, 10, 16, 30, 54, 74, 125,
  130, 135, 287
  as major cause of destitution, 54, 68
Almy, Frederic, 139, 179
American Association of Social
  Workers, 194, 204, 206
American Asylum for the Education
  and Instruction of the Deaf and
  Dumb, 14
American Charities, 138
American Civil Liberties Union, 182
American Economic Association, 151
American Female Guardian Society, 12,
  101
American Union of Associationists, 60
Associated Charities of Boston, 77–78,
  88, 127, 129, 131–32

Asylum for the Relief of Half-Orphan
  and Destitute Children, 103

Bacon, Thomas, 8–9
Baker, Ray Stannard, 124–25, 147–48
Bakke, E. W., 191
Baldwin, Roger, 182
Baltimore Female Association for the
  Relief of Distressed Objects, 13
Bannard, Otis, 174
Beard, Charles A., 196
Belgium Society of Benevolence, 128
Believers Fellowship, 270–71
Bell, Nelson, 227
Bell, Winifred, 213
Benevolent Societies of Boston, 56
Berle, Adolf A., Jr., 196
Beth Shalom, program for single moth-
  ers, 260
Between Caesar and Jesus, 151
Bonding, mark of compassion, 126, 128,
  136, 140, 142, 154–55, 160, 174, 184–85,
  196, 234, 253, 255, 271, 280, 285–86,
  292
Bonner, Arthur, 235
Booth, Ballington, 165
Booth, William, 165
Boss Tweed, 70
Boston Provident Association, 31
Brace, Charles, 35–41, 43–48, 79, 81,
  160–61, 278, 282
Bradford, William, 1–2, 275
Breeden, H. O., 169
Brook Farm, 60
Brooklyn Christian Union, 87

Brown, Ego, 290
Brown, Helen E., 118
Bruno, Frank, 174, 194

Caine, Hall, 172
Capetillo, Grace, 49–50
Carey, Henry C., 67
Carnegie, Andrew, 80
Categorization, mark of compassion, 126, 129, 131–32, 136, 140–42, 159, 226, 229, 265, 268, 280, 285, 288
"The Causes of Pauperism," 82
Chalmers, Thomas, 25–29, 31, 56–57
Charitable Association of Young Men, 13
charity coordination efforts of late nineteenth century, 157
Charity Organization Societies, 89, 91–93, 95–97, 128–29, 132, 134, 146, 148–49, 156, 158–59, 171, 174, 178–79, 278, 287
Chauncey, Charles, 5–6
Chicago Erring Woman's Refuge for Reform, 101
Chicago Home for the Friendless, 101
Chicago Orphan Asylum, 45
Chicago Relief and Aid Society, 131
Child Welfare League of America, 256
Chinese Hospital Association, 128
Chipman, Samuel, 54
The Christian, 172
Christian Aid to Employment Society, 102
Christian Century, 168–70, 196
Christian Herald, 121
Christian Maternity Home/Single Parent Association (CMHA), 258–59
The Christian Society, 151
CityTeam, x, 271, 283–84
Cloward, Richard, 221–22, 224
Coit, Stanton, 159–60
Colman, Benjamin, 3–4, 277

Columbia University Graduate School of Social Work, 178, 213, 221
communes, 60, 63, 156
compassion. *See* compassion fatigue; marks of compassion
compassion fatigue, xxv, 56, 80, 82, 97, 105, 239–40, 283
Conwell, Russell, 109
COS. *See* Charity Organization Societies
Council on Foundations, 1
Croly, Herbert, 173
Crooker, Joseph, 139

Davis, Robert, 50
De Leon, Daniel, 151
de Tocqueville, Alexis, 22, 278
"Democratic Principles in Public Assistance," 204
The Depression, 187, 189, 194, 280. *See also* New Deal
Devine, Edward T., 148, 174
Discernment, mark of compassion, 19, 40, 57, 110, 126, 132–34, 136, 140, 142, 184, 229, 265–66, 280, 285, 292
divorce, 175, 237–38, 253–54
Dix, Dorothea, 59
Dodge, Rev. E. Stuart, 122, 147
Doors of Hope, 184–85
Dorcas Society, 14
Douglas, Lewis, 192
Dunn, Michael, 119–20

early American model, 2
aid in kind, 10
avoiding stingy charity, 19
charity schools, 8
coalition-building among charity organizations, 17
family relationships emphasis, 9
neighborhoods and, 5, 10, 15, 18
obligation to change, 20
orphanages, 10, 14–15
outdoor relief, 9

pauperism, 5, 16, 22
personal involvement emphasis, 12, 15, 18
role models, 18
sermons, 3, 8
theistic charity, 15
Edley, Christopher, Jr., 23
Education Society, 14
"Efforts of Social Workers toward Social Reorganization," 203
Ely, Richard, 151–52, 280
Emergency Relief Appropriation Act of 1935, 201
employment, 5, 23, 35, 68, 92–93, 96–97, 101–2, 104–6, 111–12, 126, 130–31, 136–37, 140, 142, 163, 165, 185, 190, 198, 201, 211, 260, 268, 277, 280, 289, 292. *See also* poorhouses; work test; workhouses
Encyclopedia of Social Reform, 152, 170
entitlement, 56, 193, 204, 207–8, 214, 216, 225, 230, 234, 236–38, 241, 280. *See also* Great Society
Erring Woman's Refuge, 20, 101
Evangelical Aid Society for the Spanish, 102

Family Ministries, 283
Federal Emergency Relief Administration, 192. *See also* New Deal; Works Progress Administration
Female Benevolent Societies, 14, 31
Female Bible Society, 14
Female Charitable Association, 13
Female Charitable Societies, 11–12, 14, 278
Female Domestic Missionary Society for the Poor, 12
Female Humane Association, 12, 278
FERA. *See* Federal Emergency Relief Administration
Florence Crittenton homes, 184

Flower, B. O., 152
Folsom, Marion B., 209
Ford Foundation, 215, 245
Fragment Society, 12
Franklin, Benjamin, 50–51
Freedom, mark of compassion, 126, 137–40, 142, 182, 280, 291–92
Fremantle, William G., 151–53, 171
French Benevolent Society, 128

Garland, Hamlin, 151
German Ladies' Society, 128
Giles, Hiram H., 47
Gilman, Catheryne Cooke, 156
Gilman, Robbins, 155
Girard, Stephen, 18
God's grace, mark of compassion, 6, 108, 116, 118, 142
Gompers, Samuel, 178
Gospel Mission, x, 272
government welfare programs, 51, 67
Great Society, 211, 218–19, 221, 232–33, 235, 245, 284
Greeley, Horace, 60–67, 69, 74–75, 150, 156, 171, 224, 243
Griffiths, D., Jr., 21–22
Grimke, Thomas S., 23
Gronlund, Laurence, 151
Gurteen, S. Humphreys, 89–96, 98–99, 130, 135, 163, 198, 278

Hale, Edward Everett, 123
A Handbook of Charity Organizations, 89
handicapped persons, 15
Harding, Warren, 177
Harrington, Michael, 213, 216
Hartley, Robert M., 30–31, 35, 37, 39, 70, 278
Hatch, Alfred S., 113, 120, 248
Haveman, Robert, 233
Hearst newspaper chain, 172–73
Hebrew Benevolent Society, 15, 100

Hebrew Ladies Sewing Society, 100
Hebrew Relief Society, 15
Helping Hand agency, 101
Henry, Carl, 217
Herron, George, 151
Hillman, Sidney, 196
Holz, Richard, 165
Home for Aged Protestant Women, 105
Home for Crippled Children, 101
Home for Mothers and Infants, 100
Home for Working Women, 105
homeless children, 35
    incorrigibility, 46
    influence of overcrowding, 36
    lodging houses, 39
    placement in farmers' homes, 40,
        112, 286
homeless persons, 282, 286, 293
    access to material help, 261
    behavior problems and, 266
    shelters for, 103, 130, 163–64, 262–63,
        268–70, 272, 288
    substance abuse and, 266, 268
    work test, 288–89
Hopkins, Harry, 196, 198–99
Horwitz Benevolent Fund, 100
House of His Creation, 258
House of Industry and Home for
    Discharged Convicts, 120
House of Mercy, 31
housing, xvii, xxiv–xxv, 100, 147, 152, 156,
    161, 164, 172, 185, 195, 208, 245, 260,
    263, 265, 268–69, 289. *See also* home-
    less persons
    government projects, 177, 212
    Single Room Occupancy hotels, 265
    urban renewal, 208, 265
How the Other Half Lives, 125
Howells, William Dean, 151
Hull House, 154–55, 176, 196
Hungarian Association, 128

immigrants, xxi, 15, 37, 74, 80, 104–6, 118,
    120, 128, 137, 234
Industrial Christian Alliance, 102, 141
Institution of Mercy, 31
intemperance. *See* alcoholism
Irish Immigrant Society, 128

Jarman, Rufus, 208
Johnson, Andrew, 69–70
Johnson, Lyndon, 218–19, 228, 233–34.
    See also Great Society

Kahn, Dorothy C., 204
Kellogg, Paul, 196
Kennedy, Edward, 243–44

Ladies Benevolent Societies, 12–13, 278
Ladies' Bikur Cholim Society, 32
Ladies' Christian Union, 31
Ladies' Depository, 31
Ladies' Society for the Female Poor and
    Especially the Relief of Poor Widows
    with Small Children, 13
Lamb, Charles, 94
Lathrop, Julia, 176
Legal Services, 229–30
Lehman, Herbert, 196
Levitan, Sar, 233, 245
Lindeman, Eduard, 195–97
Loeb, Sophie Irene, 174–75
Looking Backward, 2000–1887, 150, 196
Lovejoy, Owen, 179–81
Low, Seth, 70, 88
Lowell, Josephine Shaw, 89, 95–99, 137,
    163, 174, 193, 224, 278
Lunacy Law Reform and
    Anti-Kidnapping League, 103

Machen, J. Gresham, 181
Macy, J., 46
Magdalen Benevolent Society, 152
Marcus, Grace, 204

marginal tax rate for the poor, 242–43
Maria Marthian Society, 15
marks of compassion, 123–43
    affiliation with families, 126–28
    bonding with volunteers, 128–29
    categorization of applicants, 129–32
    discernment to prevent fraud, 132–36
    employment of the able–bodied,
        136–37
    freedom to work, 137–39
    relationship with God, 140–43
marriage, 236–38, 254, 256, 258, 260, 276
Married Ladies' Missionary Society, 14
Massachusetts Charitable Fire Society,
    12
Massachusetts Society for Promoting
    Christian Knowledge, 13
Maternity and Infancy Act, 176
Mather, Cotton, 5, 17, 90, 252, 277
McAuley, Jerry, 115–22, 147–48, 185, 272
McGonegal, George, 75–76
McGuffey's Reader, 18
McMurry, Dan, 263–64, 268
Memorial Union for the Rescue of
    Homeless and Friendless Girls, 100
mentally ill persons, 59, 266–68, 287
mission movement, 113, 121
Morgenthau, Henry, Jr., 196
mothers' pensions, 174–76, 197

National Conference on Social Work,
    161, 179, 182, 195, 197, 204–5
National Council of Churches, 216,
    226–27, 245
National Federation of Settlements, 177
National Welfare Rights Organization,
    224–29, 238–39
NCC. *See* National Council of Churches
    Neighborhoods
New Deal, xxi, 99, 176, 187, 192–93, 197,
    201, 209, 219, 243
New Hampshire Missionary Society, 13

New York Association for Improving
    the Condition of the Poor, 28
New York Bureau of Charities, 158
New York Children's Aid Society, 38, 282
New York Christian Home for
    Intemperate Men, 152
New York Dispensary, 12
New York Female Assistance Society, 32
New York Foundling Hospital, 45
New York House and School of
    Industry, 31
New York Orphan Asylum Society, 11
New York State Board of Charities, 76,
    82
New York Times, 61, 68, 142, 202, 221,
    233, 239, 247, 250
New York Tribune, 60, 67, 159
Newcomb, Simon, 83–87, 89
Newton, R. M., 167–69
nineteenth century, 20–23, 33, 35, 53, 57,
    60, 80, 95, 113, 123, 126, 133, 138,
    140–42, 147–48, 150, 153, 157, 160, 162,
    168, 171, 173, 176, 185, 189, 216, 220,
    224, 238, 242, 257, 259, 277–78. *See*
    government welfare programs; mis-
    sion movement; outdoor relief;
    Social Darwinism; urban areas
North American Phalanx, 60
Nursery and Child's Hospital, 102
NWRO. *See* National Welfare Rights
    Organization

Office of Economic Opportunity, 219,
    221
Ohio Board of State Charities, 78
Olivet Helping Hand Society, 102
orphanages, 10, 14–15, 110–11, 160–61
orphans. *See* homeless children;
    orphanages
The Other America, 213
outdoor relief, 9, 25, 53, 68, 75–78,
    88–89, 97–99, 176–77

Parran, Thomas, 192–93
pauperism
    causes, 16, 54, 82–83
    English laws and, 16
    lack of in small towns, 22
    mass pauperism of 1980s, 241
    poverty and pauperism distinction,
        25, 28–29
Peabody, Francis, 21
Pennsylvania Board of Commissioners
    of Public Charities, 77
*People of Compassion: The Concerns of
    Edward Kennedy, A,* 243
Perkins, Frances, ix, 196
Philadelphia committee, 54–55
Philadelphia Society for Organizing
    Charitable Relief, 128
Phoenix Christian Family Care Agency,
    259
Pierce, Edward L., 76–77
Pierce, Franklin, 59, 173
Pierson, Jim and Anne, 258
Pittsburgh Home for Destitute Women,
    105
Piven, Frances Fox, 221–22, 224–25
poorhouses, 9, 25, 53, 67–68
Presbyterian Eye, Ear and Throat
    Charity Hospital, 100
Preston, S. O., 135–36
Principles of Political Economy, 83
Public Relief and Private Charity, 89
Pullman, George, 81

Quincy, Josiah, 52

Rauschenbush, Walter, 172
Raws, William, 121
Raymond, Henry, 61–66, 68
redistribution of wealth concept, 195,
    197
Reed, Ellery, 203

"Relief—No Man's Land and Its
    Reclamation," 205
Rhode Island Board of State Charities
    and Corrections, 77
Rich Christians in an Age of Hunger, 247
Richberg, Donald, 197
Richmond, Mary, 127, 133, 139, 156, 178
Riis, Jacob, xvi, 125, 131, 133, 137, 142–43,
    145–46, 266, 278, 282, 287
Riverside Rest Association, 102
Roosevelt, Franklin, 192–93, 196, 198. *See
    also* New Deal
Roosevelt, Theodore, 173, 175
Rosenau, Nathaniel, 104, 129, 286
Ruffner, William, 34, 58
Russell Sage Foundation, study of wel-
    fare stipend effects, 205–7

Salvation Army, 162–66, 186
Schaeffer, Francis, 227, 294
Schudson, Charles B., 50
Scots' Charitable Society, 2
Scripps-McRae newspaper chain, 172
sermons, early American model and, 3
settlement house movement emphasis,
    124
    governmental social work programs
        of the 1930s and, 185
    Hull House, 154–55
    New Deal and, 197
    professionalism of workers, 185
    young people and, 156–57
Sheltering Arms, 105
Sheppard-Towner Act, 176
Shriver, Sargent, 219–20, 222–23, 233
Sider, Ron, 247
single parenting, 237–38
    adolescents and, 237, 256–260
    adoption and, 236–37, 254, 256, 258,
        260
    affiliation and, 255, 258–60
    feminism and, 254

growth of, 254
six-fingered man, 273
Smith, Frances, 78
Soaries, Buster, 212
Social Aspects of Christianity, 151
Social Calvinists, 6
Social Darwinism. *See also* mission
  movement
  beginnings of, 82–83
  Gurteen's criticism, 90–98
  Lowell's criticism, 89, 95–98
  Newcomb's views, 83–87
  personal involvement and, 279
  Sumner's views, 83–84
Social Security Acts, 176, 197, 208
Social Universalism
  charity coordination efforts, 157–60
  literary and intellectual support, 151
  personal involvement and, 279
  push toward in 1980s, 244
  settlement house movement, 154–56
  social gospel emphasis, 151

social workers
  compassion fatigue and, 239
  Depression effect on role, 190
  professionalism of, 178–85
Society for Encouraging Industry and
  Employing the Poor, 6
Society for the Employment and Relief
  of Poor Women, 31, 102
Society for the Prevention of Pauperism,
  16, 22, 27
Society for the Purification of Italian
  Quarters, 103
Society for the Relief of Poor Widows
  with Small Children, 10
Society of Christian Socialists, 151
Spencer, Herbert, 82
St. Barnabas House, 102
St. Joseph's Night Refuge, 103
St. Mary's Training School for Boys, 101
St. Vincent de Paul societies, 15, 100

stinginess, 27, 186
Strong, Josiah, 124
substance abuse
  homeless persons and, 266–72
success of programs, 123–26, 141–43
Sullivan, John A., 173
Sumner, William Graham, 83–84, 89
Supreme Court, right to trial-like hear-
  ings for welfare recipients, 229
Swope, Gerard, 196
Sylvania Association, 60

Taylor, Rev. William M., 119
temperance movements, 148
Temporary Emergency Relief
  Administration, 192
theistic charity, 15
Thomas Wilson Fuel-Saving Society,
  100
Thompson, Robert Ellis, 161–62, 284,
  293
Tobin, James, 216
Tract Distribution Society, 14
twentieth century
  new theological aspect, 169–71
  professionalism of social workers,
    178–85
  state responsibility for relief view,
    171–72
  upbeat mood, 168

UHC. *See* United Hebrew Charities
United Female Benevolent Society of
  North Carolina (Fayetteville), 14
United Hebrew Charities, 21, 76, 101,
  104, 126, 129, 146–47, 286
urban areas. *See also* mission movement
  alcoholism, 74
  crime, xx, 73
  dividing into districts, 26–27
  drug abuse, 74, 135, 287
  growth, 12, 15, 25, 52, 73
  immigration, 73, 80

postwar factory boom, 74
relief days, 70
reluctance to leave, 146
rise of relief agencies in New York City, 28
urban renewal, 208, 265
U.S. Children's Bureau, 141, 176

van Kleeck, Mary, 182, 194–95
Vautin, Earl, 235
Volunteers of America, 164

Walpole, N. R., 137
War on Poverty. *See* Great Society
Ware, Nathaniel, 57
Warner, Amos G., 138–39
Washington Post, 246, 249–50, 256, 261–62, 288
Water Street, 113–16. *See also* McAuley, Jerry; mission movement
Watson, Frank Dekker, 170–72
Wayland, H. L., 135

welfare fraud
late nineteenth century, 76–78
prevention of, 133
Wesley, John, 3, 169
West, Guida, 228, 239
What Social Classes Owe to Each Other, 83
Whipple, Thomas, 20
White, William Allen, 196
White House Conference on the Care of Dependent Children, 173
Whittemore, Emma, 185
Whyte, William, 234
Wickenden, Elizabeth, 213–14
Widowed Mothers' Fund Association, 174
Widows' pensions. *See* Mothers' pensions

wilderness, 275–77, 279, 285, 291
Wiley, George, 224–26, 239
Williams, Walter, 212–13
Wisconsin Board of Charities and Reform, 77
Women's Christian Association of Pittsburgh and Allegheny, 105
Woodbury, Levi, 20
work test, 92, 96, 130–31, 151, 158, 271, 288–89
workhouses, 7–8, 293
Works Progress Administration
focus, 198
goals, 199–200
inefficiency of projects, 199
Russell Sage Foundation study, 205
World as the Subject of Redemption, The, 151–52
WPA. *See* Works Progress Administration
Yates, J. V. N., 54
YMCA. *See* Young Men's Christian Association
Young, Andrew W., 67
Young Ladies' Missionary Society, 16
Young Men's Christian Association, 162–64, 186
Young Women's Christian Association, 162–64
YWCA. *See* Young Women's Christian Association

Zaccheus' Kitchen, 264